Riverside X

An incredible decade in the history of Middlesbrough FC

Written by

Dave Allan, Graham Bell, Gordon Cox, Mike McGeary
and Richard Mulligan

Contents

Copyright:

Middlesbrough Football and Athletic Club (1986) Ltd, 2005.

ISBN 1-903760-03-8

The right of Middlesbrough Football and Athletic Club (1986) Ltd to be identified as the authors of this book has been asserted in accordance with the Copyright, Designs and Patents Act 1988.

Photographic acknowledgements:

The photographs in this book have been supplied by Middlesbrough Football Club, Blades Sports Photography, Getty Images, Highland Studios and North News and Pictures.

Published by:

Middlesbrough Football and Athletic Club (1986) Ltd, 2005.

created by hillprint media

Introduction

• GRAND ENTRANCE - The Ayresome Park Gates returned to view in 2005 as Boro celebrated 10 years at the Riverside

Middlesbrough Football Club this year celebrated its 129th birthday and 2005 is the 19th anniversary of reformation after liquidation. The years 1876 and 1986 will forever be the most critical in the club's history, the moments when a dream was born and when it almost died.

But 1995 is also a landmark, and will remain so for as long as fans and players put on a red shirt. It was the year that the club changed direction, with a new stadium that was the envy of supporters across the land. No longer would Boro be an also-ran, a club that warranted little coverage or interest outside of Teesside.

Prior to the Riverside era, Boro had never reached a major cup final and had spent

almost as many seasons outside the top-flight as in it. That makes the 10th anniversary of the Riverside Stadium's opening an important date in the long and increasingly successful history of the club.

Back in August 1995 it was still a dream that Boro could sign the Brazilian footballer of the year or spend more than £8 million on one player, that they could reach three successive cup finals or be the focus of worldwide media attention. Boro have come a long, long way in the 10 years since.

The Riverside decade has been marked by the erecting of the Ayresome Park gates at the new stadium, as well as the laying of the Boro Brick Road, the Boro Legends banners and concourse kiosks named after past and present stars.

Riverside X is part of that celebration – a chance to look back at a golden era in the club's history and look forward to an exciting future. The book goes back in time to the building of the stadium and the reasons behind the

Riverside X

change of location, following 92 years at Ayresome Park. It's the most comprehensive guide ever written about the club's recent history as each Riverside season is given a full review – with brilliant photographs and detailed statistics to help bring back all those great memories.

The greatest moments of the last 10 years are covered thoroughly with dedicated chapters on the Carling Cup final and European run of 2004-05, while every single Boro player of the Riverside era is profiled in a superb appendix which also includes tables, charts and graphs.

But just as important as the events on the pitch and in the boardroom, *Riverside X* allows the voice of the Boro fans to be heard. That's why supporters were asked to select their favourites of the last 10 years – and the results are a fascinating insight into how players, matches, strikes and seasons have been remembered. Here, fans in their thousands, have selected their favourite players, greatest games and goals, and – on the

flip side – most disappointing results and most controversial players.

All records are correct up to the end of the 2004-05 season, as the 10th Riverside campaign came to a close with the dramatic 1-1 draw at Manchester City which guaranteed UEFA Cup football for a second consecutive season. The writers would like to thank Steve Gibson, Juninho, Keith Lamb, Steve McClaren, Bryan Robson, Gareth Southgate and Terry Venables for their time and help, as well as the design and publishing team at Hillprint Media. Thanks also go to contributors Rob Dixon, Martyn Coyle and Catherine Bayles.

Also, many thanks to Blades Sports Photography, Getty Images and Highland Studios for the excellent photography throughout.

Dave Allan, Graham Bell, Gordon Cox, Mike McGeary and Richard Mulligan

• CHAMPIONS AT LAST - Chairman Steve Gibson celebrates Boro finally winning a major trophy as the Riverside dream comes to fruition at the Millennium Stadium in the 2004 Carling Cup final

The Stadium

• BEFORE AND AFTER - thriving docklands of the 1950s gave way to Boro's new home in 1995

The stadium's the thing. It hasn't been Juninho, Fabrizio Ravanelli, Gareth Southgate or Jimmy Floyd Hasselbaink. Not even Bryan Robson or Steve McClaren can take the major credit for the cataclysmic changes in Middlesbrough's fortunes and standing in the last decade. Quite simply, if the stadium hadn't been built none of them would have come.

Just to show how much time - and money - Boro were forced to catch up on in the 1990s, the club paid £1m for a player for the first time in 1994, the same year work began on the new stadium. Neil Cox was brought in from Aston Villa for a seven-figure sum a full 15 years after Trevor Francis became the first £1m player in England. However, within a year - and just weeks before the Riverside's first Premiership match - Boro had beaten that record by more than five times as they signed Nick Barmby from Tottenham for £5.25m. But it wasn't hyperinflation that caused such a jump in Boro's payments, it was the fact that the club now had the infrastructure and vision to be able to attract a fully-fledged 21-year-old England international with a big future.

The record fee kept going up as the club became more established domestically and then across the Continent. Soon Ravanelli swapped Champions League winners Juventus for Teesside for £7m in 1996, and then early in the new millennium £8m-plus figures were paid for Ugo Ehiogu and Italian prodigy Massimo Maccarone.

Throw in there Juninho, Alen Boksic, Mark Viduka and Paul Ince and it can be seen how Boro assembled a healthy smattering of some of the world's best players of the last 10 years. But was it really bricks and mortar that caused a club that had gone bust in 1986 to become one of the nation's highest-profile sides?

• THE WAY WE WERE - Boro's home for 92 years, Ayresome Park

At a basic level, the answer is "yes", at least according to the man who helped to make the Riverside Stadium a reality and has been with the club ever since. Keith Lamb, who became Boro's Chief Executive in 1986, said: "In my 20 years at Boro, the move to the Riverside is the thing that I've been most proud of. It has been the catalyst for everything that has followed from 1995 onwards. It was the stadium and the challenge of moving that swayed Bryan Robson to join us in 1994. When we met, he could see the opportunity of one more year at Ayresome Park before moving. The challenge was to get the team into the Premiership in time for the opening of the Riverside. I think it took him about five minutes to make his mind up after that."

The roots of the move date back to the 1980s when Ayresome Park, which had opened in 1903, began to deteriorate

rapidly, and the club had too many financial problems to afford refurbishments. The disasters at Valley Parade and Heysel in 1985, and then Hillsborough in 1989, led to the Taylor Report, which made all-seater stadia compulsory. But although change was inevitable for Boro, a move away from Ayresome Park was not.

Lamb explained: "We were slowly trying to refurbish Ayresome Park in the early 1990s because the stands were crumbling, particularly the Holgate End. We seemed to be having constant battles to keep the place open. I spent a lot of time, because of the disrepair, looking at how to redevelop. But Ayresome Park was stuck in the middle of terrace housing and there would have been a lot of planning permissions to gain. They would be difficult to overcome, even more so because we wanted to increase the capacity - a maximum of 20,000 seats would condemn us to second-class football forever.

"I presented redevelopment options to the board and started to look at the way other clubs were dealing with the ramifications of the Taylor Report and the new attitude to stadia. One was Everton, who had completely renovated Goodison Park and, at a time when we were lucky to have a staircase, they had lifts! Then another approach became apparent after seeing Walsall's new Bescot Stadium and then The New Den at Millwall. Both were magnificent buildings."

Good idea or not, the relocation scheme was a non-starter unless money could be found to facilitate a new ground, which would cost much more than the £9-10m quoted to turn Ayresome Park into a 20,000 all-seater arena. Up to this period, Boro had become renowned as a yo-yo club, having gained promotion to the top flight under Bruce Rioch and, in 1992, Lennie Lawrence. But they had quickly returned to where they had come from. There was little money to invest in a brand new stadium and all the construction of the new access roads that would go with it. Therefore an offer of assistance was met with great interest.

Lamb recalled: "Some of the board were nervous about the cost of a new stadium. Others, particularly Steve Gibson, who was then a director, were more bullish. We then received an approach from the Teesside Development Corporation (TDC) and their chairman, Ron Norman, and chief executive, Duncan Hall. Their target

Riverside X

• STARTING POINT - An early artist's impression of how the stadium might have looked

was the regeneration of Teesside and the idea was to come up with five flagship developments in the five boroughs of Teesside."

One potential site was identified next to Newport Bridge but this was discounted because it would mean construction of a new bridge over the Tees. Then the focus shifted to an area of wasteland at Middlehaven which had been earmarked as a leisure and retail park. Lamb continued: "The TDC needed a catalyst there and asked if we would be interested in relocating there. We didn't have the resources, but if they could facilitate the move, by plonking us on a site with the infrastructure already there, it could be possible. All we were responsible for was the building of the stadium - and that was

a goer for us because it was the same price as redevelopment of the old stadium."

The idea of leaving Ayresome Park was presented at board level - and splits were revealed from the off, with chairman Colin Henderson one of the biggest voices against. Gibson, on the other hand, had watched Ayresome Park deteriorate and was spurred on by the opinion that the club needed extra resources - and the prestige of a new stadium - if it was to make it back to the top flight, and this time become an established force. The inability of the club to attract Robert Lee and Gavin Peacock to Boro even with the offer of Premiership football in 1992-93 was fresh in the mind.

Gibson said: "The strength of opposition to change wasn't from supporters, it was from within the club. I was very excited by the discussions with TDC, but certain powerful individuals didn't think the club had the ability or the resource to deliver its end. But we were determined that we could. It emerged that a lot of dialogue had taken place between major shareholder Henry Moszkowicz and Colin Henderson. Henry thought my plans were too ambitious and would lead the club into financial ruin. I don't think Colin had a clue how to make the club anything more than an average First Division team and Henry was coming from the same direction. I knew it needed a big cash input to take the club to the top of the Premiership with a new stadium and manager. It was a jigsaw."

Arguments at board level became "verbally violent" but directors Graham Fordy, Reg Corbidge and George Cooke, as well as Lamb, sided with Gibson and by December 1993 he would become chairman and sole shareholder. Work began on the UK's biggest new stadium in 60 years during the 1994-95 season and would be finished just 32 weeks and £16m later, although the initial capacity of 30,000 was increased by 5,000 when the corner sections were filled in 1998. But while war had been waged and concluded at board level, hearts and minds had still to be won over among the fans who had spent a lifetime of Saturday afternoons in the Holgate End.

Lamb added: "There was a lot of protest from many supporters who felt we could not leave our spiritual home. I had a lot of public meetings, at which I made it clear we couldn't afford to fall further behind. Once fans started to see the stadium going up they seemed to all get behind it. The *Evening Gazette* backed the plan, and printed pictures every other week, and a visitors' centre was built.

"I think maybe fans saw what was happening at other stadia and started to see that they deserved the same facilities.

When they saw how it would look they knew that it was a stadium of which they could be proud."

There were plenty of envious eyes facing Boro during the last year at Ayresome, and not just because of the stadium that was being erected on the other side of town. Robson, a former Manchester United and England captain, had replaced Lawrence in 1994 to become player-manager and suddenly the club's profile was raised dramatically. He brought in Nigel Pearson, Cox and Alan Miller, and Boro were soon on their way towards a second promotion in three seasons with the introduction of forwards Jan-Aage Fjortoft, Uwe Fuchs and Jaime Moreno.

A place in the Premiership was sealed following the last ever competitive game at Ayresome Park on April 30 1995 when John Hendrie's double strike helped beat Luton Town 2-1 in front of an emotional 23,903 crowd. Boro were promoted as First Division champions a few days later and the dream had materialised as the first Riverside season would witness Premiership football.

But the hard work was only just starting as expectation grew in proportion to the excitement generated by the

• AERIAL VIEW - No not excavation work on an ancient castle, but the foundations as work on the stadium got underway

Riverside X

- GRAND TOUR - Boro boss Bryan Robson treats his former England colleague, and *Match of the Day* presenter, Gary Lineker to a first-hand view of the Riverside Stadium's construction

Gareth Southgate, Boro captain

"I have very happy memories of Ayresome Park, even though I only played there once. It was in May 1994 and I was playing for Crystal Palace on a warm afternoon. We had already been promoted to the Premiership but needed a win to guarantee the championship. I can't remember too much about the game itself but I know that I scored and that we won 3-2. Looking at the attendance of 8,638 it's amazing to consider the support the club gets now."

stadium, the manager and Premiership football. That holy trinity made it possible to lure Barmby before the start of the 1995-96 season, and the England star would guarantee a point at Arsenal during the first game of the campaign just six days before the Riverside's grand opening on August 26.

There were more than a few nerves for those who had put their heads on the block in making the Riverside move possible. Matters did not exactly go to script on the big day as the stadium's sprinkler system sprang into action and

ruined lunch for those enjoying opening day hospitality. Lamb said: "It was like with any new building - two days before, we didn't think it would be ready. We got the safety certificate on the Friday afternoon and on Saturday played Chelsea. I didn't feel relaxed on the day, and felt even worse when the sprinkler went off! From a commercial point of view it was a bit of a disaster, but what a day."

Craig Hignett and Fjortoft scored the goals in a 2-0 win in front of 28,826 spectators - the biggest Boro crowd in 14 years - and the rest, as they say, is history.

1995 96

Cellnet

Cellnet

A new stadium, the club's transfer record smashed four times over and then the arrival of the Brazilian footballer of the year. This truly was boom time for Boro. Teesside's football fans had never seen anything like this.

There was a buzz about Teesside that something extraordinary was happening. The club's image as perennial yo-yo club – a much-loved but rather unreliable friend – seemed to change almost overnight. Boro were no longer easy targets for supporters of their so-called 'bigger' rivals in north-east football. While Newcastle, resurgent under Kevin Keegan, remained the undoubted top dogs, Sunderland were being left behind, still in the time warp that was Roker Park.

But building a new stadium – no matter how impressive – was one thing. The real trick was building a team fit to grace such flamboyant surroundings. Having bought several players perfect for winning a promotion battle during his highly successful first year in management, Bryan Robson now needed to ensure he had a squad capable of staying up. But his plans were far beyond what even the most ardent fan expected. Robbo and Chairman Steve Gibson were thinking big.

Robson had already revealed his eye for the top stars during the promotion campaign, failing in attempts to lure Gary Lineker and Arsenal-bound Glenn Helder to Teesside. But with Gibson backing him to the hilt, those setbacks only served to galvanise his determination to bring real star quality to the Riverside. The signings of, first, Nick Barmby and then Juninho would stun football and light the imagination of the Teesside public. After years of apparently being happy to just muddle along, Boro really did mean business.

Throughout the summer of 1995, following Boro's promotion to the Premier League, speculation abounded that

Diary of the Decade

1995

AUGUST

4 - Boro smash their transfer record to sign Nick Barmby from Spurs for £5,250,000

26 - Boro open their account at the new Riverside stadium with a 2-0 win over Chelsea in front of 28,826 crowd.

SEPTEMBER

30 - Boro set a new attendance record of 29,462 for a 2-0 win over Blackburn

NOVEMBER

14 - Riverside hosts England U-21 v Austria U-21 game with Jamie Pollock taking part

DECEMBER

6 - Programme survey names Wilf Mannion as greatest-ever Boro player

7 - Boro become first football club in world to use revolutionary McLeod pitch cover

9 - Boro go fourth with a 4-1 home win over Manchester City

1996

JANUARY

21 - Intense speculation that Robson is about to take over from Terry Venables as England manager. But Robson rules himself out of the running. Boro beaten 5-0 by Hoddle-managed Chelsea in "battle of the England bosses"

29 - *Bryan Robson is poised to sign £4.5m Brazilian superstar Roberto Carlos at end of the season - Sun*

30 - Robson fined £750 after being found guilty of misconduct for using "foul and abusive" language to referee Paul Dawson after 1-0 defeat at Blackburn (Dec 16 95). Neil Cox and Nigel Pearson fined £500 each

FEBRUARY

1 - *Boro have failed in a British record £8.8m bid to sign Lazio striker Alen Boksic - N Echo*

8 - Branco signs from Brazil on free transfer

10 - Faustino Asprilla inspires Newcastle to a 2-1 derby win at the Riverside on his debut

17 - 4-1 home defeat to Bolton is Boro's eighth successive league defeat, equalling 42-year-old worst run. Speculation that Dion Dublin and Ian Rush are about to sign

29 - *Robson wants Rushie - D Star*

29 - Gary Walsh arrives from Man Utd for £250,000;

Barmby keeps his England squad place for match against Bulgaria

Robson had a transfer kitty of up to £10 million. To put that in perspective, that figure was more than Robson's predecessors, Willie Maddren, Bruce Rioch, Colin Todd and Lennie Lawrence had spent in the entire 10 years before his appointment.

Robson was determined to bring in superstar quality that would set tongues wagging throughout the football world. After an enquiry for Chelsea-bound Ruud Gullit came to nothing, Boro had a £5m bid accepted by Manchester United for Andrei Kanchelskis, only for the Russian winger to choose to join Everton. But Robson would not be thwarted.

After protracted and often heated negotiations with Spurs, young star Nick Barmby was signed for £5.25 million, dwarfing the club's previous record transfer for Jan-Aage Fjortoft the previous season.

• CELEBRATION TIME - Nick Barmby escapes Jan-Aage Fjortoft's clutches after scoring against champions, Blackburn

Rated one of the country's most exciting prospects – and among the best in the world by no less a figure than Pele – Barmby was the first current England international to join Boro for more than 60 years.

Barmby, however, was the only new signing in Boro's line-up for the opening game, against Arsenal at Highbury, but made the perfect start by putting his new side ahead before a late equaliser from Ian Wright. Then came a first ever game at the Riverside, against Glenn Hoddle's Chelsea, a crowd of 28,826 representing the club's biggest home gate for almost 15 years.

Robson recalls with a wry smile the build-up to the game, when a small kitchen fire caused the sprinkler system to start, ruining the food prepared in the hospitality suites and the players' lounge. "The players were supposed to be having a pre-match meal at the stadium but we had to abandon that and take them off to Norton Hall Hotel to get a bite to eat," he explains. "Obviously it wasn't the best of starts, but we got a great result by beating Chelsea 2-0. That was a wonderful result.

"Moving from Ayresome Park to a new stadium helped us to lift the profile of the club and attract star players. Full credit to the fans as well, though, because they filled the stadium. And that encouraged the chairman to go forward more than he had planned. The fans even shocked me because I knew Middlesbrough had a reasonable supporter base but to sell so many season tickets was terrific.

"A new stadium can have that affect in generating extra interest. The fans loved the atmosphere of the new stadium and that's why they have stayed with it. But the team has progressed along the way as well."

Craig Hignett took the distinction of scoring the first ever goal at Boro's new home, rifling Barmby's cross into the net, before Fjortoft struck a second on a magical day. Barmby was in scintillating form during the opening 10 games, scoring three and setting up five of Boro's first nine goals at the new stadium.

With his intelligent runs, on and off the ball, combined with close skills, the England star was the new darling of the fans ... at least for the time being. His partnership with

Riverside X

Diary of the Decade

Hignett, playing immediately behind Fjortoft was instinctive, with the two look-alike players earning a nickname of the 'The Midget Gems'.

After 10 games, Boro stood fourth. Much of the credit belonged to a rock solid defence, with Nigel Pearson marshalling Steve Vickers and Derek Whyte on either side of him and full-backs Neil Cox and Chris Morris. A hugely impressive run of five successive league wins included a 2-0 home win over Blackburn, the reigning champions. Then came the arrival of Juninho.

• BRAZILIAN BLEND - Juninho was greeted by 5,000 fans and a samba band after joining Boro from Sao Paulo

Although still little known on Teesside, he had starred as Brazil had beaten England 3-1 at Wembley the previous summer. Robson, watching in his role as coach for the national team, had seen enough to know he was the player he wanted.

Juninho recalls: "I was in talks about a new contract with Sao Paulo, but there was a big difference between what they were offering and what I wanted. Then Sao Paulo told me Middlesbrough were interested in buying me. My agent told me what Middlesbrough were offering and it was much better.

"At that time I expected to stay with Sao Paulo because they were the top club in Brazil, so I didn't expect to move

1996

MARCH

3 - Robbie Mustoe signs new four-year contract

6 - Crowd of 15,143 see Branco make his debut in reserves v Leicester. Boro lose 2-0

13 - Willie Maddren diagnosed as suffering from motor neurone disease

16 - *Juninho "learning English by playing Subbuteo" and learning new phrases such as "Na cabeca, meu filho" - on my head, son in Brazilian - D. Star*

APRIL

6 - Robson linked with Roberto Carlos for £4.5 million

9 - Jamie Pollock linked with moves to Leeds, Villa and West Ham

11 - Wilf Mannion made freeman of Redcar and Cleveland, but there is a row about £5,000 cost of ceremony

25 - Robson signs a two-year extension to his contract

MAY

14 - Emerson signed for £4 million from Porto, bringing Boro's quota of Brazilians to three

28 - Barmby named in England squad for Euro 96

JUNE

4 - Ireland debut for Alan Moore v Croatia in Euro 96 qualifier

24 - Ireland debut for Curtis Fleming v Portugal

JULY

4 - Boro smash transfer record when they pay Juventus £7 million for Fabrizio Ravanelli who is reportedly on £42,000 a week

9 - Robson ordered to appear before the FA to answer Boro's poor disciplinary record in 95-96; German court rules that Mikkel Beck is free to play for Boro after Fortuna Cologne refused to sanction his transfer

11 - Robson is reported to have made a stunning £11.5 m bid for Fiorentina's Argentine striker Gabriel Batitusta

12 - *Jamie Pollock is on his way to Arsenal for £2 million - Express; Pollock is staying put - N Echo*

16 - *Bryan Robson is ready to spend £4m on Parma's Fernando Couto - Express; Robson is set to swoop for West Ham playmaker John Moncur in a £4m swap that will see Jamie Pollock move to Upton Park - Star*

18 - Paul Wilkinson joins Barnsley on a free

22 - *Barmby to switch to Newcastle for £6 million - Sunday Mirror*

27 - Boro sign Emerson for £4 million

23 - Boro open tour of Malaysia

just two years after signing a new contract. But I spoke to Bryan Robson and he showed me the ambition Middlesbrough had and what he wanted to do. I decided to go.

"Everybody in Brazil criticised the move. They said the style of football was totally different in England and that because I was a very technical player it wouldn't suit me. I don't think anybody thought I could be a success in England."

Chief Executive Keith Lamb twice flew out to Brazil in a bid to sign Juninho, taking Robson with him on the second occasion. "Bryan made it clear that he wanted to sign Juninho, but it wasn't an easy job to get him," he says. "It took us two visits to Brazil and three months to persuade Sao Paulo that we were deadly serious about our determination to sign him."

A fee of £4.75m – far more than the £3m Boro had originally intending to spend – was eventually agreed, but Juninho revealed that Arsenal made a cheeky last-gasp bid to steal his signature. "The

day I was going to sign, an agent from Germany called my father and said, 'Don't sign for Middlesbrough because Arsenal will sign you'. I spoke to my father and said, 'With Middlesbrough the manager has come here to show his interest and that's very important to me'.

"You can speak to the chief executive or chairman but if the manager likes you, he's the one who's going to train the team and so he's the most important. I believed in Bryan Robson because his name was well known. I decided not to listen to any other offers and to sign for Middlesbrough."

The signing made Middlesbrough international news. There was bemusement that the Brazilian footballer of the year could sign for a club in the north of England that had never won a major trophy. On Teesside, the news was greeted with euphoria. A samba band and 5,000 fans welcomed Juninho to the Riverside on the day of his press conference.

A season-ticket sell-out followed, before Juninho superbly set up a goal for Fjortoft on his debut in a 1-1 draw with Leeds. More impressive Riverside results and free-flowing

• NEW ERA - Nigel Pearson and Clelsea captain Dennis Wise lead out their sides for the first ever match at the Riverside

Riverside X Diary of the Decade

• STEADY - Chris Morris played his part in Boro's solid start

displays followed, with victory over Liverpool preceding four-goal performances against Manchester City and West Ham.

On Boxing Day, Boro were fifth and knew victory at mid-table Everton could take them up to second. But the club's Christmas jinx struck once again. The team's preparation for the match was not ideal, as Robson admitted. "We forgot to bring our kit and had to have it sent specially," he revealed. It was perhaps not so surprising therefore when a 4-0 drubbing followed.

An injury crisis then contributed towards a disastrous spell that would see the club go 13 games and three months without a win. Whyte, Mustoe, Fjortoft, Morris, Juninho and Curtis Fleming all missed games, while star men Barmby and Juninho were struggling to gel.

By mid-February, when Boro fell to a shambolic 4-1 home defeat to bottom-of-the-table Bolton, fans were beginning to fear relegation may follow. The match was Boro's

1996

AUGUST

6 - Jamie Moreno released after two years on Teesside, joining Washington side DC United for £100,000

11 - Willie Maddren testimonial: Boro draw 0-0 with Inter Milan; Shepherdson Way is opened

14 - Robson resigns as Terry Venables' No.2, saying job takes him away from family for too long

17 - Ravanelli scores hat-trick on debut against Liverpool, first by any Boro player on the opening day of the season for 38 years (Brian Clough was the last)

27 - Juninho signs £1.5m deal with Nike; work starts on demolishing Ayresome Park

SEPTEMBER

9 - Jamie Pollock moves on a free transfer to Spanish club Osasuna

15 - Bernie Slaven testimonial v Republic of Ireland Select attracts just 3,537 to Riverside

17 - Craig Hignett told to put transfer request in writing. Boro announce plans for Rockliffe training ground

18 - Ravanelli scores four in 7-0 Coca Cola Cup victory over Hereford

OCTOBER

4 - Beck cleared to play for Boro after winning long battle with German football authorities and Fortuna Cologne, who tried to block the move

9 - John Hendrie moves to Barnsley for £250,000

11 - Boro linked with Parma duo Luigi Apollini and Lorenzo Menotti plus Tim Flowers and Hendrik Hertzog (Stuttgart Kickers)

14 - Robson fined £1,500 by FA for remarks made to referee Michael Riley after Nottingham Forest game

23 - Boro release Branco

30 - Nick Barmby moves to Everton for £5.75 million "with no hard feelings"

NOVEMBER

3 - Boro lose 3-1 in the Newcastle derby at St James's Park

23 - Ravanelli and Hignett grab the goals in an exciting 2-2 home draw with Manchester United

DECEMBER

4 - Boro linked with Inter Milan midfielder Paul Ince

5 - *Emerson fined £96,000 wages (six weeks' pay) after going AWOL for the third time in a month - Sun*

17 - *Robson is once again linked with strong interest in Barcelona defender Miguel Angel Nadal - Gazette; Reports that Boro reject record £12 million bid from Barcelona for Emerson*

• FLYING HIGH - Jan-Aage Fjortoft, seen celebrating his goal in the first match at the Riverside, was a key player

eighth straight defeat and a side that had looked so impressive early in the campaign now looked incapable of winning another match.

Meanwhile, the national press ran stories suggesting Juninho was struggling to settle on Teesside. He was furious with the inaccurate reports, though he admits he took time to adapt to his new life in England. "It was a lot different from where I lived in Brazil, which was more of a big city like London," he explains. "The weather and the way of life were also very different. Middlesbrough is quieter but I think a player needs to enjoy his football first of all and has to adapt to the other things like the weather and lifestyle. That's what I did. I was happy in my football and the rest followed.

"I had to adapt to my team-mates because you need to know how they like to play and they didn't know my style so the first year was about adapting. Also, I think the team was not at the level of a Premiership team. We had to improve in a few positions. It wasn't until the following year when Ravanelli and Emerson came that we achieved a better balance between midfield and attack."

Juninho doesn't agree that he could never have fitted into the same side as Barmby. He said: "My style was similar to Nick Barmby's but that doesn't mean we couldn't play together. I think if I was a manager and had quality players in my hand, I'm going to find a way to play them together. I enjoyed playing with Nick, who was a very good signing for Middlesbrough. I enjoyed playing with everybody – Curtis Fleming, Steve Vickers, Nigel Pearson, I had great relationships with them all."

To add to Boro's problems, Robson was being strongly linked as successor to Terry Venables with the national side. Beset by problems with business ventures, Venables stood down so that he could devote his energies to fighting accusations in court. Top of the FA's list to replace him were Robson and his Chelsea counterpart, Hoddle.

Robson was eventually offered the job, but turned it down. Like his Boro successor, Steve McClaren, he was combining his club managerial role by assisting Venables

Riverside X Diary of the Decade

with coaching duties during England get-togethers. Explaining his decision to stay with Boro, he said: "I wanted to get more experience under my belt as a league manager and to be a success at that. I wanted to make sure I could do a good job as a manager."

Boro became the first English team to play two Brazilians when Juninho was joined by the vastly experienced Branco for a home game with Nottingham Forest in mid-March. Capped more than 80 times by Brazil, Branco's arrival caused more excitement among the fans, but he would ultimately prove a flop. Out of shape and lacking focus, the defender would soon become a target for the boo-boys.

Thankfully, the slump in form came to an end with a battling 1-0 victory at Leeds and any remaining concerns over relegation were put to rest with a 3-1 home success over Sheffield Wednesday the following week. The latter match saw striker Andy Campbell become only the second 16-year-old to play for the club's first team.

Ultimately, the season proved a success, with a 12th place finish no mean feat for a newly promoted side. The challenge now was to build on this positive start – and Boro's dream team of Robson and Gibson were determined to go for it.

• LOCAL HERO - Jamie Pollock was part of the midfield engine room

1996

DECEMBER

18 - Robson gives trial to Slovakia left-back Vladimir Kinder

20 - Boro (12 games without a win) call off Premiership trip to Blackburn, citing 23 players ill or injured. Down to 17 fit players, Blackmore is recalled from loan at Bristol City

23 - Robson orders his players to stay away from the Riverside in a bid to halt spread of virus which caused them to call off Blackburn match. Middlesbrough council backs the decision not to play

28 - A four letter outburst from boro boss Malcolm Allison while commentating on Boro's defeat at Coventry results in him being taken off-air at half time by Century Radio bosses

1997

JANUARY

1 - Bernie Slaven takes over from Malcolm Allison as Century Radio's expert. Robson answers injury crisis with playing comeback at Arsenal - just 10 days before his 40th birthday. Boro lose 2-0, pushing them back into the bottom three and with just one win in 15 games. Speculation linking Paul Ince with a move to Boro

6 - Left-back Vladimir Kinder is brought in from Slovan Bratislava for £1 million .

8 - Goals from Hignett and Vickers see Boro beat Liverpool 2-1 in the quarter-finals of the Coca Cola Cup

11 - The club learns it is to face an imminent inquiry over the Blackburn cancellation. Gianluca Festa signs from Inter Milan for £2.7 million

14 - Boro are deducted three points and fined £50,000 by a Premier League disciplinary panel for the Blackburn controversy. Immediate appeal launched. Ravanelli predicts relegation. Steve Gibson insists under-pressure Bryan Robson is going nowhere and calls for team spirit

22 - Ravanelli tells the press he might have joined the wrong club and begs to be allowed home at the end of the season

FEBRUARY

1 - Jan Fjortoft joins Sheffield United for £700,000.

4 - Speculation linking Boro with moves for Newcastle's Pavel Srnicek and Blackburn's Shay Given

5 - Emerson's cousin Fabio (24), a midfielder, is signed on an 18-month contract. Meanwhile 18,500 Boro fans send signed postcards to the FA in protest at the docking of three points

17 - Roma rumoured to have made a £7.5 million offer for Juninho

21 - Mark Schwarzer arrives for £1.25 million from Bradford City, with Boro beating off competition from Everton

26 - Boro beat Stockport 2-0 away in Coca Cola Cup semi-final, with goals from Beck and Ravanelli

MARCH

12 - Robson's team lose 1-0 in the Coca Cola return at home to Stockport but go through to Wembley on a 2-1 aggregate

Riverside X

Season Stats 1995-96

	P	Home					Away					Pts	GD	H	A
		W	D	L	F	A	W	D	L	F	A				
Manchester Utd	38	15	4	0	36	9	10	3	6	37	26	82	+38	0-3	0-2
Newcastle Utd	38	17	1	1	38	9	7	5	7	28	28	78	+29	1-2	0-1
Liverpool	38	14	4	1	46	13	6	7	6	24	21	71	+36	2-1	0-1
Aston Villa	38	11	5	3	32	15	7	4	8	20	20	63	+17	0-2	0-0
Arsenal	38	10	7	2	30	16	7	5	7	19	16	63	+17	2-3	1-1
Everton	38	10	5	4	35	19	7	5	7	29	25	61	+20	0-2	0-4
Blackburn Rovers	38	14	2	3	44	19	4	5	10	17	28	61	+14	2-0	0-1
Tottenham Hotspur	38	9	5	5	26	19	7	8	4	24	19	61	+12	0-1	1-1
Nottingham Forest	38	11	6	2	29	17	4	7	8	21	37	58	-4	1-1	0-1
West Ham Utd	38	9	5	5	25	21	5	4	10	18	31	51	-9	4-2	0-2
Chelsea	38	7	7	5	30	22	5	7	7	16	22	50	+2	2-0	0-5
BORO	38	8	3	8	27	27	3	7	9	8	23	43	-15	-	-
Leeds Utd	38	8	3	8	21	21	4	4	11	19	36	43	-17	1-1	1-0
Wimbledon	38	5	6	8	27	33	5	5	9	28	37	41	-15	1-2	0-0
Sheffield Wed	38	7	5	7	30	31	3	5	11	18	30	40	-13	3-1	1-0
Coventry City	38	6	7	6	21	23	2	7	10	21	37	38	-18	2-1	0-0
Southampton	38	7	7	5	21	18	2	4	13	13	34	38	-18	0-0	1-2
Manchester City	38	7	7	5	21	19	2	4	13	12	39	38	-25	4-1	1-0
QPR	38	6	5	8	25	26	3	1	15	13	31	33	-19	1-0	1-1
Bolton Wanderers	38	5	4	10	16	31	3	1	15	23	40	29	-32	1-4	1-1

Left margin labels: CHAMPIONS LEAGUE / EUROPE / RELEGATED

Goals

Name	Prem	Total
Nick BARMBY	7	9
Jan-Aage FJORTOFT	6	8
Craig HIGNETT	5	7
Neil COX	2	2
JUNINHO	2	2
Chris MORRIS	2	2
Phil STAMP	2	2
Robbie MUSTOE	1	2
Jamie POLLOCK	1	2
Steve VICKERS	1	2
Curtis FLEMING	1	1
C FREESTONE	1	1
John HENDRIE	1	1
Graham KAVANAGH	1	1
Phil WHELAN	1	1

Player of the Year

Cellnet
Steve Vickers

Supporters
Steve Vickers

Appearances

	Prem	FAC	LC	UEFA	Total
Nigel **PEARSON**	36	3	5	0	44
Neil **COX**	35	2	5	0	42
Steve **VICKERS**	32	3	6	0	41
Gary **WALSH**	32	3	6	0	41
Jamie **POLLOCK**	31	3	6	0	40
Nick **BARMBY**	32	3	4	0	39
Jan-Aage **FJORTOFT**	27(1)	0	6	0	33(1)
Chris **MORRIS**	22 (1)	2	4	0	28(1)
Derek **WHYTE**	24 (1)	0	3	0	27(1)
JUNINHO	20(1)	3	2	0	25(1)
Robbie **MUSTOE**	21	0	3	0	24
Craig **HIGNETT**	17(5)	0(1)	3(1)	0	20(7)
Phil **WHELAN**	9(4)	3	3	0	15(4)
Craig **LIDDLE**	12(1)	1	2	0	15(1)
Phil **STAMP**	11(1)	0(1)	2	0	13(2)
Curtis **FLEMING**	13	1	1	0	15
John **HENDRIE**	7(6)	0	1(1)	0	8(7)
Alan **MOORE**	5(7)	0	1	0	6(7)
Graham **KAVANAGH**	6(1)	0	0	0	6(1)
Alan **MILLER**	6	0	0	0	6
BRANCO	5(2)	0	0	0	5(2)
Paul **WILKINSON**	2(1)	3	0	0	5(1)
Jaime **MORENO**	2(5)	0	2	0	4(5)
Clayton **BLACKMORE**	4 (1)	0	0(1)	0	4(2)
Keith **O'HALLORAN**	2(1)	2	0	0	4(1)
Bryan **ROBSON**	1(1)	1	1	0	3(1)
Chris **FREESTONE**	2(1)	0(1)	0	0	2(2)
Andy **CAMPBELL**	1(1)	0	0	0	1(1)
Mark **SUMMERBELL**	1	0	0	0	1
Michael **BARRON**	1	0	0	0	1

1995-96 Round-up

Premiership Manchester United	
FA Cup Manchester United	
League Cup Aston Villa	
Champions League Juventus	
European Cup Winners' Cup Paris St Germain	
UEFA Cup Bayern Munich	
PFA Player of the Year Les Ferdinand (Newcastle Utd)	
PFA Young Player of the Year Robbie Fowler (Liverpool)	
Promoted Sunderland, Derby County, Leicester City	

Line-Up

WALSH

COX VICKERS PEARSON WHYTE MORRIS

MUSTOE   POLLOCK

JUNINHO

BARMBY FJORTOFT

League Form

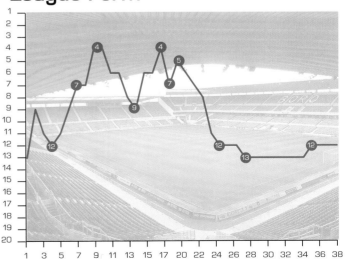

1996 97

Cellnet

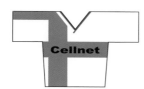
Cellnet

Doom to Boom? The title of the book produced to celebrate the 10th anniversary of Boro's rise from liquidation looked rather foolish at times during this mad roller-coaster of a season. "Doom to Boom – and back again!" mocked the club's north-east rivals. And yet cherished memories of this incredible campaign will stay in the memory long after many so-called more successful seasons have long been forgotten.

This was a season that had everything – almost. Boro *almost* won the Coca-Cola Cup, but slumped to defeat in a replay after being seconds away from winning the final. Robbo's boys *almost* won the FA Cup, but succumbed to Chelsea in the club's second successive cup final. And the club *almost* stayed up, but were relegated on the season's final day.

If all that wasn't hard enough to take, just when Boro promised to break the mould of 120 years of mediocrity, there was another painful twist – that relegation would have been avoided but for a three-point deduction imposed on the club by the FA Premier League for failing to fulfil its fixture at Blackburn in December.

Boro began that momentous season in a storm of publicity. To a squad already containing the combined abilities of Juninho and Nick Barmby, Bryan Robson added Fabrizio Ravanelli, one of Europe's most feared goalscorers, and the Portuguese league's player of the year, Emerson. Both new signings would make a huge impact on the pitch, though controversy would never be far behind either. Ravanelli, in particular, enjoyed an outstanding campaign, firing 31 goals. That included a goal-a-game cup average as Boro went for glory on two fronts, but ended up empty-handed.

The Italian international had scored against Ajax in the European Cup final two months before moving to Teesside. Having initially targeted his Juventus team-mate Gianluca Vialli, Boro turned their attention to the man known in his homeland as La Penna Bianca – The White Feather.

Diary of the Decade

1997

MARCH
26 - Appeal against three-point deduction is lost, despite the efforts of leading QC George Carman

APRIL
3 - Speculation that Everton are set to invite Robson to be their new manager.

6 - Stalemate at Wembley as Boro draw 1-1 with Leicester in the Coca-Cola Cup final

9 - Stories break that Atletico Madrid have put in an £8 million bid for Juninho. Robbo sets a 40-points safety target

13 - Another epic as Boro draw 3-3 with Chesterfield in the FA Cup semi-finals

16 - Leicester beat Boro 1-0 in the Coca-Cola Cup final replay at Hillsborough thanks to a Steve Claridge goal

22 - On the way to Wembley again after 3-0 win over Chesterfield in FA Cup semi-final replay. Beck, Ravanelli and Emerson are the scorers

MAY
8 - Blackburn 0 Boro 0 in the rearranged game - Blackburn safe but Boro still need a win at Leeds

11 - Boro relegated after a 1-1 draw at Elland Road in their final match

17 - Heartbreak again as Boro lose 2-0 to Chelsea in FA Cup Final

18 - Crowds of 50,000 line the streets of Middlesbrough to see the team come home

21 - Neil Cox agrees £1.5 million move to Bolton

27 - *Boro have joined the chase for Watford's exciting £2m-rated striker David Connolly - Gazette*

28 - *Paul Gascoigne is top of Bryan Robson's hit list - Sunday Sun*

JUNE
8 - *Manchester Utd have offered Boro £8 million plus Gary Pallister and Jordi Cruyff for Juninho - News of the World*

14 - Steve Gibson accuses Premier League officials of being "incompetent and negligent" as he finally gives up the fight to overturn controversial three-points deduction

16 - *Boro and Rangers are discussing a swap deal which would see Ravanelli moving to Ibrox and Paul Gascoigne travelling in the opposite direction - D. Mail*

19 - *Boro want Carlton Palmer to mastermind their promotion push - Gazette*

20 - *Ron Atkinson has been strongly linked with a move to Boro - Gazette*

23 - Derek Whyte signs new, three-year contract

24 - Spurs linked with move for Juninho

Emerson, an exciting box of tricks with the strength of a bull, was a sight to behold. With his long, curly black locks and ever-ready smile, Boro fans had never seen anything quite like him and it seemed for a while that the world was his oyster. But interest from his former Porto manager Bobby Robson, now with Barcelona, distracted the Brazilian from the job in hand. As the season progressed, he was too often a passenger in a side that desperately needed 11 team players.

But the real star of the show was Juninho, who took the Premiership by storm a year after his arrival in English football. Top-flight defences simply couldn't handle a player capable of beating opponents at will, with a combination of skill and electric pace. When the Brazilian wasn't scoring himself, he was usually setting up the goals, with Ravanelli the main beneficiary.

Juninho was initially delighted with his compatriot but concedes there was a problem in Emerson's make-up. "It was really important to have Emerson alongside me," he says. "A player in my position has to take risks all the time. Sometimes it works, sometimes it doesn't. When it works it normally leads to a goal or a good chance to score. When it doesn't and the opposition has a counter-attack, you have to have midfielders who are strong and can support the centre-backs. That's what Emerson did. I felt more comfortable taking the ball forward all the time and when you have confidence, the risks are less.

"Some players think that they can reach the top by talent alone. But there are plenty of examples who prove that while you must have technique and ability, you must also have discipline to reach the top. Those players who have the talent but don't reach their full potential, it's because of that."

He has only praise for Ravanelli's contribution. He added: "I played with a few Italian strikers, including Ravanelli and Christian Vieri at Atletico Madrid. I'm a player who runs with the ball and waits for players to make a run and then passes the ball.

• MIDFIELD MAESTRO - Emerson joined from Porto

Ravanelli was normally perfect at that time and he saw where I was going to pass the ball. I had Ravanelli in front and Emerson at my back and we had a great understanding. It made things easy for me."

The season opened with an unforgettable 3-3 home draw with Liverpool, Ravanelli grabbing a hat-trick on his Boro debut. When strikes from Barmby and Juninho clinched a 2-1 win at Everton in mid-September to follow four-goal home victories over West Ham and Coventry, it seemed Boro were capable of challenging football's elite at the very top of the Premier League. But the wheels were about to fall off.

A 2-0 home defeat to Arsenal the following week began a 12-game winless league run that would see Boro plummet from sixth to 17th in just three months, culminating in a dire 5-1 defeat at Anfield. Boro's problem – on the pitch, at least – appeared to be gelling the overseas superstars with the work-a-day British players who had done so well in the past. There was a definite dressing room rift between the two sets of players. Barmby, so impressive following his arrival from Spurs a year earlier, was a pale shadow of his former self and duly left for Everton in a £5.75m transfer. He moved amid rumours of a fall-out with Robson and suggestions that his style was too close to that of the outstanding Juninho.

Riverside X

Diary of the Decade

And then there was the trouble with Emerson. How many times he went AWOL is open to debate. What is clear is that his frequent and unannounced departures back to Brazil unsettled the Boro camp and made the club an easy target for the tabloid media.

Chief Executive Keith Lamb is in no doubt what unsettled the midfield power house. "Emerson started like a house on fire," he said. "He was unbelievable and took the Premier League by storm in his first seven or eight games. But Bobby Robson's move to Barcelona caused a problem because he immediately targeted Emerson. Once the player knew that Barcelona wanted him it poisoned his mind."

Despite continuing to play attack-minded football, the defeats rolled on and the crisis deepened, as Boro slumped to the bottom of the league table. Their position wasn't helped by the controversial decision to deduct three points from Boro's total after the club failed to complete the scheduled Premiership fixture at Blackburn on December 20. Robson's squad had been decimated by injuries and illness with 23 players unable to play.

Robson, who was forced to play at Arsenal on New Year's Day just days before his 40th birthday, explained that there had been no indications of the severity of the penalty. He said: "The Premier League didn't warn us that we could be deducted points. If they had done so then maybe I would have had to play some of the YTS boys or the laundry ladies. We just didn't have enough players that day." Within a month, Boro had been handed the deduction and a

● BRYAN'S BACK - Manager Bryan Robson was forced back into action due to the injury list

1997

MARCH

29 - *Ravanelli threatens to quit Boro because rumoured move to Liverpool has fallen through; Brian Deane is wanted by Boro to fire them to promotion next season - Mirror*

29 - *Everton want Bryan Robson as their new manager - Mirror*

JULY

4 - *Boro are set to fine Emerson two weeks' wages for failing to turn up for training - Journal*

7 - Juninho agrees £12 million move to Atletico Madrid

8 - Paul Merson agrees £5m move from Arsenal

9 - *Boro are locked in a £5 million auction for Derby striker Dean Sturridge - Mirror*

10 - *Monaco have entered the race for Ravanelli - Journal*

11 - Boro agree £7m deal with Everton for Ravanelli, but the player says no

12 - Club announces another season-ticket sell-out

18 - *Boro have made a bold bid for Arsenal striker Ian Wright - D Mail*

21 - Ravanelli returns to Boro to discuss his future

31 - *Robson is on the verge of signing Arsenal's David Platt for £2.5 million - D. Star*

AUGUST

11 - *Fabrizio Ravanelli was involved in a training-ground bust-up with Curtis Fleming - N. Echo*

12 - *European champions Borussia Dortmund could be ready to sign Ravanelli - N Echo*

13 - David Platt turns down Boro to stay at Arsenal

19 - *Boro are ready to replace Ravanelli with Tony Yeboah of Leeds - D. Mail*

20 - Peter Shilton joins as new goalkeeping coach

22 - *Robson wants his old mate Steve Bruce to join him at Middlesbrough - D. Star*

28 - Club announces plans to raise stadium capacity to 35,000

29 - Andy Townsend signs from Villa for £500,000

SEPTEMBER

4 - *Robson has blasted Borussia Dortmund's audacious bid to take Fabrizio Ravanelli on loan - Gazette*

6 - *Boro want AC Milan's Swedish international striker Andreas Andersson - D. Star*

6 - *Robson has stunned Everton by telling them: "I want Gary Speed" - Mirror*

22 - *Paul Merson could make a sensational return to the Premiership with Tottenham - News of World*

£50,000 fine – but not without a fight. A livid Steve Gibson and Keith Lamb called on the talents of top barrister George Carman to fight their case at appeal, but attempts at revoking the deduction proved fruitless. Gibson added: "We weren't treated fairly and it was easy for people to feel bitter and resentful."

While Boro were losing Premiership battles on and off the field, it was a different story in the cups. By March, Boro had booked their place in the club's first ever major final and had reached the FA Cup semi-final for the first time too. And realisation that Boro were on the crest of something special appeared to help the players focus on rescuing their ailing league season.

With new signings Gianluca Festa, Mark Schwarzer and Vladimir Kinder boosting the squad, four successive league wins – including a 6-1 mauling of Derby and an impressive 3-1 away victory against Leicester, their opponents in the Coca-Cola Cup final – lifted Boro out of the bottom three for the first time in three months.

Juninho says: "I don't think the football we played was too attacking. A lot of the goals we conceded were down to individual mistakes that allowed our opponents to score first, or even go two goals in front, and once that happens it make things much more difficult because the opposition have more confidence. I think that was our problem.

"If you look at the results, especially away, they were often 0-0, 1-0 or 2-0. In the cups we knew if we lost the game we were out of the competition and I think our attitude was very different from the league games."

Boro went into their Wembley showdown with Leicester full of confidence against their mid-table opponents. But a man-marking job on Juninho by the Foxes' Pontus Kaamark stifled Boro's main attacking outlet. Even so, Boro would have been full value for their victory – and a first ever major trophy - had they held onto a lead given to them in extra-time by Ravanelli. But the premature celebrations of Teesside's travelling army were cut short when Emile Heskey bungled home a last-minute equaliser.

Asked why Boro had missed their big chance, Robson recalls: "I just think it was fate. We were absolutely dominating Leicester in extra time. How we didn't score a second goal I don't know. They got a lucky break from a cross when Heskey toe-poked the ball over the line in the last minute. I don't think the team could have played any better on the day."

• PROTEST - Boro fans, at the FA Cup final, show their feelings about the Premier League's three-point deduction

Riverside X

• THRILLER - Gianluca Festa fires home against Chesterfield in the FA Cup semi-final

Diary of the Decade

1997

SEPTEMBER

25 - Ravanelli joins Marseille in £5.2 million deal

27 - Boro win 2-1 at Sunderland to extend unbeaten run to eight games

26 - Gary Walsh joins Bradford on loan

30 - *Boro are ready to pay £3.5 million for Wimbledon striker Dean Holdsworth - Sun*

OCTOBER

4 - *Bryan Robson is lining up a cut-price move for Sheffield Wednesday striker David Hirst - N Echo*

14 - *Boro are set to swoop for Liverpool's £2 million winger Mark Kennedy - Star*

1 - *Bryan Robson is urging Swiss club Grasshoppers to drop their £3m asking price for Romanian striker Viorel Moldovan - Star*

28 - Boro sign Neil Maddison from Southampton for £250,000

29 - *Benfica have made a £4 million bid to take Emerson back to Portugal - Independent*

31 - Gary Walsh sold to Bradford City for £250,000

NOVEMBER

6 - *Bryan Robson was in Italy last night to sign Juventus hitman Michele Padovano - Sun*

7 - *Boro's swoop for Padovano has failed because of the Italian's massive wage demands - N. Echo [He eventually signs for Crystal Palace]*

17 - *Boro are on the trail of Manchester United winger Ben Thornley - D. Express*

20 - *Boro want to sign Bologna's Russian international forward Igor Kolyvanov - D. Mail*

27 - Jaime Moreno re-signed on three months loan from Washington-based DC United

DECEMBER

10 - *Bryan Robson has run a personal check on Clive Mendonca - N. Echo*

14 - *Uri Geller claims his paranormal power has put Middlesbrough's soccer stars at the top of the First Division - Sunday Sun*

16 - *Boro want controversial striker Ian Wright to ensure their return to the Premiership - D. Express*

18 - Mikkel Beck voted Nationwide League player of the month for November

19 - Derek Whyte joins Aberdeen

1998

JANUARY

13 - Emerson sold to Spanish club Tenerife for £4.2 million

19 - Dion Dublin turns down a £4m move to Boro in favour of Villa

---

Juninho adds: "That was the most disappointing game I've ever played in because we were so close to glory. The emotion of the team was down after that because beforehand our confidence was very high, every player believed we could win the cup. It was such a disappointing game."

The replay at Hillsborough 10 days later was a desperate affair. Boro simply did not perform and the cup went to Leicester, courtesy of a lone strike from Steve Claridge. Either side of this devastating result came two exhausting FA Cup semi-finals against Second Division minnows Chesterfield. The Spireites looked to be heading for Wembley when they went two goals up against the shellshocked Teessiders but a brave fight-back by 10-man Boro almost clinched victory, only for a late, late equaliser to force another replay. Thankfully, Robbo's boys got it right second time around and, after 121 years without reaching a major final, they were on their way to their second inside a month.

Before then they faced five games that would decide the club's future, with just one of them at the Riverside. Ravanelli's last-minute penalty clinched three crucial points in that final home fixture, a 3-2 win over high-flying Aston Villa, but by now even the fixture schedule was conspiring against Boro, who faced playing their final four league games in the space of just eight days – Saturday, Monday, Thursday and Sunday.

• DREAM DATE - Bryan Robson and Nigel Pearson lead Boro out in the club's first ever FA Cup final

Two days after the Villa victory, a stunning display of flair and guts – with Juninho again the main instigator - saw Boro go 3-1 up at Manchester United, only for the champions-elect to claw back to level terms, costing Boro two points that would ultimately prove crucial. The controversial fixture at Blackburn was finally played as a goalless draw, meaning nothing but three points from the final game at Leeds would be enough.

Boro gave it their best shot but were clearly playing on tired legs. They were relegated as a result of a second half header from Brian Deane, a striker who Robson would later sign. Juninho's equaliser 11 minutes from time would prove to be no more than a consolation. Cue tears from fans and players alike that a season of such hope and entertainment had ended in such desperate despair. As a matter of history, they would have finished 14th had they not been deducted three points.

The end of the league season left only the small matter of an FA Cup final against Chelsea – and even that result had an air of inevitability from the moment, 42 seconds in, Roberto di Matteo smashed

the ball in off the underside of Ben Roberts' crossbar. The 2-0 defeat seemed to mean little after what had gone before. Boro were heading back to Division One.

It would be understandable if Robson regretted playing such attacking football but, eight years on, he insists that wasn't the reason for Boro's downfall. "That team was really good," he says. "Where we fell down was that the squad wasn't big enough to give people a rest during the cup runs. It was entertaining football and I wouldn't have changed that. You would maybe have liked a little bit better quality in defenders who could cope with one-versus-one situations, rather than having to deploy others to protect and cover. It was a good brand of football. I think it was tiredness after the big cup games that got us relegated.

"I still look back on losing the three points as harsh. After Keith Lamb's conversation with the Premier League on the Friday, for the Premier League to deduct three points was a scandalous decision – and I will never go back on that."

Recalling his feelings as he sat devastated on the Elland Road pitch, knowing the dream was over, Juninho admits: "It was bad moment because I knew our team was better than a lot of the teams in the Premier League. Everybody knew we could do better. Even in the last game we had chances to win but we conceded a goal and our confidence disappeared into the pitch. We weren't strong enough to remain in the Premiership. We were making a

Riverside X

Diary of the Decade

lot of mistakes and that's why we went down. In the league we thought that the next Saturday we're going to win and if we didn't, we thought we'd win the Saturday after that. But it didn't happen.

"Even so, I think that was the best season of my career. The excitement between the players and the supporters was unbelievable. Every game, especially at home but even away was very special because the supporters identified with the players and the team. If you ask the fans about their memories a lot of them will talk about that season because the team was playing such exciting football."

For Robson, it was a question of what might have been as relegation would ultimately cost him the services of Juninho, Ravanelli and Emerson, scuppering his ambition to turn Boro into a European force. "If we had been able to avoid relegation we would have been able to keep Juninho and Ravanelli," he explains. "They had ambitions to play in the following summer's World Cup tournament. They said they would have loved to have stayed but it was their World Cup ambitions that was their major reason for leaving. I can understand that.

"The club had to stand still the following season. We'd had the financial boost from two cup finals so if we had stayed up we would have been in the position for me to strengthen the squad. Relegation probably held us up by a couple of years."

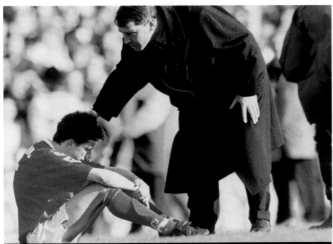

• AGONY - Robson consoles a distraught Juninho after relegation at Elland Road

1998

JANUARY

29 - *Leeds striker Rod Wallace snubs Boro at last minute - Gazette*

29 - *Tommy Johnson is ready to end his Celtic nightmare by signing for Boro for £2.3m - Mail*

31 - Craig Hignett pleads for new talks and insists he wants to stay at Boro

FEBRUARY

1 - Juninho breaks his leg in Spanish First Division game for Atletico at Celta Vigo

2 - *Merson reveals how Nigel Pearson talked him out of quitting Boro - News of World*

2 - Michael Thomas joins on loan from Liverpool

10 - Paul Merson back in international action for England B

11 - Robson ties up £2m deal for Hamilton Ricard from Deportivo Cali

12 - Boro sign Alun Armstrong from Stockport for £1.6 million

15 - Boro become the first British club to launch its own TV station

16 - Marco Branca signs from Inter Milan for £1m

25 - Boro become the first club in Britain to launch community classes in lifestyle and healthy living with the opening of the pioneering Willie Maddren Centre

MARCH

3 - Robson named Manager of the Month for February

5 - Marlon Beresford signed from Burnley for £400,000

24 - Paul Gascoigne signed from Rangers for £3.45 million

25 - Merson marks his England return with a goal in a 1-1 draw against Switzerland

APRIL

1 - Boro lose 2-0 to Chelsea in the Coca-Cola Cup final

3 - *Boro, Chelsea, Manchester Utd. and Rangers will all bid in the £16 million auction for Juventus striker Allessandro Del Piero - D. Mail*

MAY

1 - *Bryan Robson wants to take Stuart Ripley home to Middlesbrough in a £1.5m transfer - Mirror*

3 - Boro's 4-1 home win over Oxford seals promotion to the Premiership, Alun Armstrong and Craig Hignett scoring two apiece

3 - *Paul Merson insists he is staying at Middlesbrough for life - D. Mail*

9 - Fabio returns to Rio on a free transfer

11 - *Robson is ready to pounce for Chelsea striker Mark Hughes - N Echo*

Riverside X

Season Stats 1996-97

	P	Home					Away					Pts	GD	H	A
		W	D	L	F	A	W	D	L	F	A				
Manchester Utd	38	12	5	2	38	17	9	7	3	38	27	75	+32	2-2	3-3
Newcastle Utd	38	13	3	3	54	20	6	8	5	19	20	68	+33	0-1	1-3
Arsenal	38	10	5	4	36	18	9	6	4	26	14	68	+30	0-2	0-2
Liverpool	38	10	6	3	38	19	9	5	5	24	18	68	+25	3-3	1-5
Aston Villa	38	11	5	3	27	13	6	5	8	20	21	61	+13	3-2	0-1
Chelsea	38	9	8	2	33	22	7	3	9	25	33	59	+3	1-0	0-1
Sheffield Wed	38	8	10	1	25	16	6	5	8	25	35	57	-1	4-2	1-3
Wimbledon	38	9	6	4	28	21	6	5	8	21	25	56	+3	0-0	1-1
Leicester City	38	7	5	7	22	26	5	6	8	24	28	47	-8	0-2	3-1
Tottenham Hotspur	38	8	4	7	19	17	5	3	11	25	34	46	-7	0-3	0-1
Leeds Utd	38	7	7	5	15	13	4	6	9	13	25	46	-10	0-0	1-1
Derby County	38	8	6	5	25	22	3	7	9	20	36	46	-13	6-1	1-2
Blackburn Rovers	38	8	4	7	28	23	1	11	7	14	20	42	-1	2-1	0-0
West Ham Utd	38	7	6	6	27	25	3	6	10	12	23	42	-9	4-1	0-0
Everton	38	7	4	8	24	22	3	8	8	20	35	42	-13	4-2	2-1
Southampton	38	6	7	6	32	24	4	4	11	18	32	41	-6	0-1	0-4
Coventry City	38	4	8	7	19	23	5	6	8	19	31	41	-16	4-0	0-3
Sunderland	38	7	6	6	20	18	3	4	12	15	35	40	-18	0-1	2-2
BORO	38	8	5	6	34	25	2	7	10	17	35	39	-9	-	-
Nottingham Forest	38	3	9	7	15	27	3	7	9	16	32	34	-28	1-1	1-1

Goals

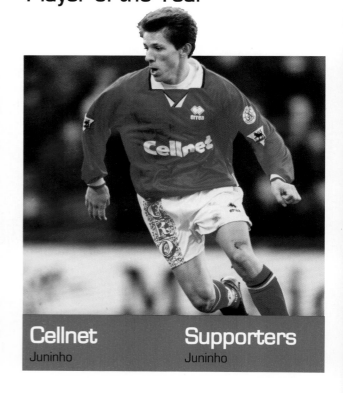

Name	Prem	Total
Fabrizio RAVANELLI	16	31
JUNINHO	12	15
Mickel BECK	5	11
Craig HIGNETT	4	7
EMERSON	4	6
Robbie MUSTOE	3	3
Phil STAMP	1	3
Clayton BLACKMORE	2	2
Gianluca FESTA	1	2
BRANCO	0	2
Nick BARMBY	1	1
Vladimir KINDER	1	1
Neil COX	0	1
Jan-Aage FJORTOFT	0	1
Curtis FLEMING	0	1
Steve VICKERS	0	1
Derek WHYTE	0	1

Player of the Year

Cellnet	Supporters
Juninho	Juninho

Appearances

	Prem	FAC	LC	UEFA	Total
Fabrizio **RAVANELLI**	33	7	8	0	48
JUNINHO	34(1)	6	7	0	47(1)
Robbie **MUSTOE**	31	7	8	0	46
EMERSON	32	5	8	0	45
Curtis **FLEMING**	30	4(1)	7	0	41(1)
Neil **COX**	29(2)	3	7	0	39(2)
Steve **VICKERS**	26(3)	5(1)	5	0	36(4)
Mikkel **BECK**	22(3)	5(1)	6(1)	0	33(2)
Craig **HIGNETT**	19(3)	6	6	0	31(3)
Derek **WHYTE**	20(1)	3(1)	3(1)	0	26(3)
Nigel **PEARSON**	17(1)	3	5	0	25(1)
Phil **STAMP**	15(9)	3(2)	4(2)	0	22(13)
Gianluca **FESTA**	13	5	4	0	22
Clayton **BLACKMORE**	14(2)	4(1)	2(1)	0	20(4)
Ben **ROBERTS**	9(1)	6	1(1)	0	16(2)
Gary **WALSH**	12	0	3	0	15
Alan **MOORE**	10(7)	1(1)	1(3)	0	12(11)
Alan **MILLER**	10	0	2	0	12
Phil **WHELAN**	9	0	2	0	11
Nick **BARMBY**	10	0	0	0	10
Mark **SCHWARZER**	7	0	3	0	10
Vladimir **KINDER**	4(2)	2(1)	1	0	7(3)
Craig **LIDDLE**	5	1	0	0	6
Chris **MORRIS**	3(1)	0	2	0	5(1)
Jan-Aage **FJORTOFT**	2(3)	0(2)	1	0	3(5)
BRANCO	1(1)	0	2	0	3(1)
John **HENDRIE**	0	0	1(1)	0	1(1)
Bryan **ROBSON**	1	0	0	0	1
Chris **FREESTONE**	0(3)	0(1)	0	0	0(4)
Andy **CAMPBELL**	0(3)	0	0	0	0(3)
Mark **SUMMERBELL**	0(2)	0	0	0	0(2)

1996-97 Round-up

Premiership		
Manchester United		
FA Cup		
Chelsea		
League Cup		
Leicester City		
Champions League		
Borussia Dortmund		
European Cup Winners' Cup		
Barcelona		
UEFA Cup		
Schalke 04		
PFA Player of the Year		
Alan Shearer (Newcastle Utd)		
PFA Young Player of the Year		
David Beckham (Manchester Utd)		
Promoted		
Bolton Wanderers, Barnsley, Crystal Palace		

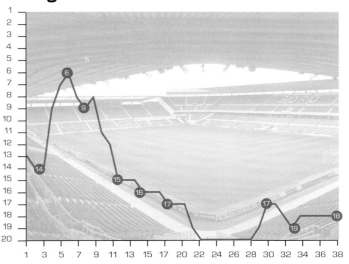

Line-Up

League Form

1997-98

The heart-breaking events of the 1996-97 season would have broken many clubs and crushed the belief of your normal football supporter. Two cup final defeats combined with the sheer injustice of being relegated via a three-point deduction might so easily have sent Boro into a downwards spiral that would have resulted in a return to the dark days of 1986. But Middlesbrough FC and its magnificent fans are made of sterner stuff.

With Chairman Steve Gibson's vision continuing to light the way, Boro bounced back in fairytale fashion. Not only did they achieve promotion back to the top flight but, against all the odds, reached a third successive cup final. It was the stuff of dreams.

It felt like the world was against the club, but the overwhelming feeling that the game's authorities had dealt Boro an unfair hand served to galvanise club, players and fans. Teesside steel was reborn. For perhaps the only time in the history of the game, Boro sold MORE season tickets following relegation, with a 30,000 sell-out crowd cramming into the Riverside week in and week out. The players responded in crusading fashion, winning promotion on a wave of euphoria in a dramatic final day win.

Boro may still have been licking the previous season's wounds – many of them self-inflicted – but Bryan Robson's side showed their mettle by overcoming the loss of star trio, Juninho, Emerson and Fabrizio Ravanelli, to continue grabbing the national headlines. Once again, it wasn't always for the right reasons. Ravanelli departed early in the campaign for a knockdown £5.2m, the enigmatic Emerson twice went AWOL before Robson's patience finally snapped and he was shipped off to Tenerife, while the shock capture of England superstar Paul Gascoigne sent the media into frenzy once again.

There appeared little hope that any player could successfully fill the void left by the departure of fans' hero, the brilliant

Diary of the Decade

1998

MAY

17 - *Boro have made a sensational £7 million bid for Everton striker Duncan Ferguson - S Mirror*

29 - *Bryan Robson is poised to launch a £2.5 million bid for Tottenham winger Ruel Fox - Star*

30 - *Blackburn winger Stuart Ripley is being linked with a return to Middlesbrough - N. Echo*

31 - *Gascoigne axed from World Cup squad after a row with Glenn Hoddle*

JUNE

5 - *Boro agree a £2.5 million fee with Man Utd for Gary Pallister*

7 - *Robson is ready to make a £5 million bid for Man Utd's Phil Neville - Sunday People*

9 - *Robson has greed a £4 million deal with Juventus for defender Moreno Torricelli - D. Mail*

10 - *Boro want Scotland midfielder John Collins to team up with Paul Gascoigne at the Riverside next season - Journal*

11 - *Robson is ready to tempt Dion Dublin from Coventry with a £20,000-a-week deal - D. Mail*

13 - *Robson has pencilled Dutch World Cup striker Patrick Kluivert into his list of summer targets - Gazette*

18 - *Boro are back on the trail of Everton's teenage central defender Richard Dunne - Gazette*

23 - *Boro are being strongly linked with Croatian international wing-back Robert Jarni - Gazette*

29 - *Middlesbrough's Brazilian legend Juninho is NOT set to return to the club - Sunday Sun*

JULY

4 - *The brilliant Juninho is unlikely ever to wear a Boro shirt again - Gazette*

7 - *Robson has ruled out a move for Arsenal's England striker Ian Wright - Gazette*

8 - *Gordon McQueen appointed first-team coach*

8 - *Boro sign Gary Pallister from Manchester United for £2.5 million and Dean Gordon from Crystal Palace for £900,000*

9 - *Robson wants to sign Man Utd striker Teddy Sheringham - Mirror*

11 - *Middlesbrough are hoping to bring Andrei Kanchelskis back to the Premiership from Italian club Fiorentina - D. Mail*

12 - *Robson has made a shock move for French World Cup striker Christophe Dugarry - People*

14 - *Robson is ready to snap up West Bromwich winger Kevin Kilbane for £2 million - Mirror; Boro announce £5m loss on 1997-98 season*

22 - *Robson censured and fined £2,500 for comments made about ref Eddie Wolstenholme following Boro's 4-0 defeat at Nottingham Forest*

Juninho. But Robson pulled off another major coup in convincing Paul Merson to leave Arsenal for Division One football. After a slow start, 'The Magic Man' started to pull the strings with a magnificent array of control, passing and individual trickery. Quite simply, Merson was a class above anything else outside the Premier League that season. At times, it seemed like he was capable of single-handedly dragging Boro back into the big time, a series of scintillating performances inspiring team-mates and fans alike.

As Bryan Robson, who also made an unsuccessful attempt to sign Merson's Highbury team-mate David Platt, recalls: "Paul Merson had a fantastic season that year and he was one of the main reasons we got promoted. He was outstanding."

Chief Executive Keith Lamb adds: "Merson was absolutely vital to us. Signing him was a statement of intent. It showed everyone that we were not going to lie down and accept relegation. His ambition was still burning bright and the move worked out well for both parties. Bryan Robson effectively resurrected his career. Paul got back into the England side on the basis of his form for Middlesbrough."

And yet Boro made a stuttering and nervous start to the campaign, scraping an opening day Riverside win over Charlton with two late goals – Ravanelli grabbing a last-minute winner before departing for Marseille – and then losing at home to also-rans Stoke City. But gradually, Boro pulled themselves together and focused on the job in hand. Mark Schwarzer's return from a long-term injury coincided with skipper Nigel Pearson recovering his fitness before his troublesome knees finally gave up the ghost. The three-man back line of Pearson, Supporters Club player of the year Gianluca Festa and ever-dependable Steve Vickers ensured the 'goals against' column remained impressive, while the promptings of Merson and the vastly experienced Andy Townsend – newly signed from Aston Villa - ensured a steady flow of goals at the other end of the pitch.

• PRESSING UP - Bryan Robson brought in Andy Townsend to galvanise Boro's midfield

While the influence of the seasoned campaigners could not be doubted, Robson was forced to put his faith in the club's flourishing youth policy. Injuries to the likes of Curtis Fleming, Vladimir Kinder and Phil Stamp gave him little option, but the teenagers flourished. Craig Harrison, Andy Campbell, Mark Summerbell, Steve Baker and Anthony Ormerod all played their part. Right winger Ormerod, just 18, marked his debut with a stunning goal at surprise early leaders Bradford City and looked set for a bright future in the game, though that potential would never be fulfiled.

Of Boro's early results, the one perhaps best enjoyed by the supporters was an impressive 2-1 win away win over local rivals, Sunderland, with Emerson showing that lightning really does strike twice in the same place. Just as he had done at Roker Park a year earlier, the Brazilian hit one of the goals of the season with a stunning long-range effort - this time at the Stadium of Light. A run of six wins in eight games during October and November lifted Boro into second. Top spot was seized for the first time in early December as Craig Hignett and Mikkel Beck began to share the attacking and goalscoring burden with Merson.

Riverside X

Diary of the Decade

Soon after, however, Boro's patience with Emerson finally snapped. Having been chased by the likes of Barcelona during his first season on Teesside, the less than glamourous footballing lights of Tenerife can hardly have been the move he had dreamed of. Indeed, a player who had looked capable of becoming one of the greats of world football would forever fail to hit the heights – never winning a Brazil cap during spells with Tenerife, Deportivo, Atletico Madrid, Rangers, Vasco da Gama and Greek side Xanthi.

Emerson's departure meant the club had now lost its three major stars in the space of six months, but Robson has no regrets about signing them. "No matter what people say, Emerson was a joy to work with," he insists. "He was a great lad around the place, he was a good trainer and everything. I think if Emerson looked back now he'd regret ever going to Tenerife. I bet he wished he had stayed and seen the club grow."

• GOALS GALORE - Marco Branca scored 10 times in 13 games after joining from Internazionale

1998

JULY

23 - *Boro are closing in on a deal to bring Italian midfield player Francesco Moriero to Teesside - Star*

25 - *Bryan Robson yesterday swooped for Argentine defender Gustavo Lombardi - N. Echo. Lombardi, signed on loan, returned to Argentina without playing a first-team game*

31 - *Robson is hoping for a breakthrough with Vicenza wide man Gabriel Ambrosetti - N. Echo*

AUGUST

3 - Boro call off Keith Gillespie's £3.5m move from Newcastle, citing an ankle injury. An angry Newcastle boss Kenny Dalglish claim he was kept in the dark about the move

10 - *Bristol City want Middlesbrough midfielder Phil Stamp and are ready to lodge a £500,000 bid - Journal*

11 - *Boro have been offered Inter Milan's £4m rated defender Fabio Galante - Journal; Boro are lining up a swoop for Colombian striker Victor Aristizabal - Journal*

13 - Club announces season-ticket sell-out

20 - Colin Cooper signed from Nottingham Forest for £2.5 million

28 - New club shop - three times the size of its predecessor - opens at the stadium

SEPTEMBER

7 - Paul Merson joins Aston Villa for £7 million

13 - Boro win 3-0 at Tottenham - Bryan Robson's first win in London in 12 attempts as manager

24 - Robson has made a £2 million swoop for Wolves' England U-21 star Steve Froggatt - *Star*

25 - *Robson is lining up a £2m bid for Vicenza hitman Pasquale Luiso - Mirror*

26 - *Moneybags club Middlesbrough are preparing an astonishing £18 million swoop for Alan Shearer - Mirror*

28 - *Boro are on the trail of Newcastle wingback Steve Watson - Gazette*

OCTOBER

6 - *Manchester United want £4.5 million-rated Boro keeper Mark Schwarzer - Star; Riverside stadium voted top of the league for disabled facilities*

7 - *Robson has put £3 million Sheffield Wednesday forward Benito Carbone under scrutiny - Sun*

10 - Paul Gascoigne checks into a clinic to treat alcohol-related problems

11 - Boro splash out £3m for Brian Deane from Benfica

15 - *Eyal Berkovic has turned down a shock move to Middlesbrough - Sun*

18 - *Robson has been secretly sounded out as a potential replacement for England coach Glenn Hoddle - People*

Ravanelli had real pride in his performance though there is no doubt he was a handful to deal with all the time. He had high standards and he expected other people to live up to the standards he set himself."

With or without Emerson, the wins kept coming. When Gibson sanctioned the signings of strikers Marco Branca and Alun Armstrong in February, it seemed that nothing could halt the Boro bandwagon. The overriding feeling that destiny beckoned was underlined with a highly impressive 3-1 home win over promotion rivals Sunderland, with Branca and Armstrong sharing the goals. Afterwards, even Wearside Boss Peter Reid conceded that Boro were the best team in the division. But then, just as it seemed nothing could go wrong, it did.

Boro had been fighting a two-pronged challenge for success, storming through to the semi-finals of the

Coca-Cola Cup. But the effort and euphoria of beating top flight Liverpool over two legs drained the players both physically and emotionally. The achievement in reaching another cup final proved a distraction from the promotion push. Boro lost focus and their rivals took advantage. Just two weeks after their dramatic semi-final victory, Robson's side lost 4-0 at Nottingham Forest, with Colin Cooper's side rubbing salt into the wound by replacing Boro at the top of the table.

Crucially, the increasingly vital Mark Schwarzer was injured for the Forest drubbing. With second choice 'keeper Ben Roberts also ruled out, veteran Andy Dibble was brought in on loan as emergency cover. The much-travelled 'keeper had enjoyed a successful loan spell with the club seven years earlier, but this time things did not go so well. The Forest defeat was a game he would rather forget, but worse was to come. Three days later, Boro

• POIGNANT MOMENT - coach John Pickering leads out the Boro team before the 1998 Coca-Cola Cup final against Chelsea

Riverside X

Diary of the Decade

embarrassingly lost 5-0 at struggling QPR, with Dibble at least partly to blame for conceding four first-half goals. Robson had to act quickly to stop the rot, signing Marlon Beresford from Burnley before the promotion drive suffered irreparable damage.

Boro needed a six-goal winning margin over Swindon Town to reclaim top spot. It seemed an unlikely prospect, but the bookies took a big hit as the home side turned on the style and hundreds of Riverside regulars enjoyed big pay-outs thanks to their pre-match confidence. Stunning strikes from Branca and Neil Maddison – the former scoring with an incredible overhead kick – were the highlights of an emphatic 6-0 victory, at generous pre-match odds of 66-1. Surely now, Boro were on their way again.

Next came the drama of a Wembley return, for the final of the Coca-Cola Cup – and a rematch with Chelsea, victor's in the previous season's FA Cup final when Boro's fortunes and spirits had been all but crushed. This time, riding on the crest of a wave and boosted by the signings of Gascoigne and yet another forward, Hamilton Ricard, Teesside believed the story would be different. Flying high in the Premier League, Gianluca Vialli's Chelsea went into the game as clear favourites. Despite dominating

• SALUTE - Curtis Fleming, right, Hamilton Ricard and Robbie Mustoe thank the Boro fans at Wembley

1998

OCTOBER

19 - Robson pledges his future to Boro by signing a new, five-year contract

21 - *Robson is attempting to lure Ajax's Finnish striker Jari Litmanen to Middlesbrough - Independent*

23 - *Boro have joined Sunderland in the chase for Everton midfielder Gavin McCann - Journal*

29 - *Boro are keen on Leeds United's unsettled midfielder Lee Sharpe - Star*

NOVEMBER

4 - Mark Schwarzer signs a six-and-a-half year contract - the longest deal offered by Robson to any player and the longest in the club's history

18 - *Boro are on the trail of West Brom striker Lee Hughes - Sun*

24 - *Robson is tracking Blackburn's Keith Gillespie - Mirror*

28 - *Robson has had a £7 million bid for Croatia World Cup star Davor Suker accepted - D. Mail*

DECEMBER

1 - *Boro have laughed off Emerson's threatened return to Teesside with a furious attack on the Brazilian midfielder - Sun*

4 - *Hamilton Ricard reveals his recipe for success . . . banana soup - Daily Sport*

8 - Robson launches club's new Internet website

10 - Vladimir Kinder told he can leave because of work permit problems

15 - *Boro have been strongly linked with Paris St Germain right back Nicolas Laspalles - Gazette*

18 - Tony Blair opens new £7 million Rockliffe Park training centre

20 - Stunning 3-2 win at Old Trafford

21 - Bernie Slaven bares his backside in Binns' window after predicting Boro could not record their first win at Old Trafford in 68 years

23 - Alan Moore transfer listed at his own request

24 - Steve Vickers signs a new three-year contract. Robson dismisses rumours that Viv Anderson is on his way back to Old Trafford to replace coach Brian Kidd

1999

JANUARY

1 - *Boro are ready to challenge Newcastle for £4m Romanian target Constantin Galca - Sunday Sun*

9 - *Defiant skipper Andy Townsend insists his side should still aim for a UEFA Cup place and says bad Christmas results were a blip in an otherwise positive season - Gazette.*

9 - *Boro are interested in Newcastle United defender Steve Howey, whose contract runs out in the summer - Gazette;* Paul Merson misses Riverside return with Aston Villa, the newly expanded BT Cellnet Riverside Stadium staging a record 34,643 attendance

possession, however, they were unable to find a breakthrough in normal time. By then, 'Gazza' had replaced Ricard for his Boro debut, but the old magic seemed to be missing. Extra-time goals from Frank Sinclair and Boro's FA Cup nemesis, Roberto di Matteo, ensured Chelsea's third cup final victory over the Teessiders.

Once again, the cup run detracted from the main aim of claiming a rightful return to the top division. Deflated by the cup final result, the players slumped to

• ON THE UP - Craig Hignett, in action against Charlton, helped Boro to promotion during his last season with the club

successive away defeats to West Brom and Sheffield United, with Merson missing a crucial penalty at Bramall Lane. Pearson, the team's emotional leader, was struggling for fitness with a knee injury that would soon end his playing career, while it was clear the spurt of new signings had disrupted the team pattern. Gascoigne and Ricard, in particular, struggled for any

semblance of form. They needed time to settle in, but that was something Boro did not have. They had already slipped to fourth, while Forest looked to have clinched one of the two automatic promotion places with a quick run of wins. The play-offs beckoned if the slump could not be reversed.

There were six games remaining to save the season. But Robson and his players weren't about to let the opportunity slip through their grasp. A thumping 4-0 home win over Bury launched a closing run of five wins and a draw. Branca, the Italian veteran who few on Teesside had heard of when he had signed two months earlier, started to look like a £1m bargain, netting a hat-trick in the Bury match and the only goal of the game in a must-win away clash with bottom-of-the-table Reading.

Four days later, the 33-year-old played in a 1-0 home win over former Boro favourite Jamie Pollock's Manchester City. The forward suffered a knee injury during the match and, despite fighting a legal battle with the club to prove he was fit, would never again start a game for the club. But Branca had already repaid his fee many times over. His nine goals in just 11 league games were essential in sealing the club's top flight return.

With Sunderland breathing down their necks, Boro knew there was little room for error. In the final away game, at Port Vale, a second minute goal from Merson and outstanding saves by Schwarzer clinched another single goal victory. Five days later, a 1-1 draw with Wolves ensured that Boro's destiny was in their own hands. A win over mid-table Oxford United in their final game would clinch second spot and promotion back to the big time. A sun-drenched capacity crowd witnessed a nervy and goalless first-half display. But the Riverside roar sprung into life after the interval. Two goals from Armstrong early in the second half broke Oxford's resolve, with Hignett adding two more to wrap up a 4-1 win. Boro were back – and, this time, no one would deny them their place in English football's top echelon.

Taking Boro back up was a special moment for Bryan Robson. "I think my proudest achievement in seven years at Middlesbrough was getting promoted immediately after getting relegated," he smiles. "To go up and also go to a cup final in the same season was a great achievement."

Riverside X

Diary of the Decade

• GET IN - Alun Armstrong celebrates in style as his two goals against Oxford help Boro back to the Premiership

That final-day win would be the last Boro appearance for goal hero Hignett and skipper Pearson. While the big defender retired on a high by leading the club to promotion for a second time, Hignett admits he was sad to be moving on, having failed to agree terms for a new contract with the club. "I had a few tears that night because I knew that would be my last game, but they were happy tears because we had been promoted," he said. "But I could go with a clear conscience, knowing I had done everything I could. The manager had said to me he was going to talk to me about a revised contract offer but he never did. He just offered me the same as before and sadly I had to turn it down."

While the likes of Merson and Branca took the plaudits, one of the unsung heroes, Robbie Mustoe, felt the season was more of a team effort. "It was up the lads who had been at the club for some time to get us out of the First Division," he said, referring to team-mates like Hignett, Pearson, Fleming and Vickers. "They picked up the pieces, fought and battled their way back to the Premiership. We shouldn't underestimate their contribution. Those players don't get the credit they deserve."

Hignett and Pearson apart, those same players would again play vital roles in helping Boro re-establish themselves among football's elite the following season, as Robson looked to build a side based on safety rather than flair.

1999

JANUARY

11 - Juninho's agent, Gianni Paladini, claims Aston Villa are the player's first choice if he leaves Madrid - but Boro still have first refusal - Gazette

12 - Manchester United could sign Mark Schwarzer to replace Peter Schmeichel - Mirror

20 - Boro are interested in Parma star Dino Baggio, but will not pay the £15 million price tag - Mail

20 - The club announces that Marco Branca's Boro career is officially over due to his knee injury

22 - Robbie Keane linked to Boro, who lose 1-0 to Ukrainian side Schaktar Donetsk in a friendly in Israel

25 - Speculation mounts that Juninho could be on his way back to England...and Boro. His dad, Osvaldo, says: "Juninho is keen to play in England. Boro have a good chance of getting him"

27 - Juninho is captured on camera leaving Villa Park after talks with John Gregory - but his future is still far from certain

28 - Relieved striker Hamilton Ricard returns from his homeland of Colombia. While he was there a freak earthquake claimed nearly 1,000 lives

29 - Boro linked to Dynamo Kiev star Oleg Luzhny, who later joins Arsenal

FEBRUARY

2 - Nineteen-year-old Paraguayan striker Miguel Dominguez, who plays in his home country for Atletico Tembetary, arrives on loan

3 - Boro travel to Hampden Park for Alan McLaren's testimonial

16 - Unsettled Ajax star Georgi Kinkladze is on Bryan Robson's shopping list - D. Mail

23 - Everton's £5 million-rated midfield ace Oliver Dacourt is reported to be the latest name on Robbo's hitlist - Daily Star. Following an Achilles problem at the beginning of the season injury-ravaged striker Alun Armstrong tears a hamstring

24 - Boro have been linked with teenagers Brazilian hotshot Rodrigo Grau and Zambian-born Cardiff striker Robert Earnshaw - Sun

27 - Boro are preparing to bring Emerson back to the Riverside - Sun

28 - Robson is considering his future in football after a poor run of results and personal problems - Sunday Express

MARCH

3 - Marco Branca arrives at Riverside for talks about resuming his playing career. But a further inspection on the knee has again highlighted the damage and shows that the Italian is not capable of withstanding the rigours of Premiership football. Boro keeper Mark Schwarzer heals his rift with the Australian football authorities and is lined up to make his comeback for the national team

4 - Midfielder Ronnie O'Brien, released by Boro, lands a place at Italian giants Juventus

Season Stats 1997-98

	P	Home					Away					Pts	GD	H	A
		W	D	L	F	A	W	D	L	F	A				
Nottingham Forest	46	18	2	3	52	20	10	8	5	30	22	94	+40	0-0	0-4
BORO	46	17	4	2	51	12	10	6	7	26	29	91	+36	-	-
Sunderland	46	14	7	2	49	22	12	5	5	37	28	90	+36	3-1	2-1
Charlton Athletic	46	17	5	1	48	17	9	5	9	32	32	88	+31	2-1	0-3
Ipswich Town	46	14	5	4	47	20	9	9	5	30	23	83	+34	1-1	1-1
Sheffield Utd	46	16	5	2	44	20	3	12	8	25	34	74	+15	1-2	0-1
Birmingham City	46	10	8	5	27	15	9	9	5	33	20	74	+25	3-1	1-1
Stockport County	46	14	6	3	46	21	5	2	16	25	48	65	+2	3-1	1-1
Wolves	46	13	6	4	42	25	5	5	13	15	28	65	+4	1-1	0-1
West Bromwich Albion	46	9	7	6	27	26	7	5	11	23	30	61	-6	1-0	1-2
Crewe Alexandra	46	10	2	11	30	34	8	3	12	28	31	59	-7	1-0	1-1
Oxford Utd	46	12	6	5	36	20	4	4	15	24	44	58	-4	4-1	4-1
Bradford City	46	10	9	4	26	23	4	6	13	20	36	57	-13	1-0	2-2
Tranmere Rovers	46	9	8	6	34	26	5	6	12	20	31	56	-3	3-0	2-0
Norwich City	46	9	8	6	32	27	5	5	13	20	42	55	-17	3-0	3-1
Huddersfield Town	46	9	5	9	28	28	5	6	12	22	44	53	-22	3-0	1-0
Bury	46	7	10	6	22	22	4	9	10	20	36	52	-16	4-0	1-0
Swindon Town	46	9	6	8	28	25	5	4	14	14	48	52	-31	6-0	2-1
Port Vale	46	7	6	10	25	24	6	4	13	31	42	49	-10	2-1	1-0
Portsmouth	46	8	6	9	28	30	5	4	14	23	33	49	-12	1-1	0-0
QPR	46	8	9	6	28	21	2	10	11	23	42	49	-12	3-0	0-5
Manchester City	46	6	6	11	28	26	6	6	11	28	31	48	-1	1-0	0-2
Stoke City	46	8	5	10	30	40	3	8	12	14	34	46	-30	0-1	2-1
Reading	46	8	4	11	27	31	3	5	15	12	47	42	-39	4-0	1-0

Left margin labels: PROMOTED · PLAY-OFFS · RELEGATED

Goals

Name	Div 1	Total
Paul MERSON	12	16
Mikkel BECK	14	15
Marco BRANCA	9	10
Craig HIGNETT	6	10
Alun ARMSTRONG	7	7
Robbie MUSTOE	3	5
EMERSON	4	4
Neil MADDISON	4	4
Anthony ORMEROD	3	3
Gianluca FESTA	2	2
Vladimir KINDER	2	2
Nigel PEARSON	2	2
Hamilton RICARD	2	2
Andy TOWNSEND	2	2
Curtis FLEMING	1	1
Jaime MORENO	1	1
Andy CAMPBELL	0	2
Chris FREESTONE	0	1
Mark SUMMERBELL	0	1

Player of the Year

Cellnet
Paul Merson

Supporters
Gianluca Festa

Appearances

	Div 1	FAC	LC	UEFA	Total
Paul **MERSON**	45	3	7	0	55
Gianluca **FESTA**	38	2	7	0	47
Mark **SCHWARZER**	35	3	7	0	45
Andy **TOWNSEND**	35(2)	3	6	0	44(2)
Robbie **MUSTOE**	31(1)	3	7	0	41(1)
Steve **VICKERS**	30(3)	3	6	0	39(3)
Mikkel **BECK**	31(8)	0(2)	6(1)	0	37 (11)
Nigel **PEARSON**	29	1	4	0	34
Craig **HIGNETT**	28(8)	1	4(1)	0	33(9)
Vladimir **KINDER**	25(1)	1	5	0	31(1)
Curtis **FLEMING**	28(3)	0	2	0	30(3)
EMERSON	21	0	4	0	25
Neil **MADDISON**	16(6)	3	4	0	23(6)
Craig **HARRISON**	16(4)	2	3(1)	0	21(5)
Marco **BRANCA**	11	0	2	0	13
Anthony **ORMEROD**	8(10)	2	2(1)	0	12(11)
Andy **CAMPBELL**	5(2)	2	3(1)	0	10(3)
Phil **STAMP**	8(2)	1	1	0	10(2)
Michael **THOMAS**	10	0	0	0	10
Mark **SUMMERBELL**	7(4)	0	1	0	8(4)
Alun **ARMSTRONG**	7(4)	0	0	0	7(4)
Steve **BAKER**	5(1)	0(1)	2(2)	0	7(4)
Paul **GASCOIGNE**	7	0	(1)	0	7(1)
Ben **ROBERTS**	6	0	1	0	7
Hamilton **RICARD**	4(5)	0	1	0	5(5)
Derek **WHYTE**	4(4)	0	1	0	5(4)
Alan **MOORE**	3(1)	0	1	0	4(1)
Craig **LIDDLE**	2(4)	0	1(1)	0	3(5)
Jaime **MORENO**	1(4)	2	0	0	3(4)
Marlon **BERESFORD**	3	0	0	0	3
Fabrizio **RAVANELLI**	2	0	0	0	2
Andy **DIBBLE**	2	0	0	0	2
Robbie **STOCKDALE**	1	1	0	0	2
Chris **FREESTONE**	0(2)	0	1(1)	0	1(3)
Clayton **BLACKMORE**	1(1)	0	0	0	1(1)
Fabio **MOREIRA**	1	0	0	0	1

1997-98 Round-up

Premiership Arsenal		
FA Cup Arsenal		
League Cup Chelsea		C FC
Champions League Real Madrid		
European Cup Winners' Cup Chelsea		
UEFA Cup Internazionale		
PFA Player of the Year Dennis Bergkamp (Arsenal)		
PFA Young Player of the Year Michael Owen (Liverpool)		
Promoted Nottingham Forest, Boro, Charlton Athletic		

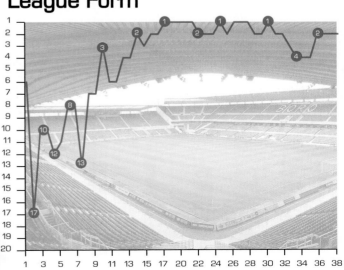

The Coca-Cola Winners 199

Line-Up

League Form

1998-99

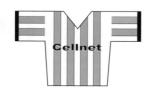

Perhaps a single player has never quite dominated a promotion campaign in the way that Paul Merson did during 1997-98. The former Arsenal man seemed like Gulliver – that's he of the travels, not the ex-Boro defender Phil – among Lilliputians as he tore Division One sides to shreds, and he achieved the rare distinction of making an England World Cup squad while outside the top flight.

On the eve of 1998-99, after all the hard work he had put in to helping Boro back to the big time, Merson seemed determined to push his side to the higher echelons of the Premiership. Going into the opening game of the season against Leeds United he said: "I can't wait to be back in the Premiership again. It's going to be hard at the start and we have got to settle in really quickly. The first stage is to stay up and then we've got to build on that. We've got a good team spirit after winning promotion but it's important that the team stays together when we are losing."

Merson, who had also suggested during a television interview that he would like to go on to manage the club, sounded like a man with a plan for the long term. But after starting the first three games of the season, in which Boro picked up two points, the recovering alcoholic and gambler was off to Aston Villa after claiming that the drinking and betting culture at the Riverside was causing him to regress. Boro were quick to deny the charges, but recouped £7m from John Gregory's Villa.

Almost a decade later and Bryan Robson still denies that the atmosphere at Boro on his watch was different to any other club. He said: "Paul had a fantastic season and he was one of the main reasons we got promoted and got to the Coca-Cola Cup final. He was outstanding, plus the club made money on him, which was great business. I think that drink and gambling was Paul's problem rather than a club problem. He had problems and I think he tried to put them on the club and his team-mates."

Diary of the Decade

1999

MARCH

9 - Paraguayan Miguel Dominquez returns home after his trial

12 - *West Brom's Lee Hughes is the latest name linked with a move to Boro - Northern Echo*

18 - Press stories say Boro are set to fly to Brazil in an attempt to sign 19-year-old teenage sensation Rodrigo Gral

19 - Keith O'Neill signs from Norwich for £700,000

21 - Defender Steve Vickers clocks up his 500th League appearance in a 2-1 win over a Nottingham Forest at the City Ground

24 - Speculation hots up in the national press that Boro are set to bring Juninho back to Teesside

26 - Juninho duly returns to the Riverside . . . but only for a friendly with Atletico Madrid; Mikkel Beck joins Derby for £500,000

APRIL

7 - *Boro are closing in on Roma's £6m-rated striker Marco Delvecchio - Sun*

10 - *Rumours are sweeping Teesside that Boro are poised to sign French dream-weaver Zinedine Zidane - Gazette*

21 - *Sheffield Utd are poised to test Boro's resolve to hang on to Andy Campbell - Gazette*

25 - *Robson wants to make Robbie Fowler Middlesbrough's record £10 million signing - People; Kevin Keegan has lined up an audacious £2 million bid to take Paul Gascoigne to Fulham - Sunday Sun; Brazilian star Emerson will definitely return to Middlesbrough in the summer - Sunday Sun*

29 - *Robson wants Paul Ince to join his old boys' brigade at Middlesbrough - Sun*

30 - *Boro are planning a £1.5m swoop for Brentford's Lloyd Owusu - Star*

MAY

4 - *Robson has sounded out Dynamo Kiev striker Sergei Rebrov about a £10 million move to the Riverside - Mirror*

9 - *Parma are bidding to snatch Juninho from beneath the noses of Middlesbrough - Sunday Sun*

16 - Boro lose 4-0 at West Ham on the last day of the season - and the Londoners pip them to a place in the Intertoto Cup

20 - *Robson is set to take a close-up look at West Brom's Lee Hughes - Gazette*

22 - *Forget Juninho - the brilliant Brazilian will almost certainly not be coming back to the Riverside - Gazette*

25 - *Emerson is set to return to Middlesbrough this week in a £3m deal - Yorkshire Post*

30 - *Boro are ready to slug it out with Leeds for Dutch striker Roy Makaay - Sunday Sun*

While Merson went off to pastures new, two old favourites were making their way back to Teesside. Gary Pallister had left for Manchester United in 1989 and returned to his hometown club for £2.5m. On his return he explained: "It's now a completely different club. If it was the old club I wouldn't have come back because it lacked ambition." However, the defender would make just 55 Premiership starts in his second spell before he was forced to retire through a knee injury in 2000-01.

More durable was another £2.5m buy Colin Cooper, the defender who had come through the ranks with Pallister before leaving for Millwall in 1991 prior to a long spell with Nottingham Forest. Now he was back where his career had started, and in 2005 he signed a one-year playing contract that would take him past his 39th birthday.

"I had some great professionals in that squad," recalled Robson. "It would be difficult to find lads that have as good an attitude as Cooper and Andy Townsend." Add to that the experience of ex-Inter Milan defender Gianluca Festa and veteran midfielder Robbie Mustoe and Boro looked to be one of the most solid teams in the top flight – which would be shown in their impressive haul of 13 clean sheets through the campaign. The flip side was that some thought Boro were now too cautious a side, a theory backed up by no less than 15 draws in 38 Premiership fixtures.

Pallister made his first Boro appearance in nine years when he started against Leicester City in the fourth game of the season, and his former England colleague Paul Gascoigne scored a great free-kick to gift Robson a first win of the season – proof that there could be life after Merson. Within days another away victory saw Hamilton Ricard cap a superb front-running performance by grabbing a brace as Tottenham were defeated 3-0. While Robson was pleased with four goals he was even more ecstatic about three clean sheets in the opening five games, particularly as a leaky defence had been seen as the main reason for relegation two seasons previously.

Robson had opted for a five-man defence with another newcomer, left back Dean Gordon, fitting in alongside Curtis Fleming, Festa, Pallister and Cooper. The £900,000 signing from Crystal Palace looked comfortable in his defending duties but was also keen to get up front as often as possible, which was certainly the case as Boro put Sheffield Wednesday to the sword at the Riverside on October 3. Mikkel Beck scored twice, just after being recalled to the Denmark international squad, and was only denied a hat-trick by a debatable offside flag.

Ricard only grabbed one on that afternoon, but it was his eighth goal of the campaign and, after the Colombian's disappointing start to his time on Teesside, Boro finally looked to have a suitable Premiership replacement for Fabrizio Ravanelli. With his unorthodox style and quick feet, Ricard was a revelation for Boro throughout the campaign. While the win over the Owls was a first at home, it would be quickly followed by victory over Blackburn Rovers, as Boro cruised into fifth in the league table despite missing forwards Alun Armstrong and Marco Branca with long-term injuries.

• LOOK WHO'S BACK - Gary Pallister returned to Teesside after a glittering Old Trafford career

Riverside X

Diary of the Decade

• TURMOIL - Bryan Robson and Paul Gascoigne appear before the cameras after the midfielder's hospital treatment

Also on target against Wednesday was Gascoigne, who looked to have put behind him the disappointment of missing out on the previous summer's World Cup squad to add much-needed creativity to Boro's midfield. But it was to be the midfielder's final game before he was admitted to hospital to battle alcohol and stress problems. In a blaze of national publicity, Gazza would spend two weeks at the famous Priory clinic as he sought to battle his demons, before returning to training with Boro on an initial part-time basis. Ahead of his return against Nottingham Forest, the England legend said: "The fans have been brilliant for me, sending me cards and good wishes. That was a big help. I'm just concentrating on doing well for Boro for now. Bryan Robson brought me here to play football and that's what I want to do."

Gascoigne would show that he was on the right lines as he grabbed a goal in his second game back, helping his side to a draw at Charlton Athletic. Another point at Highbury in front of the television cameras thanks to a goal from newcomer Brian Deane which could have been a winner but for a last-minute Arsenal equaliser, would leave Boro in seventh place going into December and eight games unbeaten in the Premiership. Deane, formerly with Sheffield United and Leeds, had arrived in October from Benfica, and was developing a tough front-line partnership with Ricard.

1999

JUNE

3 - Boro announce plans to raise stadium capacity to 35,000

4 - *Steve Bruce wants to make striker Andy Campbell one of his first signings at Huddersfield - Journal*

5 - Boro announce building of Premier League's biggest town-centre retail outlet in Captain Cook Square

17 - *Boro have lined up a £4 million swoop for French midfielder Ibrahim Ba - Mirror*

18 - *Boro have verbally agreed a £6.5 million deal to sign Wolves striker Robbie Keane - Gazette*

24 - *Boro have made a £6m bid for Spurs ace Darren Anderton - Daily Sport*

25 - *Robson has bid £6 million for Ipswich wonder-kid Kieron Dyer - Mirror*

JULY

20 - *Robson has made Stig Inge Bjornebye his second signing target at Liverpool - Mirror*

21 - *Robson ready to lure Brazilian ace Leonardo with £60,000-a-week deal - Express*

22 - Robson confirms that Robbie Keane deal is dead

30 - Paul Ince signs from Liverpool for £1 million and Christian Ziege from AC Milan for £4m

AUGUST

4 - Marco Branca fails in an attempt to reverse MFC's decision to terminate his contract

4 - *Boro have pulled out of a bid to re-sign Emerson after Tenerife unexpectedly doubled their asking price to £8 million - Mirror*

8 - *Brian Little is keen to make Andy Campbell his first signing as boss of West Brom - S People*

19 - Dean Gordon out for the rest of the season after snapping his cruciate knee ligament

28 - Boro announce that Juninho is coming "home" on loan from Atletico Madrid

29 - Boro agree £1.5m fee with Argentine side Boca Juniors for Carlos Marinelli

SEPTEMBER

6 - AC Milan midfielder Ibrahim Ba turns down the chance to join Boro

17 - Andy Townsend signs for West Brom

20 - Juninho returns to the club on loan from Atletico Madrid and a crowd of 25,602 arrives at the Riverside to see him make his return debut against Chesterfield

• DEANO-MITE! - Brian Deane is chased by Manchester United's Phil Neville in Boro's stunning 3-2 win at Old Trafford

Neither would score in a 2-2 draw with Newcastle – the goals courtesy of unsung heroes Cooper and Townsend in early December – but Deane would grab a vital home winner against West Ham United the following week. And then both would be on hand in the next league game.

On a great run, Boro had high hopes travelling to Old Trafford for a Premiership fixture a week ahead of Christmas, despite Gascoigne missing the trip through suspension. But Boro produced one of their greatest performances in recent memory as they went 3-0 up in the first hour, before late strikes courtesy of Nicky Butt and Paul Scholes created a grandstand finish.

Ricard, Gordon and Deane were the heroic goalscorers, and David Miller of the *Daily Telegraph* mused: "The main question raised by Middlesbrough's first win at Old

Trafford since 1930 is not whether Manchester United can regain the title, but whether Middlesbrough, a point behind them in fourth place, may win the championship for the first time."

Robson added: "What pleased me most was that we looked like scoring every time we went forward. We could have easily scored a fourth goal." But the glorious run would soon come to an end, with United going on to complete a Premiership, FA Cup and Champions League treble by May, and Boro sinking down the table thanks to a nightmare second half of the season. The rot began just seven days after the triumph in Manchester with a 3-1 home defeat to Liverpool. Although it was Boro's first home defeat for 12 months, it was a loss that would set a worrying trend during the following months.

A nightmare three months went by without a single win following the glorious trip to Old Trafford. Derby, Leeds, Liverpool and Sheffield Wednesday would all enjoy

RiversideX Diary of the Decade

themselves against Boro, with Manchester United also gaining revenge with a 3-1 FA Cup win in January. But the lowest point came at Goodison Park as mid-table Everton won 5-0 on a miserable Wednesday night for a deflated Boro. Ex-Riverside forward Nick Barmby opened the scoring after 45 seconds and matters would not get better for the rest of the evening. Robson said: "A lot of fans travelled to Everton and must have been very upset. Many left early and I wanted to leave with them. With the away form we have shown, we are going to be dragged into a relegation battle."

Robson locked his players in the Goodison dressing rooms for an hour after the game finished, but it would be another month before matters improved as back-to-back wins over Nottingham Forest and Southampton were achieved. A fantastic Easter saw Boro climb above the 42-point mark – and, it was hoped, Premiership safety – with a draw at Blackburn and wins over Wimbledon and Charlton. Ricard had again found his scoring boots in those five games, grabbing five goals to take his tally to 16 for the season with six games remaining.

Once again, Europe looked a possibility for Robson's side, particularly with Armstrong back from his Achilles problem and Deane back on form after a niggling injury.

• REVELATION - Hamilton Ricard enjoyed a great season leading the attack

1999

OCTOBER

1 - Paul Ince recalled to England squad for the first time in 13 months

5 - Exhausted striker Hamilton Ricard ordered to take a week off to recharge his batteries

6 - *Ambitious Huddersfield are ready to make a £1m bid for Andy Campbell - N. Echo*

17 - *Robson is considering a £4 million double raid on Crystal Palace for defender Hayden Mullins and striker Mathias Svensson - Sunday Sun*

27 - Robson officially opens the club's new retail store - the biggest outside Manchester United - in Captain Cook Square

27 - Crowd of 7,000 turns out to watch Carlos Marinelli make his debut for the reserves against Barnsley

NOVEMBER

9 - Brian Deane charged with misconduct following an incident with Paul Butler

14 - Paul Ince allegedly announces decision to quit international football after Euro 2000

28 - Former FA Chief Executive Graham Kelly completes his 200-mile charity walk to see Juninho play

DECEMBER

17 - Robson denies crisis after Worthington Cup final defeat to Tranmere; Brian Deane gets one-match ban for elbowing Paul Butler

24 - Juninho launches his official website

26 - *Robson is lining up a shock loan deal for top German striker Oliver Bierhoff - Gazette*

29 - Severe frost causes postponement of home match with Coventry

31 - Viv Anderson receives MBE in New Year's Honours List

2000

JANUARY

2 - *Bryan Robson will walk out on Middlesbrough at the end of the season - S. People*

3 - *Boro have been linked with England star Darren Anderton - Gazette*

5 - *Robson is ready to land Mexico striker Carlos Pavon - Mail; Robson has checked on Huddersfield striker Marcus Stewart - Journal*

7 - *Robson has targeted Ipswich star David Johnson - Star*

10 - Boro beat Shelbourne 3-2 in a friendly in Dublin

FEBRUARY

1 - Steve Gibson takes full control after buying out the ICI's 25 per cent shareholding

Despite the final three home games of the season coming against the three sides competing for the Premiership title – Chelsea, Arsenal and Manchester United – the manager had high ambitions. He said: "We want to finish the season on a high and end up as far up the table as possible. It is all down to the pride of the players. I also want to continue to make the Riverside a fortress." A 'fortress' the stadium certainly was as, despite the poor run, Boro had conceded just one goal at home in the first four months of 1999.

That record was improved against Chelsea – although it was a fourth goalless game in seven home fixtures – as Gianluca Vialli's side was held on April 14, and soon another fantastic win had been recorded as Gordon and substitute Townsend scored in a 2-1 defeat of Coventry City. Boro were in seventh spot in the league and just two points behind fifth-placed Aston Villa, who held the final UEFA Cup qualifying spot.

So it was with great anticipation that 34,630 crammed into the Riverside for the visit of Premiership leaders Arsenal on April 24. Robson understood the tough task ahead of his side as he admitted: "They are a very difficult side to beat and have an outstanding defensive record." But it was Arsene Wenger's forwards who impressed on an awful afternoon for Boro, but a good day for Arsenal and football as the Gunners produced a breath-taking performance to win 6-1. Marc Overmars opened the scoring with a fourth-minute penalty, and Nicolas Anelka and Kanu would grab braces with Patrick Vieira also on target. It was left for Armstrong to score his first Premiership goal in the final moments to produce a meaningless consolation. It was the club's biggest home defeat in 100 years of league football, as they conceded six goals at home for the first time since 1909.

Robson was magnanimous in defeat and said: "It was the best performance I have seen against us since I became manager

• DUAL ACTION - Steve Vickers (right) and Colin Cooper snub out Chelsea's Tore Andre Flo

but it always hurts to lose heavily." Boro somehow bounced back to gain a hard-earned point at Newcastle the following weekend, with Mustoe – who shared the supporters' player of the year gong with Ricard – scoring at St James' Park, while Manchester United won the final Riverside game of the season 1-0.

The campaign concluded in poor style as Boro were on the end of another hammering, coincidentally at the hands of West Ham United, who grabbed that fifth place in the table that had looked reachable for Robson. It was a poor finale to a wretched second half of the campaign, another which had promised so much but delivered little – although ninth place was the club's Premiership record high until 2004-05.

Mustoe added: "It was a good season, although we did have a bad run in the middle and we consolidated. I think everyone was really pleased with what we achieved, especially as it was the first season back in the Premiership."

While it was a case of ifs, buts and maybes on the pitch, matters off the park looked to be getting better and better. The club finally opened a training ground to match

Riverside X

Diary of the Decade

its Premiership prestige when the Rockliffe Park HQ was opened in October 1998. Set in 187 acres at Hurworth Place, near Darlington, Boro could impress potential signings by offering them the most up-to-date medical and sports science facilities in the Premiership as well as an indoor sports hall, plush dressing rooms and restaurant.

Steve Gibson recalled: "Fabrizio Ravanelli had made us aware of where we needed to go with his moaning about the training facilities. But our infrastructure soon caught up as Keith Lamb and Bryan travelled the world in finding out what needed to be done. They went to Italy, Spain and Germany, and Rockliffe was the result of that research."

The idea that a training ground could influence a player in joining the club was proved in 2001 when England defender Gareth Southgate moved from Aston Villa to Teesside. Southgate said: "As a professional you want everything to be right. When I joined Villa their training ground was one of the best in the country but six years on and it had fallen behind. Even now, after seven or eight years, Rockcliffe is as good as anything in the country. I have been fortunate with England to have seen a lot of facilities, and it's a match for any of them."

• NOT ANOTHER - Mark Schwarzer can't believe it as Boro are beaten 6-1 by Arsenal

2000

FEBRUARY

5 - *Robson is on the trail of French hitman David Trezeguet - Star*

10 - *Boro have joined the race for Atletico Madrid's Jimmy Floyd Hasselbaink - Mail*

14 - Boro lose 4-0 at home to Villa in Valentine's Day Massacre, a game in which Gazza breaks his arm after clash with George Boateng

16 - *Robson could be out of a job before the end of the month - Mirror*

MARCH

1 - Boro beat Newcastle 2-1 to reach FA Youth Cup semi-finals

2 - Gascoigne fined £5,000 and banned for three matches for elbowing George Boateng

4 - Dean Gordon back in action at Southampton after knee injury

7 - *Boro are ready to join the race for Bolton striker Eidur Gudjohnsen - Star*

12 - *Boro will make a £3m move for Titi Camara - Mirror*

22 - *Boro are hot on the trail of Torquay centre-back Wayne Thomas - N. Echo*

23 - Andy Campbell and Robbie Stockdale sign new four-year contracts

28 - Boro sign media partnership deal with ntl, who will take a 5.585 per cent stake in the club; Andy Campbell scores on his England U-21 debut against Yugoslavia; *Robson is targeting Hertha Berlin midfielder Sebastian Deisler as one of his summer signings - N. Echo*

30 - *Boro have run a check on Barnsley's highly-rated centre-back Chris Morgan - N. Echo*

APRIL

2 - Boro announce two-game trip to Libya

6 - *Christian Ziege has laughed off talk of a shock move to Liverpool - Sun*

12 - Boro lose 2-1 on aggregate to Arsenal in FA Youth Cup semi-final

14 - Golden Boy Wilf Mannion dies, age 81

28 - *Robson has been in talks with French World Cup star Christian Karembeu about a £5m move to Boro - Mirror*

MAY

7 - *Boro are targeting Mexican hotshot Luis Hernandez - Sunday Sun*

7 - *Robson is ready to splash out £14m on Jimmy Floyd Hasselbaink - Sun People*

9 - *Boro have stepped up their interest in Barnsley's £3m rated defender Chris Morgan - N. Echo*

11 - Robson knocks down stories that Paul Gascoigne is heading to Australia for the summer

16 - Boro undertake two-match tour of Libya, losing 1-0 to Tripoli and 2-0 to Bari

Riverside X

Season Stats 1998-99

	P	Home						Away						Pts	GD	H	A
		W	D	L	F	A		W	D	L	F	A				
Manchester Utd	38	14	4	1	45	18		8	9	2	35	19	79	+43	0-1	3-2
Arsenal	38	14	5	0	34	5		8	7	4	25	12	78	+42	1-6	1-1
Chelsea	38	12	6	1	29	13		8	9	2	28	17	75	+27	0-0	0-2
Leeds Utd	38	12	5	2	32	9		6	8	5	30	25	67	+28	0-0	0-2
West Ham Utd	38	11	3	5	32	26		5	6	8	14	27	57	-7	1-0	0-4
Aston Villa	38	10	3	6	33	28		5	7	7	18	18	55	+5	0-0	1-3
Liverpool	38	10	5	4	44	24		5	4	10	24	25	54	+19	1-3	1-3
Derby County	38	8	7	4	22	19		5	6	8	18	26	52	-5	1-1	1-2
BORO	38	7	9	3	25	18		5	6	8	23	36	51	-6	-	-
Leicester City	38	7	6	6	25	25		5	7	7	15	21	49	-6	0-0	1-0
Tottenham Hotspur	38	7	7	5	28	26		4	7	8	19	24	47	-3	0-0	3-0
Sheffield Wed	38	7	5	7	20	15		6	2	11	21	27	46	-1	4-0	1-3
Newcastle Utd	38	7	6	6	26	25		4	7	8	22	29	46	-6	2-2	1-1
Everton	38	6	8	5	22	12		5	2	12	20	35	43	-5	2-2	0-5
Coventry City	38	8	6	5	26	21		3	3	13	13	30	42	-12	2-0	2-1
Wimbledon	38	7	7	5	22	21		3	5	11	18	42	42	-23	3-1	2-2
Southampton	38	9	4	6	29	26		2	4	13	8	38	41	-27	3-0	3-3
Charlton Athletic	38	4	7	8	20	20		4	5	10	21	36	36	-15	2-0	1-1
Blackburn Rovers	38	6	5	8	21	24		1	9	9	17	28	35	-14	2-1	0-0
Nottingham Forest	38	3	7	9	18	31		4	2	13	17	38	30	-34	1-1	2-1

CHAMPIONS LEAGUE · UEFA CUP · RELEGATED

Goals

Name	Prem	Total
Hamilton RICARD	15	18
Brian DEANE	6	6
Mikkel BECK	5	5
Robbie MUSTOE	4	4
Paul GASCOIGNE	3	3
Dean GORDON	3	3
Gianluca FESTA	2	3
Vladimir KINDER	2	2
Phil STAMP	2	2
Andy TOWNSEND	1	2
Alun ARMSTRONG	1	1
Colin COOPER	1	1
Curtis FLEMING	1	1
Steve VICKERS	1	1
Mark SUMMERBELL	0	1

Player of the Year

Cellnet
Hamilton Ricard

Supporters
Hamilton Ricard/Robbie Mustoe

Appearances

	Prem	FAC	LC	UEFA	Total
Dean **GORDON**	38	1	2	0	41
Andy **TOWNSEND**	35	1	1	0	37
Hamilton **RICARD**	32(4)	1	3	0	36(4)
Mark **SCHWARZER**	34	1	0	0	35
Robbie **MUSTOE**	32(1)	1	1	0	34(1)
Colin **COOPER**	31(1)	1	1	0	33(1)
Steve **VICKERS**	30(1)	0	3	0	33(1)
Paul **GASCOIGNE**	25(1)	1	2	0	28(1)
Gary **PALLISTER**	26	0	1	0	27
Gianluca **FESTA**	25	0	2	0	27
Brian **DEANE**	24(2)	1	0(1)	0	25(3)
Robbie **STOCKDALE**	17(2)	0	3(1)	0	20(3)
Mikkel **BECK**	13(14)	0(1)	2	0	15(15)
Curtis **FLEMING**	12(2)	1	1	0	14(2)
Neil **MADDISON**	10(11)	1	1	0	12(11)
Phil **STAMP**	5(11)	0(1)	3	0	8(12)
Mark **SUMMERBELL**	7(4)	0	0(2)	0	7(6)
Marlon **BERESFORD**	4	0	3	0	7
Keith **O'NEILL**	4(2)	0	0	0	4(2)
Craig **HARRISON**	3(1)	0	1(1)	0	4(2)
Alan **MOORE**	3(1)	0	1	0	4(1)
Paul **MERSON**	3	0	0	0	3
Andy **CAMPBELL**	1(7)	0	1(2)	0	2(9)
Jason **GAVIN**	2	0	0	0	2
Vladimir **KINDER**	0(6)	0	1(1)	0	1(7)
Steve **BAKER**	1(1)	0	0	0	1(1)
Michael **CUMMINS**	1	0	0	0	1
Clayton **BLACKMORE**	0	0	1	0	1
Alun **ARMSTRONG**	0(6)	0	0	0	0(6)
Marco **BRANCA**	0(1)	0	0	0	0(1)
Anthony **ORMEROD**	0	0	0(1)	0	0(1)

1998-99 Round-up

Premiership Manchester United	
FA Cup Manchester United	
League Cup Tottenham	
Champions League Manchester United	
Cup Winners' Cup Lazio	
UEFA Cup Parma	
PFA Player of the Year David Ginola (Tottenham)	
PFA Young Player Nicolas Anelka (Arsenal)	
Promoted Sunderland, Bradford City, Watford	

Line-Up

League Form

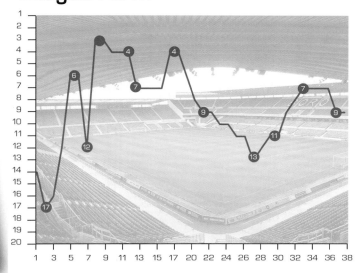

1999-00

Boro approached the dawn of the new millennium in good shape on and off the field. Following a top-10 finish in the previous campaign, Bryan Robson was more intent on fine tuning than major overhaul. The two biggest arrivals were significant captures who were to play key roles for the club.

The arrival of German international wing-back Christian Ziege cushioned the blow following the loss of Dean Gordon to a cruciate injury in only the third game of the season. Ziege had fallen out of favour at AC Milan when Robson invested £4m to rescue his career in the Premiership. All summer there had been speculation that Boro would move in for Ipswich's highly-rated Kieron Dyer, who eventually moved to Newcastle.

Robson was convinced Ziege offered better value. "I had the option of Ziege, an experienced German international, for £4m or Dyer, unproven at the top level, for £6m. Dyer is undeniably a top player but I think I got the best deal," he said shortly after the transfer was sealed. The Boro manager had been impressed by Ziege's performance for Germany in Euro 96 where he was "one of the three best left-backs in the world."

"Ziege surprised me because he was in AC Milan reserves and hadn't played for quite a time," he said. "He found himself out of the German team but then he came in and had a terrific season, winning the player of the year award."

Ziege was an instant success at the Riverside, eventually winning the club's Player of the Year award. Deadly accurate from long-range kicks, he was also a precision crosser. He got back into the German national side on the back of some fine performances at the Riverside. His stay, however, was set to be brief and, in the end, controversial.

Paul Ince had enjoyed an eventful, high-profile career with West Ham, Manchester United and AC Milan before life at Liverpool turned sour. The England midfielder had endured a high-profile fall-

Diary of the Decade

2000

MAY

18 - *Boro have joined Leicester on the trail of Lens striker Pascal Nouma - N. Echo*

21 - 25,000 attend Millennium Roman Catholic mass at Riverside

28 - *Liverpool are weighing up a £6m bid for Christian Ziege - News of World*

JUNE

1 - Boro announce 3% season-ticket rise.

6 - *Bryan Robson determined to hang on to Hamilton Ricard despite interest from Lens - Gazette.*

7 - Boro linked to Aston Villa wing-back Steve Watson (he eventually signs for Everton).

19 - *Fabrizio Ravanelli dreams of becoming Boro boss - Northern Echo.*

24 - *Boro are taking a fresh look at France striker Sylvain Wiltord - Northern Echo.*

28 - Boro target £6m Chelsea striker Chris Sutton (he eventually joins Celtic).

29 - *Blackburn are ready to bid £2m for Brian Deane - Express.*

JULY

5 - Christian Karembeu signs from Real Madrid for £2.1m

7 - Alen Boksic officially becomes a Boro player

11 - *Boro are making a stunning £6.5m bid for Leicester's Neil Lennon - Mirror*

16 - Paul Gascoigne joins Everton on a free transfer

18 - Goalkeeper Mark Crossley arrives on a Bosman-style free transfer from Nottingham Forest

19 - Australian Paul Okon signs on a free transfer from Fiorentina; Richard Piers Rayner appointed Boro Artist in Residence

23 - *Robson is set to renew his interest in Nigeria's Finidi George - Sunday Sun*

24 - Liverpool make a formal £5.5m bid for Christian Ziege

28 - Boro express interest in Real Madrid's Steve McManaman

AUGUST

3 - Bryan Robson fails in bid to bring Juninho back to Boro - he goes back to Brazil with Vasco da Gama on a season's loan.

5 - Boro complete the double signing of Coventry's Noel Whelan for £2m and Cameroon international Joseph-Desire Job, from Lens, for £3m.

6 - Robbie Mustoe is rewarded for ten years' service with testimonial match against Borussia Dortmund, which Boro lose 2-0; *Robson in the chase for Manchester United pair Henning Berg and David May - Sunday Sun.*

9 - *Robson is ready to launch a last-ditch bid to bring Steve McManaman to Boro - Northern Echo.*

out with Gerard Houllier and was anxious for a new start. The deal was attractive, with Boro paying just £1m for his signature, but did he still have the hunger and desire?

Any doubts were soon dispelled as Ince quickly became indispensable as Boro's highly-committed midfield leader. Team-mates, opponents and match officials never got a moment's peace with the motormouth skipper, who demanded the highest standards from those around him. Ince kept his family home on Merseyside and made an arduous 300-mile round journey to training, but travel weariness never impacted on his performances. "I knew Paul Ince would be a good, solid signing because I had played with him at Man United," said Robson.

• BARGAN BUY - Paul Ince proved to be one of Bryan Robson's best ever signings

Pre-season building work had increased the capacity of the Riverside Stadium by almost 5,000, to its current level of 35,100. There remains built-in capability to increase seating even further, if and when desired, by raising the level of the north, east and south stand roves to match that of the west stand.

The campaign got off to a disappointing start with a shock home defeat to newly-promoted Bradford City. But three successive wins against Wimbledon, Derby and Liverpool saw Boro join the early pacemakers. Ziege showed his star quality by scoring with trademark free-kicks as Boro turned on three-goal displays at both Wimbledon and Derby, before the Liverpool win took Boro to second with just four games played.

Top place beckoned if three points could be won at home to Leicester City in late August, but a crushing 3-0 home defeat brought players and fans alike crashing back to reality. Further poor results set the alarm bells ringing, but Robson sparked major excitement by bringing Juninho back to the Riverside.

Teesside's favourite Brazilian had endured an unhappy spell in Spain with Atletico Madrid. In February 1998, less than six months after leaving the Riverside, he had broken his leg in a Spanish First Division match at Celta Vigo. Coach Raddy Antic, with whom he had forged a strong bond, had left the club and Juninho's relationship with Atletico was rapidly deteriorating.

Robson, and chairman Steve Gibson, had kept close tabs on him and, in September 1999, took the opportunity to bring him back on a short-term contract. Robson saw it as an opportunity to assess the player's form and fitness without commitment to a major transfer fee. The player was clearly not the force he was.

"Juninho had been affected a little bit by the injury he sustained and it took a percentage away from his game," said Robson. "When I knew that I could get him back on loan it was a good way to assess him because Atletico Madrid were still asking for a big transfer fee and Juninho was on big wages at that time. You had to balance whether it was sentiment to bring him back or whether it was good business."

Riverside X

Diary of the Decade

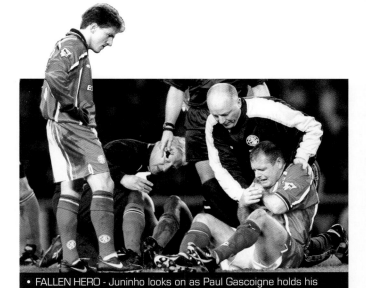

• FALLEN HERO - Juninho looks on as Paul Gascoigne holds his broken arm after swinging it wildly at Aston Villa's George Boateng

Juninho's return certainly played well with supporters. A crowd of 25,602 arrived at the Riverside to see him make his return debut in a Worthington Cup tie against Chesterfield. The attendance was probably 15,000 more than Boro would usually have expected. For many, he could do no wrong and Robson regularly attracted criticism whenever he substituted the Brazilian or left him on the bench. Another problem was that he was deployed in deeper positions where he was much less effective.

Atletico were reputedly asking £10m to do a permanent deal and Juninho has confirmed that he was keen to come back for good. "It very nearly happened," he said. "I had a problem at Atletico Madrid with the coach, Arrigo Saachi. I was not happy because I was playing one game then I was out the next. I was also unhappy with Saachi's style of management.

"I came close to leaving but at the same time I said 'No, I came here and I need to show I have the talent to succeed here'. My first six months at Atletico Madrid were wonderful but after that I got injured. It was then that my problems started.

"At that time it was only my second season with Atletico and I wanted to prove I could play whatever the system was. That's why I didn't leave. A voice inside was saying 'You need to stay and prove you can play whatever the system is and prove to Arrigo Saachi you can adapt to his style and help him get results,'"

2000

AUGUST

12 - *Ziege finally signs for Liverpool; Boro close in on Aston Villa's Ugo Ehiogu - Gazette.*

19 - Boksic scores twice on his debut as Boro win 3-1 at Coventry in opening game.

29 - Boro legend Willie Maddren dies aged 49 after his brave five-year battle against motor neurone disease.

SEPTEMBER

10 - Robson denies reports that Hamilton Ricard is on his way out of Boro

13 - *Ziege claims he received death threats at his Hutton Rudby home following his acrimonious transfer to Liverpool - Gazette*

14 - *Ricard pledges to stay and fight for his place at Boro - Northern Echo.*

15 - Former Boro keeper Gary Walsh signs on loan from Bradford to ease keeper crisis

24 - *Bryan Robson is lining up a shock £4.5m swoop for Blackburn reject Lucien Mettomo - Sunday Sun*

26 - Ricard scores hat-trick in 3-1 Worthington Cup replay win over Macclesfield.

30 - Alen Boksic hits two in 3-1 win at Southampton.

OCTOBER

4 - Magazine survey reveals Boro are England's best supported team per head of local population; *Hamilton Ricard has opened talks over a contract extension - Gazette.*

12 - Adriana Karembeu hits out at national newspaper reports that she is unhappy on Teesside.

16 - Club unveils statue to Wilf Mannion outside stadium; Boro suffer 3-1 home derby defeat to Newcastle.

19 - *Boro are making a sensational £10m double swoop for AC Milan midfielder Zvonimir Boban and Aston Villa defender Ugo Ehiogu - Gazette.*

20 - Ehiogu signs for a record £8m.

21 - Ehiogu's debut cut short after just five minutes when he tears a calf muscle in 1-0 defeat at Charlton

25 - *Boro are ready to make a renewed bid for Parma international midfielder Dino Baggio - Gazette.*

26 - *Boban has turned his back on Teesside by agreeing to spend the rest of his career at Milan - Mirror; Boro have pulled out of a £1m move for Australian defender Simon Colosimo - N. Echo.*

27 - *Boksic reveals he may quit international football - N. Echo.*

31 - *Bryan Robson has revealed how hundreds of messages of support from Boro fans have strengthemed his resolve to stay at the Riverside - N. Echo.*

NOVEMBER

1 - Death of former Boro coach George Armstrong.

2 - Boro launch new official website www.mfc.co.uk.

• TAKE THAT - Juninho takes a free-kick, watched by Christian Ziege, against Leeds United

Juninho admits it was a difficult nine months during the middle period of his Riverside career. "Bryan Robson took me back but at the same time he wasn't sure if I could be the same player again after the injury. Everybody was talking about that but I hadn't even been that badly injured. I was playing again after just three months out.

"Also, in football, you have to live with the possibility that you can be out for six to seven months and then still come back and play at the highest level. Why not? That's why I didn't like that time. People judged me because of the injury even though it was fine. It was perfect, but people thought I couldn't be the same player.

"I think Bryan Robson thought that. At that time Paul Ince and other leaders were in the team. Maybe they wanted the team to be more tactical or defensive, and they played me up front or in a more defensive position because they didn't want to change the style of play. Maybe it was because of the influence of Paul Ince and others, I don't know. But it was not a good season for me because of that."

Following Juninho's arrival, there was initially every reason to believe he could

pick up from where he left off two years earlier. When Robson temporarily moved Ziege into an attacking midfield role, the German's combination with Juninho and Ince looked extremely promising. Surely, this was a midfield to match any other for class and experience? West Ham, Watford and Everton were beaten in quick succession as the team pushed up to sixth place.

But, with Juninho struggling to make a real impact, short-term injuries to Ziege and Ince left fans in no doubt that Boro lacked depth in quality.

Planning ahead, Boro had introduced another talented South American to the squad. Carlos Marinelli was just 17 when he signed from Argentine side Boca Juniors in August 1999. One of the most naturally talented players ever to don a Middlesbrough shirt, he was labelled 'the new Maradona'. Even though Marinelli was very much one for the future, a crowd of 7,000 attended the Riverside to see the midfielder make his debut for the reserves against Barnsley.

Boro's third South American, Hamilton Ricard, was again the main attacking thrust. Unpredictable, and sometimes ungainly, he maintained his powerful partnership with Brian Deane, Ricard again top-scoring with 14 goals in all competitions and Deane grabbing 10. At this point, Ricard was busily criss-crossing the Atlantic to play for his native Colombia and, in October, the exhausted striker was ordered to take a week off to recharge his batteries.

Riverside X

Diary of the Decade

As so often, Boro performed well up to Christmas before their traditional New Year wobble. A Boxing Day defeat at Sheffield Wednesday was the start of a worrying run of five defeats in six matches, culminating in a 4-0 home loss to Aston Villa that saw the side plunge to the fringe of the relegation struggle. Just as depressing were exits from the two major cup competitions within three days in mid-December. Boro were turned over by Division Two club Wrexham in the third round of the FA Cup before a disastrous trip to Division One side Tranmere in the quarter-finals of the Worthington Cup.

Paul Gascoigne, wracked by injuries, made just seven league appearances in a constantly-changing midfield. His season came to a premature end when he broke his arm in the Valentine's Day massacre by Aston Villa that was transmitted on live TV by Sky. The arm-swinging challenge was on George Boateng – later to wear Boro colours, of course – and it cost him a £5,000 fine.

Andy Townsend, a steadying influence in the 1997-98 promotion side, had moved on to West Bromwich. Ince got back into the England squad for the first time in 13 months and Mark Summerbell enjoyed his only sustained run in the first-team during the second half of the campaign. Keith O'Neill, who had joined from Norwich late in the previous season, looked promising but was injury-prone.

• GIVEN THE ELBOW - Keith O'Neill's injuries held back his progress

1997

MARCH

6 - Chairman Steve Gibson accuses Liverpool of "lies and deceit" over alleged illegal approach for Christian Ziege.

8 - *Boro are leading the chase for Norwegian whizzkid Morten Gamst Pedersen - Gazette.*

14 - Gianluca Festa goes on transfer list at his own request.

16 - Boro fan David Golightly launches Boro Symphony in tribute to the club and Chairman Steve Gibson.

17 - *Finnish ace Jari Litmanen is being eyed up by Newcastle and Middlesbrough - N. Echo; Bryan Robson has targeted Finland defender Hannu Tihinen - Daily Mail.*

18 - Pressure mounts as Boro lose 3-0 at home to Leicester.

24 - *Greek club Panathinaikos are being linked with a surprise move for Alen Boksic - N. Echo; Bryan Robson's £3m bid for Derby defender Rory Delap has been knocked back - Express.*

DECEMBER

1 - Terry Venables approached to help Bryan Robson but claims it is "impossible" to juggle the job with TV commitments; Boro get go-ahead to build multi-million-pound four-star hotel at Rockliffe Hall.

3 - *Middlesbrough will offer Kevin Keegan £8m to take over from Bryan Robson following the breakdown of talks with Terry Venables - Sunday Mirror.*

4 - After more negotiations, Venables accepts short-term contract to become Head Coach.

8 - Alun Armstrong agrees £500,000 move to Ipswich.

10 - *Venables' first target will be Spurs winger Darren Anderton - Sunday Mirror.*

16 - Venables off to a winning start with 1-0 home triumph over Chelsea.

24 - *Terry Venables has lined up a £1.5m move for Bradford's Dean Windass - People.*

25 - *Boro are tracking Scottish wonderkid Kevin McNaughton at Aberdeen - Gazette.*

28 - *Boro have told Arsenal they can have Mark Schwarzer - if they can come up with £50m - Journal.*

2001

JANUARY

4 - Gary Pallister undergoes surgery for a chronic back problem.

8 - Ricard hits FA Cup third-round winner at Bradford.

10 - Mark Schwarzer and Paul Okon excused Australia's World Cup qualifiers to concentrate on Boro relegation fight.

13 - Boro record biggest win of season when they beat Derby 4-0 at Riverside.

16 - Transfer-listed Festa linked with Chelsea.

22 - New England coach Sven Goran Eriksson visits Rockliffe Park.

Speedy youngster Andy Campbell, who was to win the Supporters Club's Young Player of the Year award, enjoyed a purple patch early in 2000 that earned him England junior honours. He scored four goals in 13 games as Boro loitered in mid-table during early spring. His form attracted bids from Huddersfield and Sheffield United. He also scored on his England U-21 debut against Yugoslavia on March 28 and, like fellow teenager Robbie Stockdale, signed a new four-year contract.

The next generation of Boro stars also hit the headlines by reaching the semi-finals of the FA Youth Cup, losing to Arsenal over two legs. Precious few graduated to first-team recognition, however, as

Robson relied on his tried-and-tested seniors. Marinelli, who had made his debut as a substitute against Sheffield Wednesday on Boxing Day, was eligible for the youth side, who also included goalkeeper Brad Jones and midfielders Stuart Parnaby and Luke Wilkshire.

Boro's first-team was an ageing assortment, with all the problems that brings – particularly a susceptibility to injury. The over-30 brigade at the start of the campaign included Gary Pallister, Paul Gascoigne, Steve Vickers, Gianluca Festa, Deane, Robbie Mustoe, Townsend, Ince, Colin Cooper, Neil Maddison, Marlon Beresford and Curtis Fleming. That sort of experience had been the key to survival in the first year back in the Premiership, but it was clear that, sooner or later, ageing legs would have to be replaced and the squad overhauled.

Boro stuttered along in mid-table to finish a respectable 12th. A 2-0 home win over Coventry eased relegation fears in the face of an unprecedented injury list and they finished the season strongly with a five-match unbeaten run.

A 1-0 win at West Ham in their penultimate away match was particularly sweet for Ince. He had invoked the wrath of Upton Park supporters by posing in a Manchester United shirt before his move to Old Trafford was officially confirmed in 1989. "The Hammers fans have never forgiven me and I always expect some stick when I go back to Upton Park," he said. "But it makes it easier when you come away with three points."

The club was still setting attendance records, with new Riverside bests of 34,793 against Sunderland and 34,800 against Leeds United. But there was underlying unease among the supporters, as Robson struggled to strike a balance between attractive football and winning results.

Just two defeats in the final 14 games meant that, despite a disappointing 12th place finish, Boro had actually topped their previous season's points tally. The fans' frustration that this side could have achieved so much more resulted in a subdued atmosphere after the final home game – a 1-1 draw with Graham Taylor's relegated Watford – but Boro finished the season on a high at Goodison Park the following Sunday. Deane's early strike was capped by a stunning solo goal from Juninho in the

• LOCAL LAD - Mark Summerbell, pictured in action in a 1-1 draw at Sunderland, enjoyed a sustained midfield run

Riverside X

Diary of the Decade

dying minutes. "Sign on Juninho," sang the supporters. Alas, it would be a request that would fall on deaf ears, as Robson decided to look elsewhere for inspiration.

There was a controversial climax to the season when the squad made a two-match trip to Libya. The North African country was keen to change its image as a pariah state under Colonel Gadaffi, whose son was keen to make a name for himself in the game. With midfielder Phil Stamp playing in goal, Boro lost to Tripoli and to the Italian side Bari.

• THIRTY SOMETHING - Curtis Fleming was one of 12 over-30's at Boro during 1999-2000

2001

JANUARY

27 - *FIFA to debate Marco Branca's compensation claim following the ending of his contract with Boro - Gazette.*

29 - *Boro are chasing £8m-rated Brazilian and Paris St Germain striker Christian - N. Echo.*

FEBRUARY

2 - *Terry Venables wants to make Spain's top scorer Javi Moreno his first signing in a £5.6m deal - Mirror.*

9 - Terry Venables and Bryan Robson share FA Carling Manager of the Month award for January.

17 - *Boro are close to completing a detailed dossier on Brazilian striker Christian Correa Dionisio - Gazette.*

18 - *Middlesbrough are preparing an incredible £6m deal for Manchester United's Teddy Sheringham - News of the World.*

22 - Go-ahead for £59m Middlehaven development.

23 - Boro deny they are arranging to bring in Crystal Palace centre-half Fan Zhiyi.

24 - *Middlesbrough have rekindled their interest in Barcelona striker Dani - Sunday Sun.*

24 - Gianluca Festa asks to come off transfer list and pledges his future to Boro.

MARCH

1 - *Hertha Berlin are exploring ways of enticing Christian Ziege back to Germany - D. Mail.*

2 - Ugo Ehiogu hit with four-match ban for sending-off at Wimbledon.

8 - Dean Windass signs from Bradford City in a deal worth up to £1m; Boro draw 1-1 with St Johnstone in Riverside friendly.

14 - *Terry Venables could be tempted to leave Middlesbrough and return to Spain with Valencia - N. Echo.*

16 - Alen Boksic double seals Boro's first Premiership win over Newcastle at St James' Park.

16 - *Terry Venables is contemplating a move to bring Fabrizio Ravanelli back to the Riverside - D. Express.*

17 - *Boro are hot on the trail of Luton wing-back Matthew Taylor - Gazette; Boro have had a £2.5m bid rejected for Charlton striker Matt Svensson - Gazette.*

20 - *Adriana Karembeu models new away shirt designs for annual fans poll.*

21 - *Middlesbrough have been locked in talks over a £500,000 move for Millwall wing-back Lucas Neill - N. Echo.*

22 - Boro fail in bid to sign Bradford's Benito Carbone on transfer deadline day.

27 - *Tranmere have included Paul Ince on their managerial shortlist - Gazette.*

29 - *A desperate tug-of-war has broken out between Middlesbrough and Inter Milan over Slovakia striker Szilard Nemeth - D. Mail.*

Season Stats 1999-00

CHAMPIONS LEAGUE · UEFA CUP · RELEGATED

	P	Home					Away					Pts	GD	H	A
		W	D	L	F	A	W	D	L	F	A				
Manchester Utd	38	15	4	0	59	16	13	3	3	38	29	91	+52	3-4	0-1
Arsenal	38	14	3	2	42	17	8	4	7	31	26	73	+30	2-1	1-5
Leeds Utd	38	12	2	5	29	18	9	4	6	29	25	69	+15	0-0	0-2
Liverpool	38	11	4	4	28	13	8	6	5	23	17	67	+21	1-0	0-0
Chelsea	38	12	5	2	35	12	6	6	7	18	22	65	+19	0-1	1-1
Aston Villa	38	8	8	3	23	12	7	5	7	23	23	58	+11	0-4	0-1
Sunderland	38	10	6	3	28	17	6	4	9	29	39	58	+1	1-1	1-1
Leicester City	38	10	3	6	31	24	6	4	9	24	31	55	0	0-3	1-2
West Ham Utd	38	11	5	3	32	23	4	5	10	20	30	55	-1	2-0	1-0
Tottenham Hotspur	38	10	3	6	40	26	5	5	9	17	23	53	+8	2-1	3-2
Newcastle Utd	38	10	5	4	42	20	4	5	10	21	34	52	+9	2-2	1-2
BORO	38	8	5	6	23	26	6	5	8	23	26	52	-6	-	-
Everton	38	7	9	3	36	21	5	5	9	23	28	50	+10	2-1	2-0
Coventry City	38	12	1	6	38	22	0	7	12	9	32	44	-7	2-0	1-2
Southampton	38	8	4	7	26	22	4	4	11	19	40	44	-17	3-2	1-1
Derby County	38	6	3	10	22	25	3	8	8	22	32	38	-13	1-4	3-1
Bradford City	38	6	8	5	26	29	3	1	15	12	39	36	-30	0-1	1-1
Wimbledon	38	6	7	6	30	28	1	5	13	16	46	33	-28	0-0	3-2
Sheffield Wed	38	6	3	10	21	23	2	4	13	17	47	31	-32	1-0	0-1
Watford	38	5	4	10	24	31	1	2	16	11	46	24	-42	1-1	3-1

Goals

Name	Prem	Total
Hamilton RICARD	12	14
Brian DEANE	9	10
Christian ZIEGE	6	7
JUNINHO	4	5
Andy CAMPBELL	4	4
Paul INCE	3	4
Gianluca FESTA	2	2
Paul GASCOIGNE	1	1
Jason GAVIN	1	1
Gary PALLISTER	1	1
Robbie STOCKDALE	1	1
Steve VICKERS	0	1

Player of the Year

BT Cellnet
Christian Ziege

Supporters
Paul Ince

Appearances

	Prem	FAC	LC	UEFA	Total
Mark **SCHWARZER**	37	1	5	0	43
Paul **INCE**	32	0	3	0	35
Steve **VICKERS**	30(2)	1	3(1)	0	34(3)
Hamilton **RICARD**	28(6)	1	4(1)	0	33(7)
Christian **ZIEGE**	29	1	3(1)	0	33(1)
Brian **DEANE**	29	1	3	0	33
Curtis **FLEMING**	27	0	4	0	31
Gianluca **FESTA**	27(2)	1	2	0	30(2)
Colin **COOPER**	26	0	4	0	30
JUNINHO	24(4)	1	4	0	29(4)
Alun **ARMSTRONG**	22(9)	0	3	0	25(9)
Gary **PALLISTER**	21	1	3	0	25
Robbie **MUSTOE**	18(10)	1	3(1)	0	22(11)
Keith **O'NEILL**	14(2)	0	3	0	17(2)
Andy **CAMPBELL**	16(9)	0	0(2)	0	16(11)
Mark **SUMMERBELL**	16(3)	0	0(1)	0	16(4)
Phil **STAMP**	13(3)	1	1(1)	0	15(4)
Robbie **STOCKDALE**	6(5)	3	2(1)	0	11(6)
Neil **MADDISON**	6(7)	0	2	0	8(7)
Paul **GASCOIGNE**	7(1)	1	1(1)	0	8(2)
Jason **GAVIN**	2(4)	0(1)	2	0	4(5)
Andy **TOWNSEND**	3(2)	0	0	0	3(2)
Dean **GORDON**	3(1)	0	0	0	3(1)
Marlon **BERESFORD**	1	0	0	0	1
Carlos **MARINELLI**	0(2)	0	0	0	0(2)
Michael **CUMMINS**	0(1)	0	0	0	0(1)
Sean **KILGALLON**	0(1)	0	0	0	0(1)

1999-00 Round-up

Premiership
Manchester United

FA Cup
Chelsea

League Cup
Leicester City

Champions League
Real Madrid

UEFA Cup
Galatasaray

PFA Player of the Year
Roy Keane (Manchester United)

PFA Young Player of the Year
Harry Kewell (Leeds United)

Promoted
Charlton Athletic
Manchester City
Ipswich Town

Line-Up

League Form

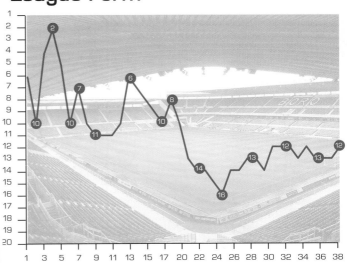

2000-01

Summer dreams. All managers have them, and Bryan Robson was no different when in August 2000 he opened his sixth full season in charge with £10m worth of new talent. Those balmy pre-seasons when the kit is pristine and the pitches as smooth and lush as bowling greens can be deceptive, however.

Few would have predicted that, within a few short weeks, Robson's Middlesbrough career would sink into crisis. Early summer had been dominated by speculation that exciting import Christian Ziege was about to jump ship to Liverpool. Reporters tracked down the German international to the beach where he dismissed the transfer chatter by insisting he was happy at the Riverside.

But the rumours refused to go away and a £5m move to Anfield was agreed just days before the big kick-off. Allegations that Ziege had been "tapped up" left a sour taste that would have implications for months ahead as Boro demanded redress from the FA.

Boro fans were optimistic, however, when Robson introduced six new signings. Joseph-Desire Job, a Cameroon international striker, signed from French club Lens for £3m, French World Cup and European Championships winner Christian Karembeu was snapped up from Read Madrid for £2.1m, Croatian star striker Alen Boksic signed from Lazio for £2.5m, and former England U-21 international Noel Whelan was brought in from Coventry for £2.25m.

Paul Okon, a highly-rated midfielder who was a regular for Australia, was signed on a free transfer from Italian side Fiorentina and Mark Crossley arrived on a Bosman-style free transfer from Nottingham Forest as cover keeper.

Robson's iconic status in world football undoubtedly helped to attract players of the calibre of Karembeu, one of the world's most decorated footballers who

Diary of the Decade

2001

MARCH

30 - *Paris St Germain are poised to lodge a £2.5m offer for Christian Karembeu - Daily Mail; Boro have failed in a bid to bring back Juninho for a third time - N. Echo.*

APRIL

1 - *Middlesbrough are weighing up a summer swoop for £8m-rated Lazio star Simone Inzaghi - Sunday Sun.*

3 - *Middlesbrough are in the queue for Manchester United striker Teddy Sheringham - N. Echo.*

9 - Christian Karembeu sent off in goalless home draw with Sunderland.

14 - Boro's 3-0 win over Arsenal is their first at Highbury for 62 years.

16 - Former Boro striker Alun Armstrong hits two in Ipswich's 2-1 win at Riverside.

19 - *Boro are running the rule over Brighton striker Bobby Zamora - D Express*

21 - Relegation fears eased with second successive 3-0 away win, at Leicester.

22 - Death of former Boro star Stephen Bell at 36.

MAY

2 - *French midfielder Stephane Zaini is set to sign for Middlesbrough from Nantes for £1m - D. Express.*

6 - Middlesbrough are tracking hot Spanish prospect Roger Garcia, of Espanyol.

7 - Manchester City's defeat at Ipswich condemns them to relegation - and means Boro are safe.

10 - *Terry Venables has made a £20m double bid for Barcelona pair Dani and Emmanuel Petit - Mirror; Middlesbrough could mount a challenge to Newcastle for £5m-rated Nottingham Forest midfielder David Prutton - N. Echo.*

11 - *Middlesbrough plan to snatch Hartlepool midfielder Tommy Miller for £1.2m - Sun.*

13 - *Middlesbrough are set to revive their interest in French striker Olivier Monterrubio - Sunday Sun*

14 - *Middlesbrough are ready to make a £2m bid for West Ham's on-loan full-back Sebastien Schemmel - D. Star.*

15 - Ex-Boro and Celtic hero Bobby Murdoch dies.

15 - *Bryan Robson will attempt to lure Brian Kidd away from Leeds if Terry Venables turns his back on Middlesbrough - D. Express.*

18 - Boro announce three-year commentary deals with Century FM and BBC Radio Cleveland.

19 - Boro sign off with a 2-1 home win over West Ham.

30 - Death of Boro Academy coach John Pickering, formerly the first team coach.

• INCE-SPIRATION - Paul Ince scored a last-gasp leveller against fellow strugglers Bradford City, but Boro were still bottom at the end of November

had also won the European Cup with his Spanish employers, and Boksic, who had also won medals galore in two spells with Lazio plus periods at Juventus and Marseille. Job had scored a hat-trick for Lens in the 1999-2000 UEFA Cup and had also helped Cameroon win the Africa Nations Cup a few months before arriving on Teesside.

How would they blend? Initial signs were encouraging. Boksic's class was immediately apparent in a 3-1 opening-day win at Coventry in which he grabbed a double. The powerfully-built Croatian boasted fantastic close skills and the vision that all world-class players possess. Job, a double-jointed box of tricks with a neat turn of speed, got the other goal and looked an exciting prospect.

The power and pace of the Premiership seemed to have caught Karembeu by surprise at first. Robson's plan had been to deploy the dreadlocked Frenchman as a raiding right wing-back to complement Ziege's known qualities on the left. But Ziege's late switch to Liverpool forced a change of thinking.

Karembeu was mostly used as a conventional midfielder, with long-serving Curtis Fleming selected at right wing-back and Keith O'Neill, until he got injured, on the opposite flank. Robson had come close to signing the versatile Chris Sutton during the summer, but the Chelsea player had chosen to go to Celtic instead. The Boro boss had also attempted to lure Steve McManaman from Real Madrid.

A notable departure was Paul Gascoigne, little seen in a Boro shirt for a year, who left for one last hurrah at Everton. "Gazza" was a constant source of headlines - usually for his off-the-field activities - and it was no surprise when he was finally offloaded. Robson is quick to defend Gascoigne's role in helping Boro back into the Premiership.

"I think at first he definitely proved to be a really good signing," he said. "Gazza came in for the last eight games of the promotion season and we won five of them. He played a big part in that. Then at the start of the next season (1999-2000) he was also excellent. Gazza had had a magnificent first half of the season at that point and people were talking about him getting back in the England team.

"Then shortly after that he got injured and his season dwindled away. He was never really the same player again then. But for the first nine months at Boro he was really successful."

The new-look squad took time to gel. Optimism was quickly replaced with worry when Boro went on a six-match winless streak following the opening victory at Highfield Road. Injuries quickly took their toll as Boro slipped further and further down the table.

Gary Pallister succumbed to a long-term back injury. Paul Okon broke his foot in only his third match, a 2-1 home defeat to Leeds, and was forced to miss the Olympics in home-town Sydney. And when Boro splashed out a club record £8m for Ugo Ehiogu to shore up a leaky defence, the curse struck again, with the player limping off just five

Riverside X

Diary of the Decade

• GALLIC GOAL - French international Christian Karembeu points the way forward after a winner against Liverpool

minutes into his debut at Charlton. By mid-September Boro did not have one fit senior keeper.

Mark Schwarzer broke his thumb in training, Crossley pulled a hamstring, Marlon Beresford underwent a cartilage operation and Sam Russell was recovering from a broken foot. When attempts to sign Chelsea reserve Mark Bosnich failed, Robson contacted Bradford City to bring back former Boro keeper Gary Walsh as emergency loan cover.

A 3-1 home win over Southampton briefly settled the nerves before the rot really set in during autumn 2000. Boro suffered eight defeats in the next nine matches to hit rock bottom in the Premiership. Robson was big enough to admit he needed help.

The man he turned to was Terry Venables, the former England manager who had apparently turned his back on

2001

JUNE

31 -   Bryan Robson is locked in a three-way battle to sign Belgian international defender Stijn Revven - D. Express.

2 -   Middlesbrough have been linked with Argentine striker Gabriel Batistuta - Gazette.

5 -   Bryan Robson announces departure as manager.

10 -   Boro are believed to be planning a £10m double swoop for Derby duo Malcolm Christie and Rory Delap - Sunday Sun.

12 -   Steve McClaren signs five-year contract as Boro's new manager.

13 -   Middlesbrough have given Steve McClaren their blessing to return to the England fold for the crucial World Cup qualifier against Germany - D. Mail.

14 -   Boro have joined the chase for Wimbledon's £6m-rated striker Jason Euell - Gazette.

17 -   McClaren is to begin a kids-only spending frenzy with the £6m capture of John Terry from Chelsea - Sunday People.

19 -   McClaren could make a plunge for Villa goalkeeper Peter Enckelman - Gazette.

22 -   Paul Ince is wanted by Italian club Brescia - Mirror.

24 -   Steve McClaren is being tipped to enter the hunt for Leicester midfielder Muzzy Izzet - Sunday Sun.

JULY

1 -   Middlesbrough have joined the hunt for Denmark defender Jacob Laursen - Sunday Sun.

26 -   Brian Deane is being lined up for a third stint at Sheffield United - Sun.

AUGUST

5 -   Boro beat Athletic Bilbao 3-0 in Curtis Fleming's testimonial.

7 -   Keith O'Neill joins Coventry.

8 -   Jonathan Greening and Mark Wilson transferred from Manchester United in joint £3.5m deal.

9 -   Boro start short pre-season tour of Holland.

11-   Launch of Boro TV Extra.

12 -   Boro lead the chase for FC Copenhagen forward Sibussio Zuma - Sunday People

13 -   Steve Vickers linked with Crystal Palace.

14 -   Strasbourg defender Habib Beye turns down a trial at Boro - BBC Online; Middlesbrough are ready to offer Andy Cole a fresh challenge - Daily Express; Boro open new ticket facility in MFC Retail town-centre store.

17 -   Marlon Beresford joins Wolves on a month's loan.

management to pursue a media career. 'El Tel' had swapped the dressing-room for the studios of ITV where he was highly prized as a guest expert.

"I said at the time that I wanted to bring a coach in," said Robson. "John Pickering was in ill health and Gordon McQueen was struggling with an ankle injury. I just felt we needed to bring someone else in to help with the role. We couldn't get other top-class coaches in. Terry was available and I had worked very well with him at international level, so that's the reason I gave him the call."

There were complications, however. Venables was committed to launching a new Saturday-night match highlights programme for ITV, so a short-term contract was agreed as a compromise. The new man adopted the title of Head Coach and took charge of team selection and tactics in consultation with Robson.

"I had known Bryan for a long time but the first time I worked with him was when I was England manager," said Venables. "I wanted him as my assistant and told him it would be great experience for him. He liked the idea although, of course, he already had so much experience as a player and was already Middlesbrough manager. We got on very well and worked very well together while with England, and had quite a successful time as we got to the semi-finals of Euro 96."

The Londoner explained the background to his contract. "Middlesbrough wanted me to sign a long deal but I had an agreement with ITV. I spoke to Brian Barwick (then head of ITV sport) and he said that he would allow me to leave for the rest of the season. I gave him my word that I would come back. But Boro still wanted a longer deal and so the idea was put on the back-burner."

Venables was appointed on December 4 2000 and made it clear that the job of keeping Boro in the Premiership was very

• NEW START - Paul Okon suffered a broken foot but his fortunes changed following Terry Venables' arrival

much a partnership. "I thought it was a big step for Bryan to take because he was bound to get criticised for bringing in someone at that stage of the season to share the responsibilities over the team. He made it clear that he wouldn't bring in anyone else - it was either me or no-one - so I decided to do it.

"It wasn't an easy situation for Bryan, the coaches or myself because no-one knew how it would work. Once I decided to do it I threw myself at the job and my only focus was to help keep Boro in the Premiership. To make our situation work we had to immediately make a decision as to who was responsible for what.

"That meant that our relationship did not become difficult. I took over the coaching and tactical side of things - how we would play. Bryan was in charge of everything else apart from that, including the signing of players. Of course we deliberated with each other about decisions, because we were both in a situation in which we wanted the best for the football club and ego had been thrown out of the window.

"Neither of us was stubborn enough to not listen to the other, and when you have that then a sharing of duties can work." Venables' first priority was to get Boro

Riverside X

Diary of the Decade

organised. He had a series of one-to-ones with the players, outlining their responsibilities by way of video analysis.

The new coach commanded immediate respect and the gamble began to pay instant dividends on the field. Dean Gordon scored the winner in a crucial first match at home to Chelsea as, slowly but surely, Boro stabilised. Having taken just 11 points from their first 17 games it was a desperately welcome victory.

"We very quickly developed a tactical plan and got a good result against Chelsea," remembers Venables. "That made a big difference because immediately people started to believe. From then on we were very strong as a group and knew that we had a good chance.

"Maybe people up and down the country had already given up on us, but we just kept on working hard to get results and on occasions we had good fortune."

Boro embarked on a 10-match unbeaten run that at least gave them a fighting chance of achieving their 40-point safety target. It wasn't always pretty, but the Venables style of keeping it tight at the back and grinding out points was mightily effective.

• FAMOUS FOOT - Dean Windass celebrates with team mates after grabbing a goal against Ipswich

2001

AUGUST

18 - *Steve McClaren has made a £3.5m bid for Bordeaux left back Patrick Bonnissel - Sunday People*

20 - Carlos Marinelli and Arthuro Bernhardt launch new Boro Junior Lions club. Boro linked with Derby midfielder Seth Johnson

23 - Boro give trial to Austrian midfielder Markus Schopp of Sturm Graz; *Bradford have turned down the chance to re-sign Dean Windass - The Sun*

31 - MFC Community Project receives £75,000 BT Innovative Lifelong Learning Award.

SEPTEMBER

1 - Allan Johnston signs from Glasgow Rangers for £600,000 as Boro deny interest in Coventry midfielder Lee Carsley

3 - Phil Stamp joins Millwall on a month's loan.

5 - Jonathan Greening and Mark Wilson feature in the England U-21 side that beats Albania 5-0 in Euro Qualifer at the Riverside; *Boro have opened talks for French full-back Patrice Cateron - Daily Star*

9 - Boro lose 4-1 at home to Newcastle, their fourth successive defeat.

10 - *Steve McClaren is to buy his way out of trouble by spending £6m on South African striker Sibusio Zuma - Mirror*

11 - David Murphy makes Boro debut in 3-1 Worthington Cup win over Northampton before 3,918 fans, the Riverside's lowest attendance for a competitive senior game. The tie also features first starts of Szilard Nemeth and Mark Wilson - all three make it on to the scoresheet.

12 - *French left-back David Di Tommaso is set to sign for Middlesbrough - tribalfootball.com*

16 - *Steve McClaren is set to sign Poland's international left-back Marek Kozminski from Italian side Brescia - Mirror*

17 - Mark Schwarzer makes his 150th Boro League appearance, at Leicester

18 - Steve Vickers joins Crystal Palace on a month's loan, while Anthony Ormerod is loaned to Hartlepool and Chris Bennion to Scunthorpe; *Bordeaux striker Christophe Dugarry is due to sign for Middlesbrough today - tribalfootball.com*

19 - Boro fail in move to bring South Africa striker Benni McCarthy on loan after the Celta Vigo player fails to gain a work permit

21 - Portsmouth give a trial to Christian Hanson

24 - PFA threatens player strike over TV payments

25 - Italian defender Antonio Benarrivo turns down the chance to join Boro on loan

26 - Gareth Southgate launches club's new international honours board at Riverside; Premier League charges Christian Ziege and Liverpool with breach of rules following the German's controversial transfer to Anfield in August 2000

"Getting regular points was great for our position but also put more and more doubt into the minds of the teams around us - we would not be shaken off." Venables said. "It's true that the first priority was to grind things out. However, there needed to be a plan of attack because it wasn't enough for us to get goalless draws every week.

"We needed to win games to stay up. I introduced some ideas about movement into our offensive play that worked very well. But the main thing was to not lose, and sometimes that meant the fans were a little disappointed by the style of play - although they didn't mind as much if we won."

• SUPERSTAR - Alen Boksic weighed in with 12 goals as Boro retained their Premiership position

Boksic's goals were crucial. Adversity brought the best out of the unpredictable striker, who weighed in with 12 league goals. Memorable strikes included a wonderful free-kick in a 2-1 win at Newcastle and a brilliant solo goal in a 3-0 away win over Leicester.

He was another player Venables brought the best out of. By nature a loner, Boksic would often sit out certain training sessions and rarely mixed with his team-mates. "Alen Boksic was a special guy with wonderful ability and exceptions had to be made for him on occasions," said Venables.

"He was different to most players and people, and sometimes he would be very low in himself. I felt that we had to do certain things in training without him, and in the long run we would get better performances from him. The other players didn't have a problem with that because I was honest with them.

"I explained to them why I felt Alen was better sitting out certain things and what benefits they would get out of that. I had a similar situation with Gary Lineker when I was at Spurs. He hadn't had a decent break and he was tired so I let him go on holiday to Tenerife during the season.

"That could have caused problems but I told the others why Gary needed the break and they understood. So sometimes while the others were practising defensive plays, Alen would be just shooting away somewhere else or doing some fitness work. But he repaid me, Bryan and everyone else with goals and great performances. In terms of talent he was up there with Paul Gascoigne, Alan Shearer and Bernd Schuster - among the best I worked with."

The revival included an incredible 3-0 victory over championship-chasing Arsenal - the only time the Gunners lost at Highbury that season. "We never relaxed until the maths was sorted," Venables added. "It was important that we didn't lose our focus, we had to stay hungry and we knew that a defeat for us and a win for a couple of rivals could be disastrous."

Okon revelled in a different role as sweeper and colleagues such as Ince, Ehiogu, Mark Schwarzer and Steve Vickers put in some towering performances as the team achieved mid-table safety.

Robson believes the early casualty list was a key factor in the pre-Christmas decline. "I think the main problem was all the best players had bad injuries in the first part of that season. We lost people like Ehiogu, Ince and 'Boks' for long periods. Terry Venables came in and gave us some pointers but I think the main reason we did so well in the second part of the season was everyone was fit and we didn't really get too many injuries."

Boro finished the season in a comfortable 14th position, with Venables earning the devoted respect of the Teesside faithful. He was cheered to the rafters when he went on

Riverside X Diary of the Decade

to the pitch following the final fixture, a 2-1 home win over West Ham.

Robson, however, was booed by sections of the Riverside crowd. "It's a tradition that players salute the fans at the last home game, but Bryan and I just walked a little way on to the pitch just to wave goodbye for the summer," said Venables. "It was very unkind what happened with Bryan, and I was very disappointed. I knew how much the club meant to him and how hard things had been for him, so to be treated in that way was uncalled for.

"We should have all - players and staff - just walked off, or even better not gone out there in the first place. But it wasn't everyone that was jeering, it was a minority, so why spoil it for everyone else? I appreciated the support I was shown, but it was both of us that had kept Boro in the Premiership so the treatment of Bryan disappointed me."

Robson remembers: "It's never nice when the fans are criticising you and they are not on your side. But that's water under the bridge now and you have just got to move on from that."

And that is exactly what he did . . .

• DOUBLE ACT - Terry Venables and Bryan Robson combined to take Boro from the bottom of the Premiership to mid-table security

OCTOBER

2001

1 - Mark Summerbell joins Bristol City on a month's loan.

4 - *Middlesbrough are chasing Australia international defender Tony Vidmar of Rangers - tribalfootball.com*

6 - *Steve McClaren is hot on the trail of Ipswich's £2m rated full-back, Jamie Clapham - Gazette*

7 - *Boro are in talks with Italian club Brescia over a sensational swap deal involving Paul Ince - Sunday Sun*

8 - *Boro have quashed speculation that they are close to completing a £2m move for Marseille star Jerome Leroy - Gazette*

12 - Franck Queudrue joins Boro on a season-long loan from French club Lens

19 - Club launches its first-ever Annual Charter Report

21 - *Leeds full-back Ian Harte is being watched by Boro - People*

23 - Boro give trial to Ajax striker Brutil Hose

25 - MFC Ladies football team agree a partnership deal with Boro. Boro buy George Camsell England shirt for £1,000

30 - Paul Ince loses appeal against dismissal at Sunderland

NOVEMBER

2 - Boro's 5-1 home win over Derby is their biggest of the season, with Carlos Marinelli hitting a double

3 - Mark Schwarzer and Paul Okon leave for Australia's World Cup qualification quest

7 - Steve Vickers' hopes of a permanent move to Crystal Palace quashed as clubs fail to agree fee

11 - *Middlesbrough target Leigh Bromby (Sheffield Wednesday) has ruled out a move to the Riverside - Sunday Sun*

13 - *Middlesbrough are seeking a way to sign Tromso striker Morten Gamst Pedersen - Journal*

15 - Steve Vickers and Curtis Fleming join Birmingham on loan for a month. Steve Baker joins Scarborough on a free transfer and Mark Summerbell joins Stockport on trial

23 - Christian Hanson joins Torquay on a month's loan.

25 - *Spanish side Espanyol are set to throw Joseph-Desire Job a lifeline - Sunday Sun*

27 - PSV Eindhoven striker Dennis Mortensen joins Boro on trial

28 - Brian Deane joins Leicester for £250,000

29 - Boro fans vote to keep existing policies on smoking restrictions at the Riverside; *West Brom have denied interest in Dean Windass - Northern Echo*

Season Stats 2000-01

	P	Home					Away					Pts	GD	H	A
		W	D	L	F	A	W	D	L	F	A				
Manchester Utd	38	15	2	2	49	12	9	6	4	30	19	80	+48	0-2	1-2
Arsenal	38	15	3	1	45	13	5	7	7	18	25	70	+25	0-1	3-0
Liverpool	38	13	4	2	40	14	7	5	7	31	25	69	+32	1-0	0-0
Leeds Utd	38	11	3	5	36	21	9	5	5	28	22	68	+21	1-2	1-1
Ipswich Town	38	11	5	3	31	15	9	1	9	26	27	66	+15	1-2	1-2
Chelsea	38	13	3	3	44	20	4	7	8	24	25	61	+23	1-0	1-2
Sunderland	38	9	7	3	24	16	6	5	8	22	25	57	+5	0-0	0-1
Aston Villa	38	8	8	3	27	20	5	7	7	19	23	54	+3	1-1	1-1
Charlton Athletic	38	11	5	3	31	19	3	5	11	19	38	52	-7	0-0	0-1
Southampton	38	11	2	6	27	22	3	8	8	13	26	52	-8	0-1	3-1
Newcastle Utd	38	10	4	5	26	17	4	5	10	18	33	51	-6	1-3	2-1
Tottenham Hotspur	38	11	6	2	31	16	2	4	13	16	38	49	-7	1-1	0-0
Leicester City	38	10	4	5	28	23	4	2	13	11	28	48	-12	0-3	3-0
BORO	38	4	7	8	18	23	5	8	6	26	21	42	0	-	-
West Ham Utd	38	6	6	7	24	20	4	6	9	21	30	42	-5	2-1	0-1
Everton	38	6	8	5	29	27	5	1	13	16	32	42	-14	1-2	2-2
Derby County	38	8	7	4	23	24	2	5	12	14	35	42	-22	4-0	3-3
Manchester City	38	4	3	12	20	31	4	7	8	21	34	34	-24	1-1	1-1
Coventry City	38	4	7	8	14	23	4	3	12	22	40	34	-27	1-1	3-1
Bradford City	38	4	7	8	20	29	1	4	14	10	41	26	-40	2-2	1-1

Side labels: CHAMPIONS LEAGUE, UEFA CUP, RELEGATED

Goals

Name	Prem	Total
Alen BOKSIC	12	12
Hamilton RICARD	4	7
Christian KAREMBEU	4	4
Ugo EHIOGU	3	3
Joseph-Desire JOB	3	3
Alun ARMSTRONG	2	2
Colin COOPER	2	2
Brian DEANE	2	2
Gianluca FESTA	2	2
Dean GORDON	2	2
Mark SUMMERBELL	1	2
Phil STAMP	1	1
Paul INCE	0	1
Noel WHELAN	0	1

Player of the Year

BT Cellnet
Alen Boksic

Supporters
Alen Boksic

Appearances

	Prem	FAC	LC	UEFA	Total
Mark **SCHWARZER**	31	3	2	0	36
Paul **INCE**	30	3	2	0	35
Curtis **FLEMING**	29(1)	3	2	0	34(1)
Christian **KAREMBEU**	31(2)	1(1)	1	0	33(3)
Steve **VICKERS**	29(1)	1	1	0	31(1)
Colin **COOPER**	26(1)	2	2	0	30(1)
Hamilton **RICARD**	22(5)	3	3	0	28(5)
Alen **BOKSIC**	26(2)	2(1)	0(1)	0	28(4)
Gianluca **FESTA**	21(4)	3	3	0	27(4)
Paul **OKON**	23(1)	2	0	0	25(1)
Ugo **EHIOGU**	21	3	0	0	24
Dean **GORDON**	12(8)	2	3	0	17(8)
Noel **WHELAN**	13(14)	0(2)	3	0	16(16)
Brian **DEANE**	13(12)	1	1	0	15(12)
Keith **O'NEILL**	14(1)	1	0(1)	0	15(2)
Robbie **MUSTOE**	13(12)	1(1)	0	0	14(13)
Phil **STAMP**	11(8)	2	0(1)	0	13(9)
Jason **GAVIN**	10(4)	0	1	0	11(4)
Joseph-Desire **JOB**	8(5)	0	1(1)	0	9(6)
Gary **PALLISTER**	8	0	1	0	9
Mark **SUMMERBELL**	5(2)	0	3	0	8(2)
Dean **WINDASS**	8	0	0	0	8
Andy **CAMPBELL**	5(2)	0(2)	1	0	6(4)
Mark **CROSSLEY**	4(1)	0	0	0	4(1)
Gary **WALSH**	3	0	0	0	3
Carlos **MARINELLI**	2(11)	0	0(1)	0	2(12)
Alun **ARMSTRONG**	0	0	1	0	1
Mark **HUDSON**	0	0	1	0	1
Stuart **PARNABY**	0	0	1	0	1
Robbie **STOCKDALE**	0	0	1	0	1
Chris **BENNION**	0(3)	0(1)	0(1)	0	0(5)
Marlon **BERESFORD**	0(2)	0	0	0	0(2)
Neil **MADDISON**	0	0	0	0	0

2000-01 Round-up

Premiership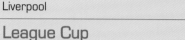
Manchester United

FA Cup
Liverpool

League Cup
Liverpool

Champions League
Bayern Munich

UEFA Cup
Liverpool

PFA Player of the Year
Teddy Sheringham (Manchester United)

PFA Young Player of the Year
Steven Gerrard (Liverpool)

Promoted
Fulham
Blackburn Rovers
Bolton Wanderers

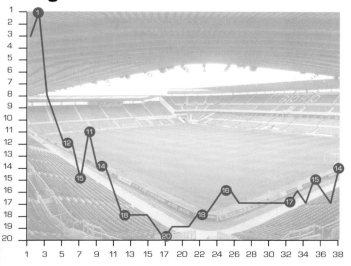

Line-Up

League Form

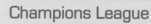

2001-02

Diary of the Decade

Events moved quickly in the summer of 2000 when Steve Gibson embarked on a wholesale change of managerial and coaching staff. The initial plan had been to install Terry Venables on a longer deal, but he could not be cut loose from his contract with ITV, where he was central to sports controller Brian Barwick's plans for the Premiership highlights package.

"Teesside Tel" left with regrets. "If I had not had the situation with ITV I would definitely have stayed because I thought that the group of players that were there – plus the backing of the chairman - could have been the start of something special. But I had given my word to ITV and I wasn't going to break that.

"Negotiations could never really get off the ground because I had done my bit – and it was that which meant I didn't stay there for longer, not the uncertainty over Bryan's future or some of the nonsense written about me not working on Saturdays.

"But the club has gone from strength to strength since then so I'm sure that the fans aren't too disappointed that I didn't stay on all these years later."

With no future for the Venables-Robson axis, Gibson decided to make a clean break. The chairman's relationship with Robson had always been close. They had both left their imprint on a football club transformed out of all recognition from the under-achieving Ayresome Park era. The parting was bound to be painful.

Chief Executive Keith Lamb offers an interesting insight into how the supporters' reaction to Robson at the final home game of the previous season influenced the decision to seek a new team commander: "At the time of his leaving it hurt him – he was a winner. He had overcome all kinds of adversities during his playing days, including two broken legs, but had still captained England and Manchester United for so long.

"Captain Marvel doesn't fail. I don't think he would necessarily have failed here beyond 2001 had the fans not displayed

2001

DECEMBER

2 - *Boro are back on the trail of Michael Ball following his touchline bust-up with Dick Advocaat - Sunday Sun*

5 - Dean Windass joins Sheffield Wednesday on a month's loan

11 - Mark Schwarzer books into hospital for a hernia operation, extending mark Crossley's first team run

12 - First stage of Middlehaven redevelopment plan nears completion

19 - Sean Kilgannon joins Dunfermline on a three-month loan

20 - Steve Vickers joins Birmingham for £500,000 while Chris Bennion joins Scunthorpe on a free transfer

21 - Boro declare war on bootleggers who have cost the club £8m in counterfeit kit and other fakes - the equivalent of combined transfer fees of Gareth Southgate and Carlos Marinelli; Barclaycard Premiership fixture with Fulham at the Riverside frozen off.

2002

JANUARY

4 - Curtis Fleming joins Crystal Palace for £100,000

5 - FA Cup third round tie at Wimbledon frozen off

7 - Joseph-Desire Job joins French club Metz on loan for the rest of the season

8 - Middlesbrough Football in the Community start girls-only sessions; Juninho weds promoter Juliana Bchara at a glamorous ceremony in his home town of Sao Paulo

10 - Paul Okon joins Watford on a free transfer

14 - Boro agree £6m fee with Argentine side Independiente for Uruguay striker Diego Forlan

15 - A 2-0 victory over Wimbledon at Selhurst Park sets up an attractive FA Cup third-round home tie with Manchester United

19 - Tow Law FC given use of Boro's luxury coach for big FA Vase trip to Ash United, Aldershot

24 - Diego Forlan eventually signs for Manchester United after Reds make late move

25 - Tragic death of Colin Cooper's son, Finlay, in a household accident overshadows FA Cup win over Manchester United

29 - Ten-man Boro complete double over Sunderland at Stadium of Light with Noel Whelan grabbing the winner

their support for Terry. At the last home game of the season, the fans gave Terry a resounding cheer and Bryan was booed. That really hurt him and was a sign that they wanted change. Sometimes the fans can influence what we do – the club has to take the fans into account. Six and a half of Bryan's seven years here were fantastic.

"Steve Gibson and I realised that Venables didn't want to stay on. We tried to keep him but he didn't want to continue in that role as it would cause more problems for Bryan. He said: 'I've done the job I said I'd do'. That left Bryan in a difficult position – which had been apparent since December.

"Bryan thought that he could overcome it and was deeply shocked when we decided to change manager. It hurt him. He wasn't used to failure, but it wasn't really failure – it was simply time for a change."

The man Gibson saw as the way forward was Manchester United assistant manager Steve McClaren. He took soundings from respected figures within the game and liked what he heard about the 40-year-old Yorkshireman, who was widely regarded as one of the brightest young coaches in Britain.

McClaren, a lower-leagues midfielder in his playing career, had built up valuable coaching experience with Oxford and Derby before helping to guide United to the highest domestic and European honours. He was also an assistant to Sven Goran Eriksson at England level. But he was also a gamble because, for all his coaching credentials, he had never managed at any level.

Gibson was tenacious in his attempts to recruit McClaren, even though he had to play catch-up to get his man. Other clubs had also been alerted to his availability and Southampton and West Ham had already interviewed him.

• NEW TEAM - Steve McClaren and assistant Bill Beswick took over in the summer of 2001

Riverside X

Diary of the Decade

The ensuing weeks were tense on all fronts. The chairman, Lamb, Robson, assistant manager Viv Anderson and coach Gordon McQueen all flew to Singapore for their traditional end-of-season soccer tournament as normal.

McClaren had been sounded out at that point, with contract details outlined during a meeting at his home. News of the meeting was leaked in the press while the Boro party was still in the Far East. When they returned, there was some straight talking to do.

The executives plus the management staff were due to attend the funeral of respected coach and Academy chief John Pickering, who had endured a long illness. Lamb takes up the story: "Steve and I felt we couldn't go to church without clearing the air.

"I came into the office on the morning of the funeral to tell Bryan we were going to change manager. It was very difficult for both of us. We all attended the funeral together and the day after Bryan and Steve sat down to discuss the details.

"We had a joint press conference at which myself, Bryan and Steve sat together. We then went out with our wives and had a few drinks and something of a wake. My view is that Steve felt that during that summer he had to put the club's best interests ahead of his personal feelings for Bryan – just as Bryan had put the club first in December. The change was in the best interest of the football club."

McClaren was installed on a five-year contract. It was not so much a wind of change as a gale. Rockliffe Park underwent a fundamental culture change that was nothing short of revolutionary.

Robson's backroom team of Anderson, McQueen and David Geddis quickly departed. In their place came Bill Beswick, a sports psychologist highly regarded for his work with Manchester United, Derby and the FA, as assistant manager and coaches Steve Harrison, Steve Round and Paul Barron.

Harrison had worked under Graham Taylor with England and came with a wealth of coaching and managerial experience at Aston Villa, Watford, Millwall, Crystal

2002

JANUARY

30 - Boro withdraw their £6m bid for Manchester United striker Dwight Yorke after club and player are unable to agree terms

31- Gianluca Festa fined after being sent off for allegedly spitting at Kevin Phillips in the derby against Sunderland. Marlon Beresford joins Burnley on loan

FEBRUARY

8 - Benito Carbone signs on loan from Bradford City until the end of the season

9 - Willie Maddren Centre celebrates its fourth anniversary

11 - Premier League names MFC as their most "localised" club, with 74 per cent of supporters living within 10 miles of the stadium; Leicester give Boro permission to talk to Muzzy Izzet after clubs agree £6m fee

14 - *Middlesbrough are closing in on £6m African star Dereck Boateng, of Panathinaikos - D. Mirror*

16 - Robbie Mustoe presented with special memento before FA Cup fifth-round tie with Blackburn after breaking the club record for all-time cup appearances (87)

17 - Boro deny stories linking Gareth Southgate to Manchester United

20 - Muzzy Izzet turns down move to Riverside

22 - Lens midfielder Michael Debeve joins on contract until the end of the season

25- Andy Campbell joins Cardiff City on loan until the end of the season

MARCH

5 - Luke Wilkshire makes full debut in 1-1 draw at Southampton

10 - Boro book place in FA Cup semi-finals after 3-0 Riverside victory over Everton

14 - Liverpool FC fined £20,000 and Christian Ziege £10,000 by Premier League after Boro complaints of "poaching". Boro decided to take the matter to the High Court

26 - Cardiff make Andy Campbell's move permanent in £1m deal and Hamilton Ricard is released to join Bulgarian side CSKA Sofia; Mark Crossley, Luke Wilkshire, Stuart Parnaby, Brad Jones and Arturo Berhnardt sign new deals

28 - Mark Summerbell joins Portsmouth on loan

APRIL

3 - Bernie Slaven pulls out of race to become the town's first directly-elected mayor

Palace, Wolves and Preston. Round had been second-team coach under McClaren at Derby and Barron, the goalkeeping coach, was another acquisition from Villa who had worked with the FA.

Modernisation became a key priority – the introduction of up-to-the-minute coaching techniques and cutting-edge sports science gleaned from study of Europe's leading clubs. When the players returned for pre-season training they were asked to embrace a new era of clinical professionalism.

McClaren admits he was close to becoming a Hammer before being won over by Gibson's persuasiveness. "I was on the verge of joining West Ham before I got a call from a journalist friend asking me if I would be interested in Boro. They were negotiating with Terry Venables and having some difficulties.

"I told him I would be interested, and the journalist put the chairman and myself in touch. I had a deadline to give West Ham a decision but delayed that by a few hours so that I could meet Keith Lamb and Steve Gibson on the M62 near Huddersfield.

"The pull of West Ham was the great crop of talent that they had, but I knew straight away that I had to join Boro, purely because of the chairman. He had such ambition, and Sir Alex Ferguson had told me that I should choose a chairman as much as the club.

"Steve spoke sense and told me that I did not have to rush my decision because it was for my first managerial job. I had never met him before. He's fiercely ambitious and competitive and if he goes after something he gets it. He makes long-term plans and that's why I signed a five-year deal. He's straightforward and a typical Northern bloke. That's why I liked him."

The squad inherited by McClaren numbered 43 players. It included well-paid senior pros who, through injury or loss of

• BAD START - Gareth Southgate made his debut as Dennis Bergkamp and Arsenal ran riot in a 4-0 win

form, had not seen first-team action for months and even seasons. Boro were ripe for a major overhaul, but moving unwanted players off the books can be a slow and frustrating business.

Managers are always judged by their signings and, with his first buy, McClaren was determined to set a trend for his new Middlesbrough breed. Boro paid what was then the second highest fee in their history when they invested £6.5m in Gareth Southgate from Aston Villa. Other clubs were put off by the asking price, but in retrospect it was a bargain.

Southgate had become unsettled at Villa following differences with manager John Gregory. "I considered my options," he said. "I could sit at Villa, where I had been unhappy and relations with the manager had deteriorated. There had also been interest from two other top ten clubs.

"West Ham came in after I had signed with Boro, but none of the other clubs could agree a fee. I have a suspicion that Villa might only have accepted the bid from Boro because they thought I wouldn't sign for them!

"Steve McClaren offered me a different kind of challenge – the opportunity to join the start of an adventure at

Riverside X

Diary of the Decade

Middlesbrough. We talked for a long time and he outlined his plans to move the club forward. He really sold the club to me and made me want to be part of it."

The turn-over on the playing staff continued apace before a ball was kicked with Christian Karembeu joining Greek club Olympiakos for £3.7m, Keith O'Neill switching to Coventry and Gary Pallister retiring from the game. Established senior pros such as Curtis Fleming, Steve Vickers, Hamilton Ricard, Brian Deane and Paul Okon quickly exited during the opening half of the 2001-02 season when it became clear they had no future under the new regime.

McClaren went back to Manchester United for the double signing of England U-21 midfielders Jonathan Greening and Mark Wilson in a £3.5m deal. Next came Scottish international Allan Johnston from Rangers for £600,000.

Supporters, naturally, were waiting to be won over. And the McClaren era got off to a disastrous start with four

• BACK OF THE NET - Franck Queudrue, on loan from Lens, scores against Sunderland

2002

APRIL

4 - *Boro will decline the chance to enter next season's Intertoto Cup - mfc.co.uk*; Gianluca Festa and Benito Carbone launch new MFC Travel facility; *Leicester boss Dave Bassett has indicated Muzzy Izzet could still be tempted to move to Middlesbrough - Northern Echo*

5 - Craig Dove signs new two-year contract

6 - *Boro are in the hunt for Udinese midfielder Luis Helguera - News of the World*

10 - *Wolves boss Dave Jones is set to make a second move for Paul Ince - Daily Express*

14 - Heartbreak for Boro as Gianluca Festa own goal gives Arsenal victory in FA Cup semi-final at Old Trafford

17 - Robbie Stockdale makes his Scotland debut against Nigeria at Pittrodrie

24 - Stewart Downing makes full debut in defeat at Ipswich

MAY

2 - Boro agree £2.5m deal with Lens for loan star Franck Queudrue

10 - Robbie Stockdale and Allan Johnston called up for Scotland's Far East tour

15 - Death of former Boro chairman George Kitching. Jonathan Greening receives late call-up for England U-21 Euro finals squad

17 - Club announces season-ticket price freeze for 2002-3

18 - Marlon Beresford and Anthony Ormerod to be released in the summer

21- Boro vow to fight on after High Court rejects claims for damages over Christian Ziege affair; *Fulham want to bring Juninho back to the Premiership - Daily Express*

22 - Benito Carbone has his contract terminated at Bradford City

25 - *Derby and Cardiff are in a tug-of-war for Robbie Mustoe - Gazette*

26 - *Boro are looking at Brazilian striker Rodrigo - News of the World*

27 - *Roma midfielder Diego Fuser is being targeted by Middlesbrough - fromtheterrace.co.uk*

29 - *Boro are favourites to land Benni McCarthy - Gazette; Sunderland's Kevin Phillips is being strongly linked with a move to Boro - Gazette*

30 - *Middlesbrough want to bring Nick Barmby back to the North-East - Star*

31 - *Cameroon midfielder Marc Vivien Foe claims Boro are trying to tempt him to Teesside - Gazette*

• CUP STAR - Noel Whelan celebrates scoring in the 2-0 FA Cup win against Manchester United

total harmony in the dressing-room. It wasn't just that he was paid more than anyone else (and in many cases, vastly more) but that he contributed so little to the team's spirit. The best-paid guy happened to be the least committed."

Boksic top-scored that season with a measly eight league goals. No-one else managed more than four. Yet bit by bit, and despite another alarming run of four defeats around Christmas, the team scraped itself off the floor. Results were ground out. The football was unspectacular but the fans could forgive that if it meant staying in the Premiership.

The defence was key. Southgate and Ugo Ehiogu resumed their centre-back partnership from Villa days and Franck Queudrue, signed on loan from Lens, looked better and better as the season wore on. Robbie Stockdale, given an extended run on the other flank, produced some of the best football of his Boro career.

In the middle, 33-year-old Robbie Mustoe – recalled by McClaren after finding himself out of favour under Venables - found huge reserves of energy and Ince demonstrated immense motivational and leadership skills. Benito Carbone, signed on loan from Bradford City for the

straight defeats against Arsenal, Newcastle, Bolton and Everton. From the very first couple of months the campaign developed into a grim battle for survival.

Boro went into the home match with West Ham on September 15 bottom of the table and desperate for a point of any description. The 2-0 win restored an important degree of hope.

One of McClaren's main problems was the lack of a regular goalscorer. So much rested on the shoulders of their enigmatic Croatian, Alen Boksic, who seemed to perform only when it suited him. Southgate said revealingly in his book, *Woody and Nord:* "We didn't know whether we wanted Alen in our team or not. I felt we were a better side with Alen leading the attack but there was another view that in matches where we had our backs to the wall, he could be a passenger.

"This was especially true for away games. What was indisputable was during Alen's time at the club it was impossible to have

• WHAT A WIN - Alen Boksic scored the only goal as Manchester United were beaten at Old Trafford

Riverside X

Diary of the Decade

• BRILLIANT BENI - Loan signing Benito Carbone helped Boro in the second half of the season

final three months of the campaign, offered a new attacking outlet and undoubtedly contributed to Boro's survival.

In the end, it was comfortable. The team rose as high as ninth during the final weeks, which included a 1-0 win at Old Trafford on McClaren's first return to United. And there was also the consolation of a thrilling FA Cup run that climaxed in a semi-final defeat to Arsenal.

Only an unlucky own goal by Gianluca Festa denied Boro a second FA Cup final appearance. Along the way there was a memorable 2-0 fourth-round home win over Manchester United and victories over Blackburn and Everton.

McClaren's first season at the Riverside was a stressful baptism to management. "There were sleepless nights," he said. "But I did not doubt myself. I have to thank the staff around me for that. We had come together through the adversity and it really bonded us. We never doubted the players because we knew the talent was there to get through it."

2002

JUNE

9 - *Fiorentina striker Daniele Adani will be Boro's next target - Sport First*

12 - *Boro have abandoned their latest attempt to land Celta Vigo striker Benni McCarthy*

16 - *Boro are poised to make a £6m move for Derby striker Malcolm Christie*

21 - *Gareth Southgate wants a transfer and wants urgent talks with Steve McClaren - D. Express*

22 - *Ipswich midfielder Matt Holland is a £6m target for Boro - Mail*

23 - *Boro will step up their interest in Muzzy Izzet - Sunday Sun*

26 - *Boro strongly linked with Leeds striker Robbie Keane - Gazette*

29 - *Robbie Mustoe is set to sign for Derby County - Gazette*

30 - *Middlesbrough are close to landing Celtic midfielder Alan Thompson - Sunday People*

JULY

1 - Paul Ince turns down new two-year contract to join Wolves

2 - *Bayern Munich have issued a "hands-off" warning to Boro over Owen Hargreaves - Teamtalk*

3 - Massimo Maccarone becomes Boro's £8.15m record signing; Robbie Mustoe turns down a one-year deal to end his 12-year stay at the club; Boro agree a £3.8m fee with Atletico Madrid to re-sign Juninho

4 - Gareth Southgate unveiled as new Boro skipper

5 - Dial-a-Phone unveiled as new shirt sponsors

6 - *Spurs are ready with a renewed bid for Alen Boksic - Gazette*

7 - Steve McClaren dismisses speculation linking him with Leeds United; *Middlesbrough have stepped up their interest in Norwegian starlet Martin Wiig - Sunday Sun; Boro and Tottenham are in the hunt for Senegal World Cup star Henri Camara - N. Echo*

8 - Death of former Boro and England star Ralph Birkett, aged 89;

9 - 17,400 fans endorse moves to bring back Juninho on club's official website

10 - *Middlesbrough have bid £2.8m for Inter Milan's Grigoris Georgatos - D. Star*

11 - *Boro step up their efforts to bring Juninho back to the Riverside; Steve McClaren is expected to take Spanish midfielder Luis Helguera on trial - N. Echo*

14 - *Middlesbrough are in the hunt for £3m Italy midfielder Antonio Asta - Sunday Sun*

Season Stats 2001-02

	P	Home					Away					Pts	GD	H	A
		W	D	L	F	A	W	D	L	F	A				
Arsenal	38	12	4	3	42	25	14	5	0	37	11	87	+43	0-4	1-2
Liverpool	38	12	5	2	33	14	12	3	4	34	16	80	+37	1-2	0-2
Manchester Utd	38	11	2	6	40	17	13	3	3	47	28	77	+42	0-1	1-0
Newcastle Utd	38	12	3	4	40	23	9	5	5	34	29	71	+22	1-4	0-3
Leeds Utd	38	9	6	4	31	21	9	6	4	22	16	66	+16	2-2	0-1
Chelsea	38	11	4	4	43	21	6	9	4	23	17	64	+28	0-2	2-2
West Ham Utd	38	12	4	3	32	14	3	4	12	16	43	53	-9	2-0	0-1
Aston Villa	38	8	7	4	22	17	4	7	8	24	30	50	-1	2-1	0-0
Tottenham Hotspur	38	10	4	5	32	24	4	4	11	17	29	50	-4	1-1	1-2
Blackburn Rovers	38	8	6	5	33	20	4	4	11	22	31	46	+4	1-3	1-0
Southampton	38	7	5	7	23	22	5	4	10	23	32	45	-8	1-3	1-1
BORO	38	7	5	7	23	26	5	4	10	12	21	45	-12	-	-
Fulham	38	7	7	5	21	16	3	7	9	15	28	44	-8	2-1	1-2
Charlton Athletic	38	5	6	8	23	30	5	8	6	15	19	44	-11	0-0	0-0
Everton	38	8	4	7	26	23	3	6	10	19	34	43	-12	1-0	0-2
Bolton Wanderers	38	5	7	7	20	31	4	6	9	24	31	40	-18	1-1	0-1
Sunderland	38	7	7	5	18	16	3	3	13	11	35	40	-22	2-0	1-0
Ipswich Town	38	6	4	9	20	24	3	5	11	21	40	36	-23	0-0	0-1
Derby County	38	5	4	10	20	26	3	2	14	13	37	30	-30	5-1	1-0
Leicester City	38	3	7	9	15	34	2	6	11	15	30	28	-34	1-0	2-1

UEFA CUP CHAMPIONS LEAGUE

RELEGATED

Goals

Name	Prem	Total
Alen BOKSIC	8	8
Noel WHELAN	4	7
Szilard NEMETH	3	6
Paul INCE	2	3
Colin COOPER	2	2
Carlos MARINELLI	2	2
Robbie MUSTOE	2	2
Franck QUEUDRUE	2	2
Ugo EHIOGU	1	2
Benito CARBONE	1	1
Brian DEANE	1	1
Gianluca FESTA	1	1
Jonathan GREENING	1	1
Allan JOHNSTON	1	1
Gareth SOUTHGATE	1	1
Robbie STOCKDALE	1	1
Luke WILKSHIRE	1	1
Dean WINDASS	1	1
Mark WILSON	0	1

Player of the Year

BT Cellnet
Gareth Southgate

Supporters
Gareth Southgate

Appearances

	Prem	FAC	LC	UEFA	Total
Gareth SOUTHGATE	37	6	1	0	44
Jonathan GREENING	36	3(1)	1	0	40(1)
Robbie MUSTOE	31(5)	6	1(1)	0	38(6)
Paul INCE	31	4	1	0	36
Robbie STOCKDALE	26(2)	6	2	0	34(2)
Franck QUEUDRUE	28	6	0	0	34
Ugo EHIOGU	29	2	2	0	33
Mark SCHWARZER	21	3	1	0	25
Alen BOKSIC	20(2)	2(1)	1	0	23(3)
Noel WHELAN	18(1)	5	0	0	23(1)
Mark CROSSLEY	17	3	1	0	21
Carlos MARINELLI	12(8)	3(2)	1(1)	0	16(11)
Colin COOPER	14(4)	1	1(1)	0	16(5)
Allan JOHNSTON	13(4)	2(1)	1	0	16(5)
Szilard NEMETH	11(10)	2(2)	2	0	15(12)
Benito CARBONE	13	0	0	0	13
Dean WINDASS	8(19)	3(3)	1	0	12(22)
Gianluca FESTA	8	3(1)	0	0	11(1)
Curtis FLEMING	8	0	0	0	8
Jason GAVIN	5(4)	1(1)	1(1)	0	7(6)
Hamilton RICARD	6(3)	1	0(1)	0	7(4)
Luke WILKSHIRE	6	1	0	0	7
Brian DEANE	6(1)	0	0	0	6(1)
Mark WILSON	2(8)	1(1)	2	0	5(9)
Phil STAMP	3(3)	1(2)	0	0	4(5)
Joseph-Desire JOB	3(1)	0	0(1)	0	3(2)
David MURPHY	0(5)	0(1)	2	0	2(6)
Michael DEBEVE	1(3)	1(1)	0	0	2(4)
Stewart DOWNING	2(1)	0	0	0	2(1)
Steve VICKERS	2	0	0	0	2
Paul OKON	1(3)	0	0	0	1(3)
Andy CAMPBELL	0(4)	0(1)	0	0	0(5)
Mark HUDSON	0(2)	0	0	0	0(2)
Marlon BERESFORD	0(1)	0	0	0	0(1)
Dean GORDON	0(1)	0	0	0	0(1)

Line-Up

2001-02 Round-up

Premiership — Arsenal

FA Cup — Arsenal

League Cup — Blackburn Rovers

Champions League — Real Madrid

UEFA Cup — Feyenoord

PFA Player of the Year — Ruud van Nistelrooy (Manchester Utd)

PFA Young Player of the Year — Craig Bellamy (Newcastle Utd)

Promoted — Manchester City / West Bromwich Albion / Birmingham City

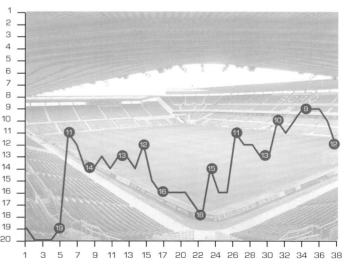

League Form

2002-03

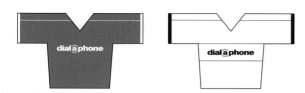

It was the crack of dawn in the UK, but already early afternoon in Shizuoka, Japan. England had just been eliminated from the 2002 World Cup thanks to a freak goal from Brazil's Ronaldinho that flew over goalkeeper David Seaman and ended the hopes of Sven Goran Eriksson's side before breakfast had been digested. But while it was the three Rs - Ronaldo, Rivaldo and Ronaldinho - that caught the headlines, the Brazilian with the best grasp of English was former Boro star Juninho and that was why, after the final whistle, 'The Little Fella' was grabbed by the British media to reflect on England's defeat.

Now 29, the brilliant midfielder was playing in his first World Cup and had started the first four games of the tournament before sitting out the quarter final against England.

But he would return for the final, coming on as a substitute to win a medal that must have more than made up for the domestic disappointments of 1997 with Boro.

While Boro fans would have been pleased to see Juninho back on their TV screens more than two years after his last Riverside game, little did they know that he would soon be signing for a third spell on Teesside. And, although he was on England duty, Three Lions coach Steve McClaren made his first move just moments after Brazil had achieved victory.

Juninho, still an Atletico Madrid player although he had spent much of the previous two years on loan back in his home country, recalled: "At the end of the England versus Brazil game Steve asked me if I would consider coming back to Middlesbrough. I said, 'Why not? Start the conversation and we will see what happens'. In the end I decided to come but this time not on loan, on a four-year contract. When you go somewhere on loan you are not really part of the club. That's why I wouldn't like to go on loan to any club again because I've had a bad experience."

Diary of the Decade

2002

JULY

15 - *Middlesbrough are targeting Celtic star Alan Thompson - D. Star*

16 - *Paris SG midfielder Edouard Cisse has set his sights on moving to Middlesbrough - Planet Football*

23 - *Cash-strapped Leicester have offered Muzzy Izzet to Boro for at cut-price - Evening Gazette*

26 - Juninho agrees a four-year deal with Boro after £3.8 fee agreed with Atletico Madrid; *Leeds want Gareth Southgate to replace Rio Ferdinand - News of the World*

AUGUST

1 - End of BT sponsorship deal sees Boro's home revert to "Riverside Stadium"

4 - *Jesper Blomqvist expects to become a Middlesbrough player within 48 hours - Sunday Sun*

5 - George Boateng signed from Aston Villa for £5m, bringing Steve McClaren's summer spending to £19.45m

7 - Tony Vidmar signs on a free transfer from Rangers; Juninho scores in comeback friendly against Alaves, with other new signings Massimo Maccarone and George Boateng also on target

2 - Geremi signs on a year's loan from Real Madrid

10 - Steve McClaren elects to stay on as Sven-Goran Eriksson's right-hand man

11 - Juninho tears cruciate ligament in friendly with Italian side Modena

16 - *Middlesbrough have turned down the chance to sign Brazilian World Cup star Ricardinho - N. Echo*

22 - Juninho will fly to USA for knee surgery

23 - *Alen Boksic is being lined up for a move to Real Madrid - Sun*

28 - Gianluca Festa and Phil Stamp released

29 - *Middlesbrough boss Steve McClaren is lining up a bid for Italian defender Emanuele Brioschi - D. Mirror*

SEPTEMBER

7 - Gareth Southgate wins his 50th England cap in friendly with Portugal

10 - Tony Vidmar signs on a free transfer after being released by Rangers; Nemeth (2) and Maccarone destroy Sunderland 3-0 at the Riverside

15 - *Middlesbrough are keeping tabs on Reading striker Darius Henderson - Sunday Sun*

18 - *Joseph-Desire Job has been taken off the transfer list - D. Express*

20 - *Middlesbrough are in the hunt for Icelandic teenager Sigurdur Donys - Express*

While the deal took some time to finalise, the second occasion Keith Lamb convinced the Brazilian to sign on a permanent basis was a much easier process than in 1995. Lamb said: "We were in the position of knowing him, his father Oswaldo and his family. It only took a long time because it was complicated for him to negotiate an exit from Atletico rather than negotiate a deal with Boro. He wasn't desperate to get away, but simply wanted to come back to Boro."

The £3.8m deal was just one of several designed to get the club buzzing again following a disappointing previous season that had been undermined by poor crowds.

Steve Gibson said: "Of course I was concerned that attendances dipped. This club only exists for the town and its people. If it appeared we were losing the approval of our supporters then it was clear we had to take some action - and that's what we did in the summer."

Each area of the field benefited as Gibson provided the cash that made the club the third highest spenders in the Premiership in the summer of 2002. A massive £19m was spent on Juninho, defender Franck Queudrue, midfielder George Boateng and the exciting young Italian striker Massimo Maccarone. The latter became the club's record signing at £8.15m from Empoli after impressing against England in the European U-21 Championships, while Boateng moved from Aston Villa and Queudrue made a permanent move from Lens after his successful loan spell.

Unfortunately Juninho would not be able to join his new teammates until March 2003 after suffering a horrendous cruciate ligament injury on a pre-season tour of Italy.

But Geremi - on loan from Real Madrid for a season - was able to start the opening game of the campaign at Southampton after a whirlwind signing. McClaren recalled: "Geremi was a player I came

• GREAT START - Massimo Maccarone celebrates a goal following his record £8.15m transfer

across when I was with Manchester United and we played Madrid on a couple of occasions. He always impressed me either in midfield or as full-back. I literally couldn't believe it when I got the call from an agent asking if we'd be interested in taking him on loan. I didn't need any convincing - I agreed straight away. Managers love calls like that - most calls are a waste of time but that's one I'll never forget."

The new boys didn't make an immediate impact in the goalless game at St Mary's, but just seven days later and Maccarone showed why he had been the talk of Europe over the summer. He scored two headers against Fulham in what would eventually be a 2-2 draw, and in the following home game an injury time strike from Joseph-Desire Job would see off Blackburn Rovers.

Two successive away defeats against Manchester United and Everton would follow, but a fantastic run of four wins in five games would see Boro rise to third place in the table by early October after adopting a diamond-shaped midfield which brought the best out of Boateng. The great run reached its zenith with a superb 3-0 win at Tottenham Hotspur, in which Maccarone, Geremi and Job were on target - with experienced coach Steve Harrison describing it as "the best away performance I've ever seen".

Riverside X

Diary of the Decade

A few weeks later, on November 4, and another fantastic display saw Gareth Southgate score the late winner against top-of-the-table Liverpool. It was the sixth win of the season - but a disastrous winter would see Boro win only seven matches over the rest of the campaign. McClaren said: "Our falling away showed that it was too early for us to be thinking about Europe. We were delighted with the start we made, but we knew that it would be hard to sustain because we didn't have the squad to cope with injuries. The Christmas period sorts teams out and we faded after that."

Even a Boxing Day win over Manchester United - thanks to goals from Alen Boksic, Szilard Nemeth and Job in front of 34,673 - could not inspire an immediate turnaround as four losses followed in the next five games in January.

But the first month of 2003 was more notable for four signings off the field rather than the dismal performances on it.

McClaren seemed determined to add some younger legs into his squad after the search for experience during his previous forays into the transfer market. Michael Ricketts was one player that had attracted the attention of a number of

- GOODBYE - Alen Boksic, in action during the 3-0 win at Spurs, retired midway through the season

2002

SEPTEMBER

22 - *Boro have targeted Torino forward Cristiano Lucarelli and South African striker Siyanonga Nomvete to replace Massimo Maccarone - Sunday Sun*

26 - Members of North Korea 1966 World Cup team visit Riverside for match with Leeds United

29 - Maccarone, Geremi and Job score in 3-0 win over Spurs at White Hart Lane

OCTOBER

4 - *Dean Windass wants to stay at Boro for the rest of his career - N. Echo*

5 - Ugo Ehiogu wins England recall for Euro Championship qualifiers with Slovakia and Macedonia

12 - *Steve McClaren is contemplating a move for Dutch winger Kevin Bobson - N.Echo; Middlesbrough are lining up a £6m bid for Brazilian starlet Diego Ribas da Cunha, "the new Pele" - Sunday Sun*

17 - FA announce that Riverside could be the venue for a senior England international for the first time

23 - *Boro are considering a New Year move for Celtic striker John Hartson and have made a fresh approach for Lazio midfielder Dino Baggio. They have also contacted representatives of AS Roma striker Gabriel Batistuta - Tribal Football*

26 - Mark Schwarzer presented with special memento to celebrate his 200th Boro appearance

28 - *Middlesbrough will make a New Year bid to land Leeds defender Danny Mills - Sun*

NOVEMBER

1 - Steve McClaren steps down as England coach to concentrate on his career at Boro

9 - *Boro are set to make an audacious £5m triple swoop for Derby pair Danny Higginbotham and Malcolm Christie and Brondby winger Thomas Lindrup - Gazette*

10 - *Middlesbrough are in the hunt for Barcelona star Michael Reiziger and Parma defender Matteo Ferrari - Sunday Sun; Steve McClaren has been given £6m to land Bayern Munich's Owen Hargreaves - S. People*

12 - Jonathan Greening named in England training squad ahead of Macedonia international

13 - Dean Windass joins Sheffield United on a month's loan; former Boro star Gary Gill seriously injured in road accident

15 - *Sugababes, Liberty X and Busted appear at Riverside in BBC Children in Need concert; Steve McClaren is lining up a £1m deal for Senegal defender Ferdinand Coly - D. Mail*

• LEADER - Gareth Southgate was impatient for success

McClaren needed even more firepower. The player he chose was Derby County's England U-21 ace Malcolm Christie, whose subtle talents had so impressed in the Premiership before the Rams' relegation in 2001-02.

And Boro's boss made it two purchases from Pride Park as he also bought Chris Riggott, a highly-rated central defender who, at just 22, was a year younger than Christie. While still in their early 20s the two had amassed over 200 league games between them for Derby - which made them seem excellent value both now and for the future. A slightly more vintage addition to McClaren's collection was the midfielder Doriva who arrived on loan from Celta Vigo, and would join Juninho among the Brazilian ranks at the Riverside. But while the 30-year-old would have to wait more than two months before his debut, the English lads were thrown in at the deep end.

Ricketts and Riggott would both start Boro's first game since the window was closed, and helped Boro to an impressive 1-1 draw with Liverpool at Anfield, in which Geremi gave McClaren's side the lead. That pair was joined by Christie in the starting XI for the following match - away at basement side Sunderland on February 22 - with Riggott scoring twice from defence and his ex-Derby pal grabbing the killer third in the 59th minute.

While Ricketts' Boro career would prove to be a disappointment, he impressed his new boss during the early weeks at the Riverside. "In January we were struggling to score - we needed some presence in attack," recalled the boss. "We went on a great run that got us back up the league. Michael was a presence during that time, and I hoped that he would build on that.

"It's always a disappointment when a player doesn't fulfil their potential and he was one of them. We thought we could get good things out of him, but we were wrong. He had made his England debut the previous year but has struggled since then - these things happen for various reasons but usually it's down to the player. Buying any player is a gamble, but he did little after those first few matches."

With new and old firing on all cylinders, the good times continued over the next fortnight with Juninho finally able to make his third 'debut' for the club. Just days after his

Premiership clubs after so impressing during his first top-flight season with Bolton Wanderers during 2001-02. Hitting 12 Premiership goals and picking up his first England cap, the forward seemed to have the lot - pace, strength, skill and an eye for goal - and that was why McClaren was willing to prise the player from the Reebok Stadium just hours before the transfer window slammed shut.

But £2.5m Ricketts wasn't the only striker purchased on January 31. Although Maccarone had scored twice in January and Nemeth had four goals to his name, Boksic announced his retirement at the end of the month - which meant

Riverside X

Diary of the Decade

comeback in the reserves was witnessed by a massive 19,450 crowd, he came on as a half-time substitute against Everton, and grabbed the 74th minute equaliser in a 1-1 Premiership draw on March 1. Then a Riverside record 34,814 saw Boro beat Newcastle United 1-0 thanks to a Geremi header, and the Cameroon ace would also nick a stunning winner at Leeds United next time out.

• NEW BOYS - Michael Ricketts, Chris Riggott and Malcolm Christie signed during the transfer window

2002

NOVEMBER

16 - *Alen Boksic will end his Boro career next summer by signing for Hajduk Split - Gazette*

22 - Former Boro star Jamie Pollock announces his retirement at the age of 28

24 - *Middlesbrough are on the trail of Piacenza stopper Gianluca Lamacchi and Lens star Ferdiand Coly - Sunday Sun*

26 - High Court decides Liverpool and Christian Ziege have case to answer over controversial transfer from Boro

30 - Joseph-Desire Job fractures skull in 1-0 defeat to West Bromwich at The Hawthorns

DECEMBER

4 - *Boro have again been linked with Barcelona striker Dani - Gazette*

5 - *Middlesbrough could revive their interest in Bayern Munich's Owen Hargeaves - D. Star*

2003

JANUARY

6 - Jamie Pollock joins TFM as presenter

7 - Dean Windass turns down request from Chelsea's Carlo Cudicini to support his appeal against his sending-off in the FA Cup defeat at Stamford Bridge

8 - Juninho and Benito Carbone nominated for FA Premier League's Ten Seasons Award, celebrating a decade of the new division; *McClaren wants the go-ahead to spend his way out of Boro's injury crisis - Express*

9 - Boro reveal they have enquired about Derby's Chris Riggott and Malcolm Christie

11 - *McClaren wants to sign Leeds midfielder Seth Johnson - Gazette*

12 - McClaren praises subs Whelan and Maccarone for great fightback against Southampton at the Riverside; *Geremi has warned Boro that he is unlikely to stay next season - Sunday Sun*

12 - *Boro and Sunderland are in the hunt for Italian hitman Dino Fava Passaro - Sunday Sun*

13 - *Boro target Malcolm Christie says it would be a huge wrench to leave Derby - Express;* Dean Windass joins Sheffield United on loan until the end of the season; Boro become only the second club in Britain to win an anti-racism award

14 - *Derby have rejected a Boro bid to take Christie and Riggott on loan - D. Mail*

15 - *Boro could be dragged into a tug of war with Leeds for Malcolm Christie - Gazette;* Boro will turn to Aberdeen centre-half Russell Anderson if their move for Riggott breaks down - D. Star

By the time Boro had drawn with Charlton, thumped West Bromwich Albion - Christie scoring in both games - and drawn with Manchester City, they were eight games unbeaten since the January arrivals had signed. Dreams of a highest ever Premier League finish and even a first ever European qualification were alive and kicking. But a 2-0 home defeat to Arsenal began a poor end to the season with four losses in the last five games, although Maccarone ended his first Riverside season

as he had started it with a home double as Spurs were thrashed 5-1. Christie, Juninho and Nemeth had made it 3-0 in the first half, and in the last game of the season Ricketts grabbed his first Boro goal - coincidentally at the Reebok Stadium against former club Bolton.

So four points more than in his first season, McClaren had also taken his side a position higher in the Premiership table. Each of the new signings had paid off to varying extents - Maccarone was top scorer with nine goals - while 2001 recruit Jonathan Greening had shone on the right of midfield, earning player of the year titles from fans and sponsors.

- IN FORM - Jonathan Greening edges past Liverpool's Danny Murphy during a 1-1 draw at Anfield

With an increasingly young squad, maybe Boro could look forward to an exciting future, but one character was sick of hearing about 'the future' and demanded answers from his boss. Skipper Southgate recalled: "I was delighted with some of the players we had brought in but it was the second year in which we had not progressed as I would have hoped. At the end of 2002-03 I was at a low point, particularly as Manchester United had been linked with me regularly in the newspapers. Paper talk unsettled me because I hoped the phone might ring based on those rumours - but it's something out of your own control.

"It seemed to be speculation but my thinking was that, at 32 or 33 years old, the chance would not come up again. I remember that I discussed things with Steve McClaren and he said to me that the club still had ambition and he wanted me to be part of it. The point for me was that it has to be now or never."

McClaren also recalls the meeting between skipper and boss, and said: "We spoke at the end of the first two years and, like me, he was very disappointed. The job was bigger than either of us imagined. He had been linked with other clubs and that made him unsettled.

"I said that I had no problem with his ambition, but I asked him to stick with us because years three and four would be when we would break through. If that hadn't happened we couldn't stand in his way. He was

Riverside X

Diary of the Decade

• MAGNIFICENT SEVEN - Szilard Nemeth grabs one of seven goals during 2002 - 03, against West Brom

patient. No one came in for him or made an offer, and I was glad. They would have had to offer big money because Gareth was, and is, irreplaceable."

While the phone didn't ring for Southgate, the manager's hopes of keeping hold of seven-goal Geremi ended when Russian billionaire Roman Abramovich took over Chelsea in July and made the Cameroon ace one of his first signings. But McClaren attempted to snap Geremi up again in 2005 and believes he could one day return. He said: "Geremi lifted us throughout the season and was influential with his goals, free kicks and performances. I was disappointed when he decided to leave because he liked it here - but no one knows what might happen in the future."

2003

JANUARY

16 - *Bill Beswick has voiced concerns that Gareth Southgate is in danger of burn-out - Times*

17 - *Coventry midfielder John Eustace joins on a month's loan; Boro have launched a shock bid to land Spurs striker Les Ferdinand - D. Star*

19 - Boro extend away losing streak to eight matches with 1-0 defeat at Fulham

20 - *Seth Johnson is on his way to Boro for £4m - Mirror; Brian Clough is recovering from a liver operation*

21 - *Boro and Fulham have joined the race for Michael Ricketts - Telegraph*

26 - *Spurs are lining up a bid for Alen Boksic - S. Mirror*

27 - *Seth Johnson's proposed Boro move has collapsed - News of the World ; Boro are lining up a shock move for AC Milan striker Jon Dahl Tomasson - Sunday Sport*

30 - FA announced that Riverside will host England's World Cup qualifier with Slovakia on June 11; *Romania midfielder Paul*

Codrea has set his sights on moving to Boro - N. Echo

31 - Boro beat the Transfer Window clock to sign Malcolm Christie and Chris Riggott from Derby for a combined £3m fee, Michael Ricketts from Bolton for £2.5m and ex-Brazilian international Doriva from Celta Vigo on a free. Carlos Marinelli joins Torino on loan until the end of the season

FEBRUARY

1 - Controversy over postponement of Riverside derby with Newcastle because of snow

2 - *Alen Boksic has stunned Boro by quitting the club - News of the World*

8 - Geremi free-kick strike in 1-1 draw with Liverpool at Anfield is Boro's first away goal in 13 hours, ending run of eight straight defeats on their travels13 - Andrew Davies turns down the chance to play for Wales U-20

14 - *Boro are tracking Roma keeper Francisco Antonioli - Sunday Sun*

22 - New boys Malcolm Christie and Chris Riggott (2) make instant impact in 3-1 away win over Sunderland

28 - Noel Whelan joins Crystal Palace on loan; *Middlesbrough are keeping tabs on Chievo Verona midfielder Eugenio Corini Otar*

MARCH

1 - Juninho scores on senior return following cruciate op in 1-1 home draw with Everton

8 - Jason Gavin joins Sheffield United on a week-long trial and Mark Crossley returns to Stoke on loan

Season Stats 2002-03

	P	Home						Away						Pts	GD	H	A
		W	D	L	F	A		W	D	L	F	A					
Manchester Utd	38	16	2	1	42	12		9	6	4	32	22		83	+40	3-1	0-1
Arsenal	38	15	2	2	47	20		8	7	4	38	22		78	+43	0-2	0-2
Newcastle Utd	38	15	2	2	36	17		6	4	9	27	31		69	+15	1-0	0-2
Chelsea	38	12	5	2	41	15		7	5	7	27	23		67	+30	1-1	0-1
Liverpool	38	9	8	2	30	16		9	2	8	31	25		64	+20	1-0	1-1
Blackburn Rovers	38	9	7	3	24	15		7	5	7	28	28		60	+9	1-0	0-1
Everton	38	11	5	3	28	19		6	3	10	20	30		59	-1	1-1	1-2
Southampton	38	9	8	2	25	16		4	5	10	18	30		52	-3	2-2	0-0
Manchester City	38	9	2	8	28	26		6	4	9	19	28		51	-7	3-1	0-0
Tottenham Hotspur	38	9	4	6	30	29		5	4	10	21	33		50	-11	5-1	3-0
BORO	38	10	7	2	36	21		3	3	13	12	23		49	+4	-	-
Charlton Athletic	38	8	3	8	26	30		6	4	9	19	26		49	-11	1-1	0-1
Birmingham City	38	8	5	6	25	23		5	4	10	16	26		48	-8	1-0	0-3
Fulham	38	11	3	5	26	18		2	6	11	15	32		48	-9	2-2	0-1
Leeds Utd	38	7	3	9	25	26		7	2	10	33	31		47	+1	2-2	3-2
Aston Villa	38	11	2	6	25	14		1	7	11	17	33		45	-5	2-5	0-1
Bolton Wanderers	38	7	8	4	27	24		3	6	10	14	27		44	-10	2-0	1-2
West Ham Utd	38	5	7	7	21	24		5	5	9	21	35		42	-17	2-2	0-1
West Bromich Albion	38	3	5	11	17	34		3	3	13	12	31		26	-36	3-0	0-1
Sunderland	38	3	2	14	11	31		1	5	13	10	34		19	-44	3-0	3-1

UEFA CUP CHAMPIONS LEAGUE

RELEGATED

Goals

Name	Prem	Total
Massimo **MACCARONE**	9	9
GEREMI	7	7
Szilard **NEMETH**	7	7
Malcolm **CHRISTIE**	4	4
Joseph-Desire **JOB**	4	4
Ugo **EHIOGU**	3	3
JUNINHO	3	3
Alen **BOKSIC**	2	2
Jonathan **GREENING**	2	2
Chris **RIGGOTT**	2	2
Gareth **SOUTHGATE**	2	2
Franck **QUEUDRUE**	1	2
Noel **WHELAN**	1	2
Michael **RICKETTS**	1	1
Stewart **DOWNING**	0	1
Carlos **MARINELLI**	0	1
Mark **WILSON**	0	1

Player of the Year

Dial-a-Phone	Supporters
Jonathan Greening	Jonathan Greening

Appearances

	Prem	FAC	LC	UEFA	Total
Jonathan **GREENING**	38	1	0	0	39
Mark **SCHWARZER**	38	1	0	0	39
Gareth **SOUTHGATE**	36	1	0	0	37
GEREMI	33	1	0	0	34
Franck **QUEUDRUE**	29(2)	1	1	0	31(2)
Ugo **EHIOGU**	31(1)	0	0	0	31(1)
George **BOATENG**	28	0	0	0	28
Massimo **MACCARONE**	26(8)	0	0	0	26(8)
Joseph-Desire **JOB**	22(6)	1	0	0	23(6)
Stuart **PARNABY**	21	1	1	0	23
Szilard **NEMETH**	15(13)	1	1	0	17(13)
Colin **COOPER**	14(6)	0(1)	2	0	16(7)
Alen **BOKSIC**	13(5)	0(1)	0	0	13(6)
Robbie **STOCKDALE**	12(2)	0	1	0	13(2)
Tony **VIDMAR**	9(3)	1	2	0	12(3)
Malcolm **CHRISTIE**	11(1)	0	0	0	11(1)
Luke **WILKSHIRE**	7(7)	0	2	0	9(7)
JUNINHO	9(1)	0	0	0	9(1)
Mark **WILSON**	4(2)	1	2	0	7(2)
Michael **RICKETTS**	5(4)	0	0	0	5(4)
Carlos **MARINELLI**	3(4)	0	2	0	5(4)
David **MURPHY**	4(4)	0	0	0	4(4)
Chris **RIGGOTT**	4(1)	0	0	0	4(1)
Noel **WHELAN**	2(13)	0(1)	1	0	3(14)
DORIVA	3(2)	0	0	0	3(2)
Dean **WINDASS**	0(2)	1	1	0	2(2)
Andrew **DAVIES**	1	0	1	0	2
Mark **CROSSLEY**	0	0	2	0	2
Allan **JOHNSTON**	0	0	2	0	2
Jason **GAVIN**	0	0	1	0	1
Stewart **DOWNING**	0(2)	0	0(1)	0	0(3)
Craig **DOVE**	0	0	0(2)	0	0(2)
John **EUSTACE**	0(1)	0	0	0	0(1)
Jamie **CADE**	0	0	0(1)	0	0(1)
Brian **CLOSE**	0	0	0(1)	0	0(1)

2002-03
Round-up

Premiership
Manchester United

FA Cup
Arsenal

Carling Cup
Liverpool

Champions League
Milan

UEFA Cup
Porto

PFA Player of the Year
Thierry Henry (Arsenal)

PFA Young Player of the Year
Jermaine Jenas (Newcastle Utd)

Promoted
Portsmouth
Leicester City
Wolverhampton Wanderers

Line-Up

League Form

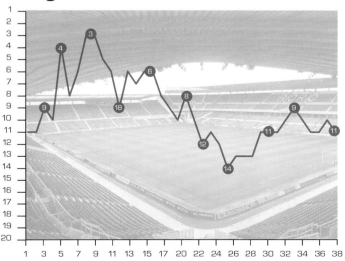

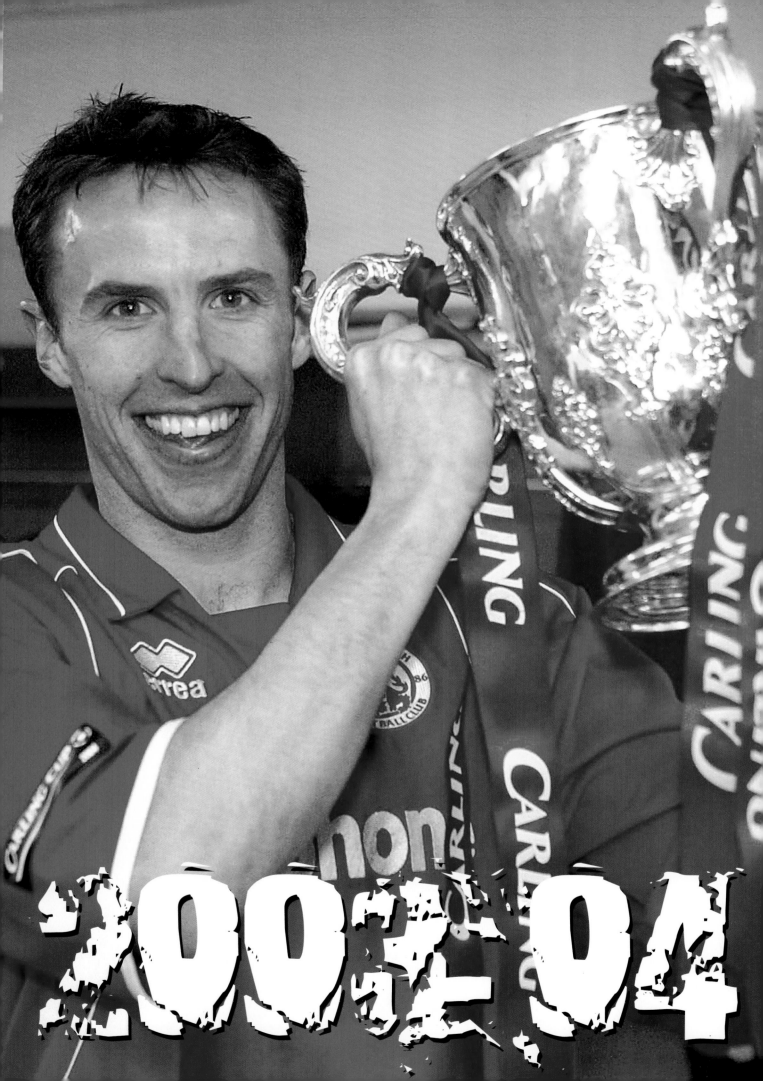

High Premiership finishes are all very well, but will the achievement of fourth or fifth spot in the table be remembered forever by a club's fans?

The season 2003-04 will undoubtedly be regarded as Boro's most successful to date because, quite simply, they finally lifted a major piece of silverware. At last, after 128 years of existence, the club joined the ranks of those with a major trophy in the cabinet.

It was the Carling Cup that was lifted, at the Millennium Stadium in Cardiff on Sunday, February 29 following a 2-1 win over Bolton Wanderers. The game began in exhilarating style with Joseph-Desire Job opening the scoring after two minutes and Bolo Zenden soon making it 2-0 from the penalty spot. With 72,634 in attendance, Kevin Davies pulled one back for Bolton in the 21st minute, but Boro held on to their lead and Mike Riley's final whistle produced scenes never before seen in the club's history.

Gareth Southgate lifted the trophy and chairman Steve Gibson was among those celebrating with the players on the Millennium Stadium turf. The Carling Cup run began in the rather less glamorous surroundings of Brighton's Withdean Stadium and only an extra-time goal from Malcolm Christie put Boro through.

Wigan Athletic, Everton and Tottenham Hotspur were then dispatched before a semi-final against Arsenal in January. The first leg saw Juninho hit a winner at Highbury while Zenden seemed to have all but wrapped up the club's third appearance in the League Cup final in eight years when he opened the scoring at the Riverside in the 69th minute.

Arsenal's Edu pulled one back eight minutes later but a late own goal from Jose Antonio Reyes guaranteed Boro's first trip to the Millennium Stadium - which had hosted major finals since Wembley's temporary closure in 2000.

While Job and Zenden scored the goals in the final, Southgate felt that the team was helped by an unsung 'twelfth man'. The

Diary of the Decade

2003

MARCH

9 - *Middlesbrough have been linked with an audacious swoop for West Ham star Paulo Di Canio - Sunday Sun; Alen Boksic is interesting the backers of a new league in Qatar - S. Express*

15 - *Steve McClaren plans to make on-loan Real Madrid midfielder Geremi a permanent signing - Sun*

23 - *Middlesbrough are lining up Atalanta midfielder Ousmane Dabo - Sunday Sun*

28 - *Steve McClaren has ruled out bids for Chievo midfielder Eugenio Corini and West Brom playmaker Jason Koumas - N. Echo*

31 - *Boro are monitoring the progress of Boavista midfielder Jose Bosingwa - Gazette*

APRIL

2 - *Newcastle are planning an audacious £2m swoop for Gareth Southgate - D. Express*

9 - *Emerson wants to return to the Riverside - D. Mirror*

11 - *Boro are preparing to fight Aston Villa and Leeds for Sunderland's Kevin Phillips - D. Mail*

13 - *Middlesbrough have resurrected their interest in Austrian international Markus Schopp of Brescia and made enquiries about Auxerre's World Cup winger Khalilou Fadiga - Sunday Sun*

17 - *Middlesbrough are planning a summer move for Blackburn's Keith Gillespie - D. Mail*

20 - *Middlesbrough are tracking Crystal Palace forward Julian Gray - Sunday Sun; Rivaldo has emerged as a summer target for Boro - News of the World; Steve McClaren wants to grab Blackburn Rovers skipper Garry Flitcroft - People*

22 - *Boro are being linked with Hearts midfielder Scott Severin - Evening Gazette*

23 - *Middlesbrough and Everton are in a tug of war for Sunderland forward Kevin Kilbane - N. Echo*

MAY

3 - *Mark Viduka is a summer target for ambitious Boro - Gazette*

7 - *Middlesbrough have been linked with Sheffield United midfielder Michael Brown - D. Express*

11 - *Valencia are on the trail of Jonathan Greening - Sunday Sun*

13 - *Franck Queudrue picks up a five-match ban for his red card in 2-1 defeat at Bolton, his third sending-off of the season*

15 - *Colin Cooper is wanted by Sunderland - S. Mirror*

18 - *Brazilian winger Rodrigo has begged Steve McClaren to play him alongside Juninho at Middlesbrough - News of the World; Middlesbrough have been offered Brescia strike duo Igli Tare and Luca Toni - Sunday Sun*

skipper said: "The fans played a major role in the win. The first big thing I remember about the day was travelling through the area of Cardiff that our supporters were in on the way to the stadium. It was a real lift to see all that red and it really got everyone going. The scenes when we had won will never be forgotten by the players or the fans that were there.

"We could go on to win the league or European Cup but will not be able to top the outpouring of emotion on that day. It was terrific to be involved. I had been there for three years and it felt wonderful, so I can only imagine what it must have been like for fans who had followed the team for a lifetime."

After spending such vast amounts in the summer of 2002 and January 2003, it should have been no surprise that Boro were now among the top sides in the country.

But the summer transfer window ahead of 2003-04 was a quieter affair for McClaren and Gibson - at least in terms of fees.

International stars Gaizka Mendieta, Danny Mills and Zenden each joined the club on loan for the season from Lazio, Leeds United and Chelsea respectively. Mendieta had been one of the most celebrated players in Europe a few seasons before when he inspired Valencia to two consecutive Champions League finals in 2000 and 2001. The first was lost to Real Madrid and he then scored in the 2001 final against Bayern Munich, before again suffering defeat - this time on penalties. In the summer of 2001 he moved to Lazio for £28.9m, but endured a difficult season before returning to Spain on loan with Barcelona in 2002-03. However, the Catalans did not make the move permanent and McClaren grabbed the opportunity to sign a world-class midfielder.

"We were absolutely delighted to have signed him," said McClaren at the time. "I came across him many times in European competition when I was with Manchester United and he was at Valencia. He was undoubtedly one of Europe's best players at that time. We had spent all summer searching for a quality player to replace Geremi on the wide right and believed Mendi would bring creativity to our play, while also contributing to our scoring. Eventually we would sign him the following summer on a free transfer - we just couldn't believe the deal that we got."

Mendi would score just twice in his 31 league appearances in 2003-04, but his creativity was there for all to behold - as was the case with Dutch international Zenden. The ex-PSV and Barcelona star was well known to Premiership crowds after two seasons with Chelsea, while the third loanee was Mills - who had played all of England's games in World Cup 2002. The right-back was known for his fiery temper and ability in almost equal measure, but he seemed a great signing as financially-troubled Leeds attempted to get as many players as possible off their payroll.

• KEY ACQUISITION - Gaizka Mendieta

Riverside X

Diary of the Decade

• ON THE BALL - Danny Mills joined on a season's loan from Leeds

Carlos Marinelli grabbed the first goal of the Premiership year when he opened his account just 10 minutes into the Fulham game at Craven Cottage, in what would be his last appearance for the club after four inconsistent seasons. But the West London side would win 3-2 - thanks, in part, to a penalty miss from Malcolm Christie - and worse was to come the following week when Boro were thrashed 4-0 at home to Arsenal. The first point was gained in a 1-1 draw at Leicester City, but defeats three and four came against Leeds United and then Bolton.

Southgate said: "It looked like a disaster, but then somehow we got a result against Everton and then Malcolm Christie scored the winner in extra time against Brighton in the Carling Cup and then scored another as

2003

MAY

28 - *Manchester United will make another move to sign Gareth Southgate - D. Mail*

30 - *Steve McClaren is lining up a £4m bid for Fulham midfielder Sean Davis - D. Mirror; Villa full-back Ulises de la Cruz claims he is a target for Middlesbrough - Sport First*

JUNE

1 - Tony Vidmar and Arturo Bernhardt released

3 - *Steve McClaren is planning an ambitious double bid for Blackburn's David Dunn and Barcelona's Marc Overmars - Gazette*

9 - *Manchester City have joined the chase for Geremi - Gazette*

11 - Riverside stages its first senior international since 1937 when England (with Gareth Southgate) beat Slovakia (with Szilard Nemeth) 2-1 in a Euro 2004 qualifier watched by a capacity crowd

16 - *Boro are tracking Sporting Lisbon hot shot Mario Jardel - Gazette*

18 - *Middlesbrough are showing interest in Ray Parlour - D. Mail; Manchester United are ready to snatch Geremi from under Boro's noses - Gazette*

20 - *Birmingham City are ready to offer Mark Crossley a two-year deal - N. Echo*

21 - *Boro are tracking West Ham winger Trevor Sinclair - Gazette*

22 - *Bayern Munich and Borussia Dortmund are tracking Franck Queudrue - Sunday Sun*

23 - *Middlesbrough have been offered Lyon midfielder Marc-Vivien Foe on a free transfer - N. Echo*

24 - *Boro are ready to challenge Newcastle for Feyenoord midfielder Brett Emerton - Gazette*

25 - *Middlesbrough have switched their attentions to Arsenal midfielder Edu - N. Echo*

28 - *Michael Ricketts aims to be the fittest man on Teesside next season - Gazette*

29 - *Middlesbrough are back on the trail of French midfielder Ousmane Dabo - Sunday Sun; Jonathan Greening is a shock target for Arsenal - D. Star; Middlesbrough have been linked with Roma striker Marco Delvecchio - Sunday Sun*

JULY

5 - *Steve McClaren wants Sheffield United's Michael Brown - N. Echo*

6 - Ugo Ehiogu diagnosed with a cruciate injury; *Boro are front-runners to sign Leeds United misfit Olivier Dacourt - D. Star*

8 - *Middlesbrough have joined the race for Newcastle winger Nolberto Solano - D. Star*

13 - *Steve McClaren wants Newcastle star Gary Speed - People; Middlesbrough are back in the hunt for Sedan striker Henri Camara - Sunday Sun*

• CORKER - Massimo Maccarone scored a fantastic goal against Birmingham, and is congratulated by (left) Doriva, Juninho and Jonathan Greening

we beat Southampton in the Premiership. It just shows how a cup win can inspire a team."

That Everton victory - the seventh game of the season - came on September 21, and Boro were soon embarking on an 11-game unbeaten run which included wins over Aston Villa, Manchester City, Tottenham and Wolves. Amazingly the period also included a streak of four goalless scorelines in five games with Boro sharing bore draws against Liverpool, Portsmouth, Charlton Athletic and, in the Carling Cup, Everton. In fact a club record was equalled as Boro avoided conceding a goal in seven consecutive games as they matched the feat of the 1987-88 side, which had included a young Colin Cooper, now 36 years old and still going strong on Teesside.

Boro's unbeaten run came to an end against those old foes from Manchester

United, with Sir Alex Ferguson's team leaving the Riverside with three points after a 1-0 win on December 28, courtesy of a Mills own goal. The New Year began in fine style with win a over Fulham which heralded the arrival of a new star on the Boro scene. His name was Stewart Downing, and the young left winger had spent the previous few weeks on loan at Sunderland but was recalled because of injuries to several first-teamers. While only 19 years old, the Pallister Park kid was confident enough to snatch the ball from the likes of Mendieta to take free kicks as he sought to establish himself for his hometown club.

Notts County were also comfortably beaten in the FA Cup as Boro made it two wins in two in 2004, before crashing back to Earth with a 4-1 thumping by Arsenal.

Southgate picked up an injury in that match - a big worry as it was the first of four meetings with the Gunners in the space of less than four weeks, as they had also been drawn together in the Carling Cup semi-final and the FA Cup fourth round. Southgate said: "I missed the first leg of

Riverside X

Diary of the Decade

the semi-final and didn't even travel to London because I was working so intensely on the injury. I watched the game on television and it was a bit scary. Our defence was all over the place because of injury, and even though they put out a weakened team they had such a mental hold over us because of the thrashings they had given us. But we managed to get a 1-0 win."

Despite first-leg victory, Southgate was negative about his side's chances of progressing - especially after a 4-1 defeat in the FA Cup four days later. He said: "I didn't think that would be enough of a lead, and I was concerned when I saw the side they picked for the second leg which included Patrick Vieira, Ashley Cole, Edu and Jose Antonio Reyes, who made his debut. I knew it would be a hell of a game even if Thierry Henry, Robert Pires and Freddie Ljungberg didn't play. Arsenal gave us a cracking game. I remember it being a fantastic atmosphere. We got ahead late in the game but they pulled one back which could have made things very awkward for us."

So Arsenal had been thwarted at last - despite having scored four goals in three of the five games between the clubs in 2003-04. But McClaren's team also had other big sides in their sights - and Leeds were put to the sword

• BACK OF THE NET - Joseph-Desire Job scores in the home win over Fulham

2003

JULY

15 - Alan Wright pulls out of Boro training try-out to join Rangers

16 - Loan star Geremi joins Chelsea

21 - Doriva signs one-year contract

22 - *Middlesbrough target Scott Parker has penned a new five-year deal with Charlton - N. Echo;* Colin Cooper signs new one-year deal

25 - Luke Wilkshire joins Bristol City for £100,000

26 - Massimo Maccarone suffers ankle ligament damage in friendly at Hull

27 - *Middlesbrough could be ready to swoop for Brazilian striker Jardel - Sunday Sun*

29 - *Inter Milan have confirmed Boro's interest in French midfielder Stephane Dalmat - Gazette; Boro's number one summer target, Brazilian midfielder Flavio Conceicao, has dramatically snubbed a move to the club - Gazette; Steve McClaren is making a £2m swoop for NAC Breda winger Kevin Bobson - D. Mirror*

AUGUST

4 - *Steve McClaren could be lining up a deal for Inter Milan midfielder Giorgios Karagounis - Gazette;* Alan Wright signs one-year contract after being freed by Aston Villa

5 - Noel Whelan joins Millwall on loan; *Middlesbrough are lining up a move for Sheffield United midfielder Michael Tonge - D. Star*

13 - Mark Crossley joins Fulham for £500,000 with Carlo Nash (Manchester City) lined up as replacement deputy keeper

23 - Danny Mills signs on a year's loan from Leeds and Gaizka Mendieta joins from Lazio for a similar period

29 - *Steve McClaren has made a shock move for Heerenveen striker Romano Denneboom - D. Mirror; Steve McClaren has refused to pay £3m for Lazio midfielder Christian Manfredini - N. Echo*

31 - Bolo Zenden signs on a year's loan from Chelsea; Stuart Parnaby suffers cruciate ligament injury in 3-2 home defeat to Leeds

SEPTEMBER

3 - Andrew Davies selected for England U-21

24 - Malcolm Christie scores extra-time winner over Brighton in Carling Cup

OCTOBER

3 - Knee injury in training puts Joseph Job out for four months

4 - Hernan Crespo's late goal seals Chelsea's 2-1 win at the Riverside

12 - *Middlesbrough's hopes of luring striker Eidur Gudjohnsen from Chelsea have been dashed - Sunday Sun*

17 - Arrival of Captain Cook replica ship HM Bark Endeavour at Middlehaven

24 - Robbie Stockdale joins West Ham on a month's loan

at Elland Road on January 31 with Zenden, Job and Michael Ricketts each scoring in a 3-0 win. Just 18 months previously, the West Yorkshire side had apparently wanted to recruit McClaren as they searched for a return to the Champions League, but now they were heading for relegation.

• ON THE WAY - Juninho beats off the challenge of Arsenal's Kolo Toure in the Carling Cup semi-final

Another club with a link to Boro's boss would be next to taste defeat as McClaren's men upset the apple cart with a 3-2 win at Old Trafford, courtesy of a Juninho double and a late strike from Job. An unfortunate defeat at Newcastle wasn't the best way to prepare for the Carling Cup final at the end of February, but the win over Bolton was also followed up by a 3-1 defeat at Birmingham City - with McClaren complaining that Boro should not be forced to play a league match so soon after the biggest game in the club's history.

Hopes remained high that Boro could go on a run that would secure the club's best Premier League finish, but inconsistency was a problem during the run-in for a second successive campaign. Impressive home wins over Tottenham, Birmingham, Bolton and Southampton left Boro within four points of fourth-placed Liverpool with five games remaining. But a toothless display at relegation-bound Wolves dented hopes of a record-breaking finish. When that was followed up with a 2-1 home defeat to fellow Euro-chasers Aston Villa, the season was all over bar the shouting. Indeed, it would end with a humbling last defeat at Portsmouth, with Yakubu helping himself to four of the goals. McClaren said: "The cup win probably didn't help our chances of a high league position - tiredness caught up with us and we maybe lacked the incentive to slog our guts out. We had already made it into Europe and it caused a loss of focus."

Despite a poor finish from the team there were plenty of plusses in the squad, with Mendieta initially struggling for consistency on the left wing but coming into form in the New Year, winning fans over with a series of exciting displays. While having to adapt to the pace of English football, Mendieta's quality often stood out. Zenden also took time to settle, but the midfield was kept together by the ever-dependable George Boateng and Players' Player of the Year, Doriva.

Juninho seemed to revel in his first full season since returning to Teesside and, with eight Premiership goals in his 31 appearances, was just one strike behind top scorer Szilard Nemeth. The Brazilian was selected Player of the Year by supporters, but the club legend was to make his last-ever Boro appearance on April 24 against Villa, with a thigh injury ruling him out for the rest of the season and a move to Celtic taking place in August. McClaren explained: "We had brought Juni in to provide a spark that would help us beat opponents, and he had a burning ambition to win things with the club. But he broke his leg in his first pre-season and was out for the best part of a year, and that was a massive disappointment. He lost half a yard because of the injuries he suffered, and that was ultimately why we let him go. He still had it in the brain and feet and he was still an effective player, but he just couldn't get away from defenders."

Riverside X

Diary of the Decade

While established international players were the main Premiership focus, there was plenty bubbling just beneath the surface. Downing scooped the Supporters Club Young Player of the Year, while James Morrison followed him by making his Premiership debut. Young full-back Tony McMahon showed what an impressive crop of talent was progressing at the Riverside as he lifted the FA Youth Cup in April following a fantastic win over Aston Villa. Youth team skipper Andrew Davies was another Academy graduate who made his way into the first team, but after making 10 appearances he broke his right leg in March and was on the sidelines for months.

Southgate and Ugo Ehiogu also missed chunks of the season through injury, with the latter out for seven months with a posterior cruciate ligament problem as well as a number of other minor ailments. And there was heartache for skipper Southgate who missed the closing stages of the campaign with a knee injury that also caused him to miss Euro 2004 - which would have been the England star's fifth consecutive major international tournament.

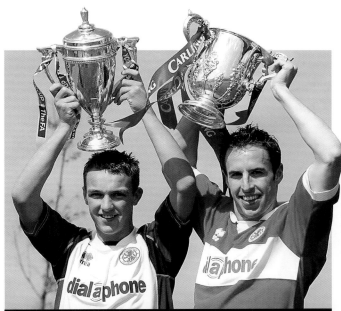

• CUP WINNERS - Tony McMahon and Gareth Southgate show off the FA Youth Cup and Carling Cup trophies

2003

OCTOBER

26 - *Steve McClaren is eyeing Inter Milan striker Obafemi Martins - News of the World*

30 - Stewart Downing joins Sunderland on loan

NOVEMBER

1 - Steve McClaren celebrates 100 matches as Boro manager in 2-0 league win over Wolves at Riverside

2 - *Marc Overmars could be set for a Premiership return with Middlesbrough - News of the World*

4 - Malcolm Christie breaks a leg in training ground accident

29 - *Lazio hotshot Simone Inzaghi is a January transfer target for Boro - Gazette*

DECEMBER

3 - Boro beat Everton in penalty shoot-out to reach Carling Cup quarter-finals

4 - *Boro could be in the running to sign Brazilian superstar Rivaldo - N. Echo*

6 - Colin Cooper celebrates 700th match for club and country

10 - *Boro are planning to offer £2m for Blackburn striker Andy Cole - Gazette*

11 - Stewart Downing recalled from loan at Sunderland to answer Riverside injury crisis

13 - Goalless home draw with Charlton is Boro's record-breaking seventh successive clean sheet

14 - *Boro have turned down a £500,000 bid from Wigan for Stewart Downing - News of the World*

17 - Boro penalty winners again with Carling Cup quarter-final triumph at Spurs

23 - *Steve McClaren will be first on the phone if Manchester United decide to sell £4m-rated Nicky Butt - D. Mirror*

28 - *Chelsea want Steve McClaren to be Sven Goran Eriksson's No. 2 at Stamford Bridge - The People*

2004

JANUARY

1 - *Boro have re-entered the race to land in-demand Preston striker Ricardo Fuller - N. Echo*

2 - *Boro may face competition from Leeds for Porto striker Edgars Jankauskas - D. Mail*

7 - *Middlesbrough want striker Dmitri Bulykin from Dinamo Moscow - Sun*

13 - *Boro are targeting Liverpool striker Emile Heskey - Gazette*

14 - *Sheffield Wednesday are chasing Boro centre-back Colin Cooper - Star*

Riverside X

Season Stats 2003-04

	P	Home					Away					Pts	GD	H	A
		W	D	L	F	A	W	D	L	F	A				
Arsenal	38	15	4	0	40	14	11	8	0	33	12	90	+47	0-4	4-1
Chelsea	38	12	4	3	34	13	12	3	4	33	17	79	+37	1-2	0-0
Manchester Utd	38	12	4	3	37	15	11	2	6	27	20	75	+29	0-1	3-2
Liverpool	38	10	4	5	29	15	6	8	5	26	22	60	+18	0-0	0-2
Newcastle Utd	38	11	5	3	33	14	2	12	5	19	26	56	+12	0-1	1-2
Aston Villa	38	9	6	4	24	19	6	5	8	24	25	56	+4	1-2	2-0
Charlton Athletic	38	7	6	6	29	29	7	5	7	22	22	53	0	0-0	0-1
Bolton Wanders	38	6	8	5	24	21	8	3	8	24	35	53	-8	2-0	0-2
Fulham	38	9	4	6	29	21	5	6	8	23	25	52	+6	2-1	2-3
Birmingham City	38	8	5	6	26	24	4	9	6	17	24	50	-5	5-3	1-3
BORO	38	8	4	7	25	23	5	5	9	19	29	48	-8	-	-
Southampton	38	8	6	5	24	17	4	5	10	20	28	47	-1	3-1	1-0
Portsmouth	38	10	4	5	35	19	2	5	12	12	35	45	-7	0-0	1-5
Tottenham Hotspur	38	9	4	6	33	27	4	2	13	14	30	45	-10	1-0	0-0
Blackburn Rovers	38	5	4	10	25	31	7	4	8	26	28	44	-8	0-1	2-2
Manchester City	38	5	9	5	31	24	4	5	10	24	30	41	+1	2-1	1-0
Everton	38	8	5	6	27	20	1	7	11	18	37	39	-12	1-0	1-1
Leicester City	38	3	10	6	19	28	3	5	11	29	37	33	-17	3-3	0-0
Leeds Utd	38	5	7	7	25	31	3	2	14	15	48	33	-39	2-3	3-0
Wolves	38	7	5	7	23	35	0	7	12	15	42	33	-39	2-0	0-2

Goals

Name	Prem	Total
Szilard NEMETH	9	9
JUNINHO	8	9
Joseph-Desire JOB	6	8
Massimo MACCARONE	6	7
Bolo ZENDEN	4	7
Gaizka MENDIETA	2	3
Michael RICKETTS	2	3
Malcolm CHRISTIE	1	2
Jonathan GREENING	1	1
Carlos MARINELLI	1	1
Gareth SOUTHGATE	1	1

Player of the Year

Dial-a-Phone
Juninho

Supporters
George Boateng

Appearances

	Prem	FAC	LC	UEFA	Total
Mark SCHWARZER	36	1	7	0	44
George BOATENG	35	2	6	0	43
Franck QUEUDRUE	31	2	7	0	40
Bolo ZENDEN	31	2	5(1)	0	38(1)
Gaizka MENDIETA	30(1)	1	6	0	37(1)
Danny MILLS	28	2	7	0	37
Gareth SOUTHGATE	27	1	6	0	34
JUNINHO	26(5)	0(1)	5(1)	0	31(7)
Joseph-Desire JOB	19(5)	2	1(2)	0	23(7)
DORIVA	19(2)	0	4(1)	0	23(3)
Jonathan GREENING	17(8)	0	4	0	21(8)
Szilard NEMETH	17(15)	1(1)	2(2)	0	20(18)
Chris RIGGOTT	14(3)	1(1)	4(1)	0	19(5)
Ugo EHIOGU	16	1	2(1)	0	19(1)
Massimo MACCARONE	13(10)	0(2)	5	0	18(12)
Colin COOPER	17(2)	0	0(1)	0	17(3)
Michael RICKETTS	7(16)	2	3(1)	0	12(17)
Stewart DOWNING	7(13)	2	1(1)	0	10(14)
Stuart PARNABY	8(5)	1	0(2)	0	9(7)
Andrew DAVIES	8(2)	0	0	0	8(2)
Malcolm CHRISTIE	7(3)	0	0(1)	0	7(4)
Alan WRIGHT	2	0	0	0	2
Brad JONES	1	1	0	0	2
Carlos MARINELLI	1	0	0	0	1
Carlo NASH	1	0	0	0	1
Robbie STOCKDALE	0(2)	0	0	0	0(2)
James MORRISON	0(1)	0(1)	0	0	0(2)

2003-04 Round-up

Premiership
Arsenal

FA Cup
Manchester United

Carling Cup
Middlesbrough

Champions League
Porto

UEFA Cup
Valencia

PFA Player of the Year
Thierry Henry (Arsenal)

PFA Young Player of the Year
Scott Parker (Chelsea)

Promoted
Norwich City
West Bromwich Albion
Crystal Palace

Line-Up

League Form

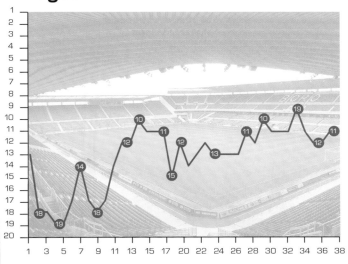

98

2004/05

Diary of the Decade

The former England striker placed the ball just on the edge of the penalty spot and took a couple of steps back. It was just before 5pm on the last day of the 2004-05 season – with all other Premiership matters settled other than which side would fill the final UEFA Cup berth.

And now at the City of Manchester Stadium, in the second minute of injury time at the end of Boro's 38th league game, Manchester City's Robbie Fowler had the chance to ruin their European hopes.

With the scores poised at 1-1, Franck Queudrue had been convicted of handball by referee Rob Styles and Fowler simply had to convert to grab three points for City to leapfrog Boro to take seventh spot in the Premiership table. The forward took a short run-up and kicked far to the right. But the long limbs of goalkeeper Mark Schwarzer were able to get low and stop the goalbound shot, with the Australian then pouncing on the ball, cradling it for dear life, with the widest of smiles as Fowler desperately tried to make amends.

Mobbed by his team-mates, the big Aussie had saved the season in the dying seconds – a Hollywood scriptwriter couldn't have penned it better. Schwarzer said: "It's up there as the most important save I've ever made because by making that save at that stage, we made it into Europe again. To think the race for seventh went down to that penalty is unbelievable, but we deserved it. It's a massive achievement to make Europe again – at a club like this we are in a position where we can keep re-writing the history books year on year."

While Schwarzer was the hero on the final day, there was no shortage of standout performers during the campaign with young Stewart Downing providing 19 goal assists, George Boateng a lynchpin and Bolo Zenden a revelation in central midfield after moving in from the left. Jimmy Floyd Hasselbaink scored an impressive 16 goals with Gareth Southgate again outstanding in central defence.

2004

JANUARY

16 - *Steve McClaren is set to do battle with Manchester United for Mark Viduka - Sun*

17 - Mark Schwarzer receives crystal memento to mark his 250th Boro appearance

20 - Juninho scores winner in first leg of Carling Cup semi-final against Arsenal at Highbury

FEBRUARY

2 - Brazilian World Cup winner Ricardinho signs short-term contract until the end of the season

3 - Boro beat Arsenal 2-1 in Carling Cup semi-final return at the Riverside

11 - Two-goal Juninho stars in 3-2 league victory over Man United at Old Trafford

17 - Stewart Downing makes his England U-21 debut v Holland U-21 at Hull

29 - Boro win Carling Cup with 2-1 win over Bolton at Cardiff, their first major trophy

MARCH

7 - Thousands greet Carling Cup heroes on victory tour of Middlesbrough

12 - Boro agree out-of-court settlement with Liverpool over controversial Christian Ziege transfer

14 - *Steve McClaren is facing a summer-long battle with Manchester United for the services of Gareth Southgate - Star*

16 - Andrew Davies breaks a leg in reserve game

18 - Stewart Downing signs new four-year contract; Steve Gibson awarded freedom of Middlesbrough

20 - Gareth Southgate makes 600th career league and cup appearance in dramatic 5-3 home win over Birmingham; *Boro are said to be tracking Spanish international striker Diego Tristan at Deportivo La Coruna - Gazette*

APRIL

2 - Training ground knee injury wrecks Gareth Southgate's Euro 2004 chances

11 - Colin Cooper recalled from loan at Sunderland to cover for injuries

19 - Boro beat Aston Villa 1-0 to win the FA Youth Cup for the first time; death of George Hardwick, aged 84

30 - Ugo Ehiogu signs two-year contract extension

MAY

1 - *Boro have been scared off by Leeds' £10m tag on striker Alan Smith - D. Mail*

9 - *Newcastle are read to launch an audacious bid for Danny Mills - S. Mirror*

14 - Steve McClaren returns as England coach to replace the ill Brian Kidd; Sam Russell joins Darlington on free transfer

18 - David Murphy released

19 - Players' Player of the Year Doriva signs new one-year contract

That all helped achieve UEFA Cup football for a second consecutive season and, although Steve McClaren had again attracted some top names for the 2004-05 campaign, Europe was eventually only reached against the odds. After starting "like a house on fire", in the words of forward Mark Viduka, Boro's chase for a Champions League spot and then a UEFA Cup place was hampered by an injury list of epidemic proportions.

The excitement of an historic first European season was underway before the first ball was kicked in anger, as McClaren added to an already successful squad. In came Viduka from Leeds United in a £4.5m deal, with fellow striker Hasselbaink arriving from Chelsea on a free transfer. McClaren explained: "A conscious decision was made that we needed to bring in players who would help us to get more goals. We were strong defensively, but needed a goalscorer who could get into double figures. We chased Yakubu, but he was out of our price range, and had been after Viduka since January and finally got him. Hasselbaink was another one of those calls that came out of the blue.

"We thought about him at the end of the season but he was at Chelsea and we thought it might be difficult. It wasn't a possibility until a few weeks later when it became a reality. A lot of hard work went in to it, particularly from Keith Lamb. Patrick Kluivert was also mentioned, particularly as we had a few Dutch players, but we ultimately decided against."

Midfielder Ray Parlour was another free signing from Arsenal, with Dutch international full-back Michael Reiziger swapping Barcelona's Nou Camp for the Riverside. Zenden and Gaizka Mendieta – each on loan at Boro the previous season – were now both permanent employees of the club, with Mendieta the playmaker set to take over from Juninho following the Brazilian's departure for Celtic.

Viduka, who had made the Champions League semi-finals in 2001, was one of

the new signings who was setting high targets for his first Boro season. "I think this club should be aiming for a Champions League spot," he said. "With the players we have here we should be aiming for the top six at least. The team is capable of that. The next three years of my career are the most important as I really want to win something personally and on a team level."

The excitement of the transfer window was matched by events on the pitch as McClaren's men drew 2-2 against Newcastle United on the opening day of the Premiership campaign. Hasselbaink was on target that day and wasted no time in scoring his second Boro goal as the Teessiders took an amazing 3-1 lead at Highbury the following weekend against champions Arsenal.

The Gunners had not been defeated in the league in almost 18 months, but would somehow kick into gear to eventually win 5-3. But Boro's confidence would not be

• LETHAL - Jimmy Floyd Hasselbaink celebrates his controversial late equaliser against Newcastle

Riverside X

Diary of the Decade

• NEW RECRUIT - Midfielder James Morrison makes his full debut against Manchester United

dented and three Premiership wins on the bounce followed before the club's first-ever European game. Czech champions Banik Ostrava provided the opposition at the Riverside, but by now Boro were firing on all cylinders as Hasselbaink scored his fourth of the season, and Viduka bagged two to make it five goals in four games. A 1-1 draw was enough in the return leg to send Boro into the group stages of the UEFA Cup, but there was to be even more success in domestic competition.

Youngster Downing made his first league start of the season against Manchester United at Old Trafford – and scored a fabulous goal that put his side ahead. Also in the side that day were teenage full debutants Tony McMahon and James Morrison, with the likes of Viduka, Hasselbaink, Reiziger, Ugo Ehiogu and Queudrue – amazingly, to name just a few – missing. Southgate recalled: "When James and Tony made their full debuts at Old Trafford I think everyone thought that anything could happen. In that

2004

MAY

21 - Portsmouth striker Yakubu is a Boro target - Gazette
22 - Tottenham are about to make a shock £2m swoop for Gareth Southgate - D. Mirror
23 - Middlesbrough could sacrifice Juninho to make way for Man Utd's Ole Gunnar Solksjaer - S. Express
25 - Boro will move for freed Arsenal striker Sylvain Wiltord - D. Mail
26 - Steve McClaren is interested in Wolves striker Henri Camara - Express
29 - Middlesbrough will pull out all the stops to sign Patrick Kluivert - Express
31 - Boro are eyeing Aston Villa full-back Mark Delaney - Express

JUNE

1 - Steve McClaren has made a surprise move for Leicester striker Paul Dickov - D. Mirror
9 - Boro are eyeing Paris St Germain full-back Bernard Mendy - Gazette
13 - Lazio defender Massimo Oddo is a target for Middlesbrough - S. Mirror
16 - Chelsea's Mario Melchiot is favourite to become Boro's new right-back - Gazette
23 - Michael Ricketts joins Leeds
24 - Robbie Stockdale signs for Rotherham on free transfer
27 - Rangers defender Michael Ball is a target for Middlesbrough - S. Mirror
30 - Middlesbrough are lining up a £4.25m bid for Bayern Munich midfielder Owen Hargreaves - D. Express

JULY

1 - Malcolm Crosby becomes new reserve team manager
5 - Michael Reiziger signs on a free transfer from Barcelona
6 - 888.com named as new main sponsor; Joseph-Desire Job signs new two-year contract
8 - Mark Viduka signs from Leeds for £4.5m
9 - Jimmy Floyd Hasselbaink signs on a free transfer from Chelsea
12 - Danny Mills signs for Manchester City
23 - Ray Parlour signs on a free transfer from Arsenal
29 - Jonathan Greening joins West Bromwich for £1.25m

AUGUST

2- Bolo Zenden agrees new one-year deal
7- Gareth Southgate agrees two-year contract extension
12- Steve McClaren to continue as England coach in 2006 World Cup campaign
17- Riverside hosts England U-21 v Ukraine U-21
22- Amazing 5-3 defeat at Arsenal after Boro were 3-1 ahead
23- Massimo Maccarone joins Parma on loan
25- Juninho joins Celtic on a free transfer

situation the senior players need to try and make it as comfortable as possible for them to make that step up. It was a big ask of them but they responded to it with such maturity, and if they can deal with that they will be able to deal with anything."

The game ended 1-1 but it was an impressive performance that caught the imagination on Teesside as well as through the country, and while youth was given its day at Old Trafford the next match would see 32-year-old Hasselbaink grab a superb hat-trick at Blackburn Rovers as Boro won 4-0.

By the time Zenden and Chris Riggott scored in the 2-0 win over Liverpool in late November, Boro were fourth in the league and unbeaten in seven Premiership games. Wins would also follow against

Manchester City, Aston Villa and Norwich City, with Boro fifth in the table at the turn of the year and looking favourites to qualify from their UEFA Cup group after victories over Lazio, Egaleo and Partizan Belgrade. A record Riverside crowd of 34,836 saw the Norwich game on December 28, but – as in seasons past – the coming of January would signal a downturn in fortunes.

McClaren added: "It's all ifs and buts, but if players like Viduka and Boateng had been fit in January and February then we might have finished much closer to those top sides that we'd been up with earlier in the season. We regularly scored two goals per game before Christmas and for a long time after that we struggled to get one goal."

Manchester United and Chelsea would beat Boro within the first four days of 2005, and the former would also brush McClaren's team aside 3-0 in an FA Cup fourth-round match at the end of January. Wayne Rooney scored a couple of sublime goals, and a 1-0 defeat of Blackburn in early February would be Boro's solitary Premiership win in 2005 by the time they travelled to Crystal Palace on April 2. A record of four consecutive losses travelled with them – including a humiliating 3-1 home reverse to relegation-threatened Southampton and two defeats at the hands of Sporting Lisbon as they were knocked out of Europe at the last-16 stage.

All of a sudden the likes of Liverpool, Bolton Wanderers, Tottenham Hotspur, Aston Villa and Charlton Athletic looked more likely to clinch a UEFA Cup spot – with the top seven in the Premiership destined for Europe thanks to Champions League qualifiers Chelsea, Manchester United and Arsenal taking up the FA Cup and League Cup spots.

However, Queudrue headed home the winner at Selhurst Park, and a steady run until the end of the season left them in prime position for Europe as they travelled to Manchester for the final day's heroics. "Crystal Palace was a big win and other results went our way that afternoon, and all of a sudden we were back in with a shout," explained McClaren. "With six or seven weeks of the season to go we were not in good condition. We had injuries and there was no sign of players coming back. But

that's when the team rallied and the focus seemed to return. If we had lost against Palace that would have been it for us."

• TOUGH GUY - Forward Mark Viduka uses his strength against Lazio

Riverside X

Diary of the Decade

• KEY MOMENT - Franck Queudrue celebrates a vital winner at Selhurst Park as Boro chase Europe

They would lose just once in the final eight matches, with home wins over West Bromwich Albion and Tottenham and brave draws at Liverpool and Newcastle. That last run of games seemed to sum Boro's season up as resolve triumphed over adversity on the injury front. Viduka, who had been out since Boxing Day, returned for the Palace game but lasted just 10 minutes before suffering a recurrence of a torn hamstring that would see him miss the rest of the season.

Schwarzer injured his back in the warm-up prior to the Arsenal match and would be replaced by Brad Jones, his fellow Aussie then missing the final weeks of the season with chicken pox. Ehiogu, who had been restricted to a handful of starts before the run-in, returned to the squad for the Arsenal match, and no sooner was he back in contention than fellow defender Riggott suffered a knee injury in training that ruled him out for the rest of the season. With Reiziger already missing, right-back Stuart Parnaby then suffered a groin injury ahead of the West

2004

SEPTEMBER

1 - *Steve McClaren has ruled himself out of the Newcastle vacancy - N. Echo*

12 - *Sunderland want to take Malcolm Christie on loan - News of the World*

16 - Boro beat Banik Ostrava 3-0 at home at Riverside in club's first-ever UEFA Cup match

20 - Death of Brian Clough, aged 69

OCTOBER

14 - Boro fined £4,000 following crowd disturbances at Euro away tie in Banik Ostrava

15 - Jimmy-Floyd Hasselbaink scores hat-trick in 4-0 win at Blackburn

21 - Boro beat Egaleo 1-0 in UEFA Cup Group E match in Athens

NOVEMBER

4 - Boro beat Lazio 2-0 in UEFA Cup Group E match at Riverside

5 - Brad Jones joins Blackpool on loan

13 - Police investigate allegation that Bolton's El-Hadji Diouf spat at Riverside fans

16 - *Boro are set to swoop for Newcastle keeper Steve Harper - Star*

21 - *Middlesbrough are lining up a £3m move for Norwich keeper Robert Green - News of the World; Steve McClaren wants AIK Stockholm midfielder Derek Boateng - Star*

24 - James Morrison signs new four-year contract

30 - FA reject Franck Queudrue appeal against sending-off at Tottenham

DECEMBER

5 - *Boro are in the hunt for Bayern Munich defender Sammy Kuffour - S. People*

11 - Last-gasp goal by Stewart Downing secures point in 2-2 draw at Southampton

12 - *Middlesbrough are lining up a move for Hibs defender Ian Murray - S. People*

14 - *Middlesbrough are planning to swoop for Newcastle full-back Olivier Bernard - N. Echo*

15 - Boro beat Partizan Belgrade 3-0 in UEFA Cup Group E match at Riverside

19 - *Steve McClaren is set to bid £6m for Chelsea midfielder Joe Cole - S. Mirror*

24 - *Boro are on the verge on landing Portsmouth midfielder Amdy Faye - Star*

JANUARY
2005

1 - Massimo Maccarone switches his loan from Parma to Siena

5 - *Manchester United want Mark Schwarzer - Sunday Sun*

8 - *Geremi could be on the verge of a shock Boro return - Gazette; Steve McClaren has failed in a bid to take Manchester United's Phil Neville to the Riverside - Star*

9 - *Middlesbrough are lining up a swoop for Fulham keeper Edwin van der Sar - Sunday Sun*

Brom game and replacement Colin Cooper was forced off in the first half with a hip problem.

Youngster Andrew Davies returned from a loan spell with Queens Park Rangers and played three times in that position before an ankle knock. And then there were those with long-term problems that meant they couldn't feature in the closing stages of the season – including Mendieta, whose damaged cruciate ligament meant he did not play after October. Forward Malcolm Christie played just twice all season, while Joseph-Desire Job was in and out throughout the second half of the campaign.

Again, it was resolve, mixed in with a little flair, which helped Boro to get the right result at City in that nailbiting climax. Hasselbaink provided the colour with his fantastic free-kick to put Boro a goal up in the first half, but City's Kiki Musampa equalised just seconds after the interval. The home crowd,

buoyed by new boss Stuart Pearce, encouraged their team forward and most of the game was played in Boro's final third.

But Southgate and Ehiogu were inspired in the centre of defence, with Boateng and Doriva providing much-needed cover – especially after City's England goalkeeper David James joined the home side's attack for the closing stages. But, despite the euphoria, Southgate admitted some feelings of disappointment at the end of a rollercoaster season. He said: "We virtually achieved what we hoped for but the truth is that we wanted to finish in the top six, so we were disappointed we didn't manage that. We set out to qualify for Europe for the first time through the league and in the end the table shows we did that by a three-point margin, although the real story isn't quite as straightforward as that."

But the club skipper was delighted with the contribution made by the young players who had been fast-tracked

• HERO - Mark Schwarzer saves brilliantly from Robbie Fowler's penalty as Boro again qualify for the UEFA Cup

Riverside X

Diary of the Decade

from Academy and reserve-team football to the first team to help the Premiership and European cause. No less than six Academy graduates made their full debuts during the season –with Darlington-born Morrison and McMahon, originally of Bishop Auckland, becoming first choices in their respective positions for a spell. Southgate said: "I'm very conscious of what a great Academy we have here, and Dave Parnaby and Ron Bone have set up something very special. They have had the success with the youth teams that has seen two FA Youth Cup finals in a row, and a win, and what we now hope to achieve is to get players through to the Premiership – so what a year it was."

But it was Boro-born Downing, from Pallister Park, who stood above the rest and, despite Hasselbaink's goals, the majesty of Southgate and graft of Boateng, the 20-year-old was voted Boro's Players' Player of the Season, as well as making the shortlist for the national PFA Young Player of the Season. With five Premiership strikes and a haul of goal assists, he helped inspire the push for Europe with his left-wing displays and in February 2005 won his first England cap against the Netherlands. "At first it was just a bonus for me to get into the team, but after that there were so many great occasions for me, especially winning my first cap," said Downing, who was linked with the likes of Manchester United and Tottenham Hotspur after his brilliant year. "The only thing I'm thinking about is helping Boro have another great season. I've ignored all the speculation and the fans can too. I'm committed to staying with Boro – there's no reason why we can't push on for a Champions League place next season."

Within 48 hours of the triumphant display in Manchester, Boro already looked to have added the next piece of the jigsaw with the signing of Yakubu – a target from the previous season – for £7.5m.

JANUARY
2005

11 - *Middlesbrough are targeting Celtic defender Bobo Balde - D. Mail*

12 - *Boro are set to renew their interest in Steed Malbranque - Gazette*

13 - *Former Everton midfielder Olivier Dacourt tops Steve McClaren's wish list - Guardian; Chelsea keeper Carlo Cudicini is a surprise target for Middlesbrough - N. Echo*

16 - *Boro have joined the hunt for Charlton midfielder Jason Euell and are hoping to re-sign Mark Crossley from Fulham - S. Mirror*

22 - Boro pegged back to 4-4 at Norwich after leading 4-1

28 - Mark Schwarzer signs new three-year contract

FEBRUARY

9 - Stewart Downing makes full England debut v Holland

11 - Broken foot rules out Malcolm Christie for the rest of the season

20 - *Boro are keeping tabs on Espanyol's Argentinian goal ace Maximiliano Rodriguez - Sunday Sun*

24 - Hasselbaink goal seals 2-1 home victory over Grazer AK and a place in UEFA Cup's last 16

27 - Danny Graham's first goal for Boro rescues a point in 2-2 home draw with Charlton; *Steve McClaren has sent scouts to watch Blackpool deadball specialist Jamie Burns - News of the World*

MARCH

2 - James Morrison ruled out for two months after double hernia surgery

4 - Andrew Davies turns down a permanent move to Queen's Park Rangers

10 - Boro lose 3-2 at home to Sporting Lisbon in UEFA Cup Group of 16

23 - Carlo Nash joins Preston in £175,000 deal

APRIL

1 - Boro and Everton fined £8,000 by FA for pitch fracas in 1-1 draw at Riverside on January 16

5 - Mark Viduka ruled out for rest of season after comeback from hamstring injury lasts just 11 minutes in 1-0 win at Crystal Palace

12 - *Man Utd star Darren Fletcher is top of Steve McClaren's wanted list - Sun; Boro are considering a bid for Deportivo striker Walter Pandiani - Times*

13 - *Boro are joining the race for Sporting Lisbon youngster Joao Moutinho - N. Echo*

17 - *Middlesbrough are closing in on Juventus midfielder Stephen Appiah - Sunday People; Boro are leading the chase for Grazer AK midfielder Rene Aufhauser - S. Mirror*

22 - *Steve McClaren is chasing Croatian central defender Igor Tudor from Juventus - D. Express*

22 - Misery for Bryan Robson on first Riverside return as West Brom are beaten 4-0 by Boro

MAY

15 - A 1-1 draw at Manchester City guarantees a highest - ever Premiership finish of seventh, and a UEFA Cup place

16 - Boro agree £7.5m fee with Portsmouth for striker Yakubu

Season Stats 2004-05

	P	Home W	D	L	F	A	Away W	D	L	F	A	Pts	GD	H	A
Chelsea	38	14	5	0	35	6	15	3	1	37	9	95	+57	0-1	0-2
Arsenal	38	13	5	1	54	19	12	3	4	33	17	83	+51	3-5	0-1
Manchester United	38	12	6	1	31	12	10	5	4	27	14	77	+32	0-2	1-1
Everton	38	12	2	5	24	15	6	5	8	21	31	61	-1	1-1	0-1
Liverpool	38	12	4	3	31	15	5	3	11	21	26	58	+11	2-0	1-1
Bolton Wanderers	38	9	5	5	25	18	7	5	7	24	26	58	+5	0-0	1-1
BORO	38	9	6	4	29	19	5	7	7	24	27	55	+7	-	-
Manchester City	38	8	6	5	24	14	5	7	7	23	25	52	+8	3-2	1-1
Tottenham Hotspur	38	9	5	5	36	22	5	5	9	11	19	52	+6	1-0	0-2
Aston Villa	38	8	6	5	26	17	4	5	10	19	35	47	-7	3-0	0-2
Charlton Athletic	38	8	4	7	29	29	4	6	9	13	29	46	-16	2-2	1-0
Birmingham City	38	8	6	5	24	15	3	6	10	16	31	45	-6	2-1	0-2
Fulham	38	8	4	7	29	26	4	4	11	23	34	44	-8	1-1	2-0
Newcastle United	38	7	7	5	25	25	3	7	9	22	32	44	-10	2-2	0-0
Blackburn Rovers	38	5	8	6	21	22	4	7	8	11	21	42	-11	1-0	4-0
Portsmouth	38	8	4	7	30	26	2	5	12	13	33	39	-16	1-1	1-2
West Bromwich Albion	38	5	8	6	17	24	1	8	10	19	37	34	-25	4-0	2-1
Crystal Palace	38	6	5	8	21	19	1	7	11	20	43	33	-21	2-1	1-0
Norwich City	38	7	5	7	29	32	0	7	12	13	45	33	-35	2-0	4-4
Southampton	38	5	9	5	30	30	1	5	13	15	36	32	-21	1-3	2-2

(left margin labels: CHAMPIONS LEAGUE, UEFA CUP, RELEGATED)

Goals

Name	Prem	Total
Jimmy Floyd HASSELBAINK	13	16
Bolo ZENDEN	5	8
Mark VIDUKA	5	7
Joseph-Desire JOB	4	7
Stewart DOWNING	5	6
Szilard NEMETH	4	6
Franck QUEUDRUE	5	5
James MORRISON	0	4
George BOATENG	3	3
Chris RIGGOTT	2	3
Danny GRAHAM	1	2
Malcolm CHRISTIE	1	1
Michael REIZIGER	1	1
DORIVA	0	1

Player of the Year

888.com
Stewart Downing

Supporters
Bolo Zenden

Appearances

	Prem	FAC	LC	UEFA	Total
Bolo ZENDEN	36	1(1)	1	10	48(1)
Gareth SOUTHGATE	36	1	0	10	47
Jimmy Floyd HASSELBAINK	36	2	0	5(2)	43(2)
Franck QUEUDRUE	31	2	1	9	43
Mark SCHWARZER	31	2	0	10	43
Stewart DOWNING	28(7)	2	2	8(1)	40(8)
Ray PARLOUR	32(1)	2	0	6	40(1)
Chris RIGGOTT	20(1)	1	2	8	31(1)
George BOATENG	25	0	0	4	29
Szilard NEMETH	18(13)	0	1	6(2)	25(15)
DORIVA	15(11)	2	2	7(1)	26(12)
Michael REIZIGER	15(3)	2	0	4(1)	21(4)
Stuart PARNABY	16(3)	0	0	4(1)	20(4)
Mark VIDUKA	15(1)	0	1	3(1)	19(2)
Colin COOPER	11(4)	1	2	3	17(4)
Joseph-Desire JOB	10(13)	1(1)	2	4(2)	17(16)
Tony McMAHON	12(1)	0(1)	0(1)	4	16(3)
James MORRISON	4(9)	2	2	4(1)	12(10)
Ugo EHIOGU	9(1)	1	1	0	11(1)
Gaizka MENDIETA	7	0	0	0(1)	7(1)
Brad JONES	5	0	0	0	5
Andrew DAVIES	2(1)	0	2	0	4(1)
Carlo NASH	2	0	2	0	4
Malcolm CHRISTIE	2	0	0	0(1)	2(1)
Mark WILSON	0	0	1	0	1
Danny GRAHAM	0(11)	0(2)	0(2)	1(1)	1(16)
Matthew BATES	0(2)	0	0	0	0(2)
Jason KENNEDY	0(1)	0	0	0	0(1)
Adam JOHNSON	0	0	0	0(1)	0(1)
David WHEATER	0	0	0	0(1)	0(1)

2004-05 Round-up

Premiership Chelsea		
FA Cup Arsenal		
Carling Cup Chelsea		

Champions League
Liverpool

UEFA Cup
CSKA Moscow

PFA Player of the Year
John Terry (Chelsea)

PFA Young Player of the Year
Wayne Rooney (Manchester United)

Promoted
Sunderland
Wigan Athletic
West Ham United

Line-Up

League Form

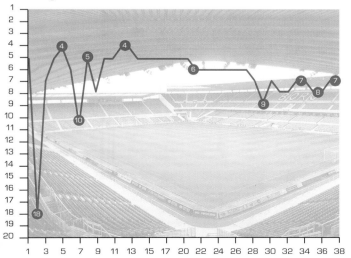

The Future

Cup finals, promotion, relegation, big signings, big losses. There's been a bit of everything during the last 10 years of Middlesbrough Football Club. The highs of Cardiff in 2004 as well as the lows of Elland Road in May 1997. The joy of Juninho's arrival at the Riverside and the disappointment of three cup final defeats.

Fans have certainly had their value for money since the Riverside first opened its doors 10 years ago, in terms of the brilliant players who have graced the Teesside turf as well as the drama that has followed the club up and down the land and across Europe. When the club first announced plans for a change of venue could even Chairman Steve Gibson have truly imagined that a Champions League winner and Italy international such as Fabrizio Ravanelli would soon be wearing a red shirt? Could even the most optimistic fan have dreamt that World Cup star Alen Boksic would spend three years in Middlesbrough, or that established England defender Gareth Southgate would choose Boro ahead of other high-profile suitors?

A culture change has certainly taken place, and the club seems determined that the future will be even brighter than the shining lights of 1995-2005. Despite claiming a European spot for a second consecutive season at the City of Manchester Stadium on the final day of 2004-05, there was never any

danger that the club would rest on its laurels.

Within 24 hours of Jimmy Floyd Hasselbaink's goal and Mark Schwarzer's save, the Nigeria international Yakubu was being shown round the club's Rockliffe Park training facility before agreeing a £7.5m move to the Riverside from Portsmouth. The player, whose Premiership scoring record was only beaten by Thierry Henry during his two years at Portsmouth, made it quite clear that his lofty personal targets could be reached with his new club.

• OPTIMISTIC - Steve McClaren sees a bright future at the Riverside Stadium

Alan Keen,
MP for Feltham & Heston and Boro Fan

"The team we have now is the most successful one we have had, certainly since I started watching. Steve McClaren could not have won things without Steve Gibson giving the solid backing to build a team. Gibson, as the crowd regularly confirm, has made the team move on from the dark old days. We've got a great future."

• KEEPING IT LOCAL - Homegrown players (left to right) David Wheater, Jason Kennedy, Andrew Taylor, Adam Johnson, Colin Cooper and Danny Graham, make the bench for the trip to Sporting Lisbon in March 2005. Also pictured are masseur Dave French and kitman Alex Smith

"I chose to come to Middlesbrough because they have ambition," said Yakubu, who joined alongside Emanuel Pogatetz, the Austria international who was a £1.8m summer capture from Bayer Leverkusen. "They have reached the UEFA Cup for two seasons and they want to do more, they want to get into the top four and the Champions League and with the players we have we can do that. With the experienced players we have and the strikers we have here, I think I can get better. I want to become the best striker in the world."

While Yakubu spoke to the assembled national media – gathered in their dozens at Rockliffe Park training complex – Boro's Chief Executive, Keith Lamb, looked on and might well have thought back to his first days at the club when his players were clearing dog dirt from their haphazard 'training ground'. Then again, Lamb has

had plenty of time to move on from such sentimental musings, after all the same man oversaw the building of the Riverside, the wooing of Bryan Robson and the trip to Brazil to snap up Juninho almost a decade before.

Complacency has never grabbed Lamb or Gibson, the two men both equally willing to back their manager in bringing the best players possible to the football club. "The club is still growing," said Lamb. "Every year we learn, and try to improve what we've got. We try to increase our resources and every penny raised goes back to the football club to invest. Hopefully the squad will be stronger each year. I hope that the fans see that at the start of every season, and will continue to do so.

"The ambition is as strong as ever. In fact it's on a broader front as we always want more. Back in 1986 it was simply survival – it's now a top-six finish and winning another trophy. It's been an interesting journey and long may it continue."

RiversideX

Football has certainly shifted since Boro's players stepped out to play Chelsea in August 1995. While the Premiership was already established, the true ramifications of its creation have taken some years to become apparent, which is also true of the growing influence of European football. The cash available to those sides that finish in European positions means they have the resources to stretch ahead of the Euro have-nots, with those not in the Premiership left even further behind.

That means, while the board is willing to back the football department of the club, Europe is now a necessity if growth is to be continued. Top players are lured by the chance of showing their skills at European level, and it is not enough to simply flash the cash. Gibson added: "Consistent European football is now this club's target and the whole structure of the club is set up to enable us to break into the top six. That's easy to say but harder to do. What we are working towards, year on year, is being able to achieve a place in the top six and then maintain it. We're hoping to be in Europe more often that not. The first target has to be the UEFA Cup but we also want to be able to challenge for a Champions League spot, too."

That desire is matched on the field, and not least by talismanic skipper Southgate, the man who identified Boro's potential when he moved from Aston Villa in 2001. He thinks that the narrative of his Riverside career has every chance of a happy ending, and is now enjoying regular European football and Premiership success having given the club a chance during a rocky first couple of years. But he also sees scope for improvement, with an eye on breaking England's status quo. He said: "We've won one League Cup but that only makes a professional want to win two League Cups or an FA Cup. Players always want more, and with the backing and ambition of the chairman then who knows where things could end? It's difficult to know the answer to that because if we reach the highest levels of the league we would then be competing with clubs with much bigger resources. But there are examples of clubs that have done that over a number of years, such as Deportivo La Coruna in Spain."

• NEW BOY - Emanuel Pogatetz joined the club for £1.8m

Bob Mortimer,
comedian

"I would love a manager to play the young local lads as a matter of course rather than just in emergencies. I'm a purist in that way because I grew up when the majority of our players came from the North East. There's so many pressures on a manager not to lose a single game that it's much easier to sign big players and keep them in every week.

"I would love us to be treble winners and to see all the children from every single part of the country wearing Boro shirts."

• PERFECT BLEND - Jimmy Floyd Hasselbaink, Mark Viduka and Bolo Zenden were the finished article when they arrived at Boro, while Stewart Downing and Tony McMahon have come through the ranks

"I'm pleased that there has been steady progress. We have improved each year that I've been here in terms of results and the quality of the squad. There has been a development with establishment in the Premiership, then the top 10 and last season the top seven. Ultimately we want to become a top-four club."

Boss McClaren also feels that rubbing shoulders with the big boys is a possibility.

He said: "Making it into the top five will be very tough – but it can be done as Everton showed in 2004-05. The club is set up for that and can make a go of it."

It seems unlikely that Boro, no matter how successful, will not be able to compete financially with Roman Abramovich's millions at Chelsea or the vast resources of Manchester United and Arsenal. That makes the promising work of the Academy over recent years all the more important as Boro seek to 'grow our own trees'. In 2004-05 no less than six Academy graduates made the

Riverside X

• FLYING THE FLAG - The Riverside faithful will continue to play a major role in any success Boro enjoy in the future

step up to first-team football, with Tony McMahon and James Morrison becoming regulars and Danny Graham scoring his first Premiership goal. Stewart Downing has become an England international, adjudged to be worth much more than the reported £6m that Tottenham offered for his services in July 2005 – with Boro keeping the player not just because of the unsuitable offer but also because the winger remains a key part of the club's future.

McClaren, now in his fifth season with the club, feels that by investing in youth the club has a chance of being able to outsmart the other pretenders to the Big Three. He said: "Financially I think it's important to bring through players from the Academy – just think about how much would have to be spent on Stewart Downing, Tony McMahon and James Morrison. It frees up cash for us in the transfer market, but it's also fantastic because it means so much to the players themselves and to the fans, and shows the Academy has been so successful. We are looking at a core of five and six as a nucleus of local players who can make it at Boro."

So while the feeling, on a national level, is that football clubs are becoming more distant from the fans, perhaps the opposite is true in Middlesbrough. The most recent Riverside season proved that a Premiership club can prosper when giving local youth the chance to shine. As Gibson concludes, no matter how successful, the club should never forget its roots as it heads into the next 10 years and beyond.

He said: "We wanted Premiership football for the town and now we are an established Premiership club. Next season could be the most successful in Middlesbrough's history. Prospects have never been greater in my lifetime. Just look at what we've achieved in the last two years, look what we did in the close season, look at the atmosphere we enjoyed at some very big games last season. It is probably the strongest we've ever been in every department of the team in the club's entire history. We've never been so strong, it's never been more exciting."

Carling
Cup Final

• CUP DEFENCE - Ugo Ehiogu and Gareth Southgate hold the Carling Cup aloft

Steve Gibson famously feared making a "prat" of himself as he was lifted shoulder-high by the Boro players on the Millennium Stadium turf after their Carling Cup final victory over Bolton. But if anyone could be forgiven for getting carried away when the 128-year wait for a major trophy came to a glorious end, it was the man the Teesside public hail as the best chairman in the game.

With memories on Teesside still raw from three recent failures on the big stage, the waves of delight flowed into an ocean of relief. Before experiencing the agony at Cardiff, the Boro faithful had so many times allowed their hopes to be raised and then dashed before they trudged back up the A19 in misery.

Boro had already lost one Wembley showdown to Chelsea, the 1990 Zenith Data Systems Cup final, before a double

Wembley whammy as the Riverside Revolution kicked into gear. The first two major finals came towards the climax of one of the most amazing seasons in the history of this or any other club.

Bryan Robson's star-studded team of 1996-97 were hurtling headlong towards relegation, having slumped from sixth-place in late September to rock bottom on January 11 after a disastrous run of just one win in 16 Premiership games. Cup competitions were a different matter, however. Freed from the shackles of more mundane domestic issues, the sublime talents of Juninho, Emerson, Fabrizio Ravanelli and co flourished.

Final number one of the Riverside era was the first of two Coca-Cola Cup dates at Wembley. From day one of his reign, Robson had always stressed that winning a first ever major trophy was his aim. Less than three years into his first managerial role he got that chance. Boro breezed past Hereford, Huddersfield, Newcastle and Liverpool, before seeing off Stockport County in a two-legged semi to reach a final against Leicester City at Wembley.

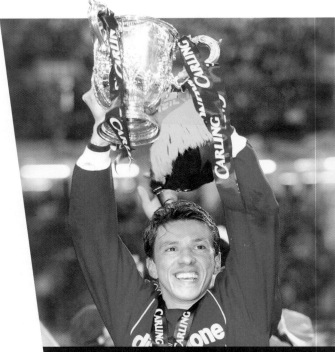

• DELIGHT - Juninho finally wins a trophy with his beloved club

More than 35,000 hopeful fans travelled down from Teesside, with Boro unbeaten in five Premiership games and the goals and the confidence flowing once again. That run included a Juninho-inspired 3-1 drubbing of the Foxes at Filbert Street. A repeat performance would do nicely. "Two cups and we're staying up" was the optimistic refrain from the Boro faithful. But the game was scoreless after 90 minutes, Swedish international Pontus Kaamark shackling dangerman Juninho with a tireless man-marking job.

"It was frustrating because when you have a guy on your back all the time people don't give you the ball," recalls the Brazilian. "But if they didn't give me the ball I couldn't play. I asked the players to pass the ball to me even if the guy is on my back so I could try to make things happen."

Five minutes into extra-time, the tiny playmaker got his wish and darted into the box before the ball fell to Ravanelli. The

massed ranks in the Boro end erupted into ecstasy as the Italian slammed the ball into the net. But with just two minutes remaining, Emile Heskey scrambled an equaliser for Martin O'Neill's side. It was rough justice for Boro.

"I just think it was fate at the end of the day," says Robson. "We were absolutely dominating Leicester in extra time of that first game. How we didn't score a second goal I don't know. They got a lucky break from a cross when Heskey toe-poked the ball over the line in the last minute. I don't think the team could have played any better in that game because we absolutely dominated Leicester."

The replay at Hillsborough was settled by a single goal, a Steve Claridge volley 10 minutes into extra-time. But for Juninho, the cup had been lost at Wembley. "That was the most disappointing game I've ever played in because we were so close to glory then they equalised in the final moments," he says. "The emotion of the team was down after that because beforehand our confidence was very high, every player believed we could win the cup."

Less than a week later Juni and his team-mates had to pick themselves up for another massive game, the FA Cup semi-final against the minnows of Chesterfield at Old Trafford. Chester City, Hednesford Town, Manchester City and Derby County had already fallen victim to Boro and on paper the game looked like a walkover, but it turned out to be one of the best semi-finals of all-time – for the neutrals, at least.

It was the game that had everything – a controversially disallowed goal, two penalties and a 10-man Boro comeback after Vladimir Kinder was sent off. When Boro went two goals down, one of the biggest ever cup shocks was on the cards and the Second Division side looked on course for the FA Cup final.

But the Teessiders' luck would soon change. With a little help from referee David Elleray – who disallowed a Jamie Hewitt shot which appeared to have crossed the line – Boro earned a replay and this time made no mistake, a happy return to Hillsborough bringing a 3-0 win and a final date with Chelsea.

By the time the final came, Boro already knew their league fate – relegation. And the three-point deduction for failing to fulfil a fixture at Blackburn Rovers generated

Riverside X

• BIG DAY OUT - Fabrizio Ravanelli beats Frank Sinclair in the 1997 FA Cup Final, but Boro would ultimately come out second best.

huge hostility from the Boro ranks at Wembley. As FA chief executive Graham Kelly introduced the royal party to the players, a cacophony of whistles and chants of "Three points, three points" was all that could be heard by the massive worldwide TV audience.

At that point the Boro fans knew nothing of the drama of just a few hours before as a fight involving Neil Cox and Ravanelli had spiced up their side's morning. "It was clear that there were a few of the lads who did not want to play First Division football and that seemed quite mercenary to the rest of us," says Craig Hignett. "The whole situation was not very good for team spirit."

Ravanelli has his own version of events. He recalled: "It was only an exchange of views with one team-mate. This individual, as well as one or two other English players, had always tried to antagonise and provoke me. I never reacted to any such provocations until a point where it became inevitable."

With relegation confirmed just days earlier and the camp bitterly divided, Boro's preparations were in disarray. Just 43 seconds into the game, Italian midfielder Roberto Di

Matteo ghosted passed Emerson as though he wasn't there and lifted the ball over rookie goalkeeper Ben Roberts via the underside of the crossbar to make it 1-0.

"We were all so disappointed with relegation and the atmosphere was not perfect for preparing for a cup final," says Juninho. "The arguments on the morning of the game could have taken our emotional control away. That was a key reason we went into the game and conceded a goal within a minute. When you start 1-0 down it's hard to get a result, especially in a cup final."

The gamble of playing a half-fit Ravanelli then backfired as the White Feather raised the white flag after 23 ineffective minutes, limping off clutching his hamstring. Despite the setback, Boro should have been on level terms by half-time after Gianluca Festa had a headed goal wrongly ruled out for offside by referee Stephen Lodge. Boro battled gamely in search of a way back before Eddie Newton scored the only goal of the second half from close range to give Chelsea a 2-0 win to end a season of such huge hope in abject misery.

• GREAT START - Bolo Zenden crosses for Joseph Job's opener after less than two minutes

Cup final number three came in March 1998, an amazing third successive major cup final appearance for Boro after a 122-year drought. Inspired by Paul Merson, a rebuilt Boro side was storming its way back to the Premiership at the first attempt. Barnet, Bolton, Sunderland and Reading were all brushed aside before a two-legged Coca-Cola Cup semi-final against Liverpool.

A narrow 2-1 defeat at Anfield left the tie within Boro's grasp. Back at an electrified Riverside, the Merseysiders had no answer as Merson's penalty and a goal from new boy Marco Branca - all within the first four minutes - gave Robson's men a 3-2 aggregate lead.

Having hit three crucial goals on the road to Wembley, Hignett – stalling over a new contract offer at the time - was left out of the squad in favour of new signing Paul Gascoigne. It may have been an unfamiliar feeling for Higgy, who had started the two previous finals, but it was very much déjà vu for his team-mates as Chelsea triumphed again.

Mark Schwarzer was in superb form, repelling a series of Chelsea attacks. Boro fans had to wait until the 48th minute for their side to get a shot on target. Gascoigne

Riverside X

was introduced with the game still goalless on 64 minutes, but he was clearly struggling for match fitness as the game headed into extra-time. Frank Sinclair made the breakthrough for the Blues in the 95th minute, heading home an expert cross from Dennis Wise. Di Matteo, whose goal had broken Boro hearts less than a year earlier, smashed in a 22-yarder on 107 minutes to seal the victory. Gazza later gave his runners-up medal to the unfortunate Hignett.

And so to Cardiff's stunning Millennium Stadium on Leap Day 2004. Brighton, Wigan, Everton, Spurs and Arsenal had stood in Boro's way and although McClaren's men twice needed penalty shootouts, Gaizka Mendieta and Franck Queudrue hit decisive goals to see them through. With Wembley Stadium under reconstruction, Boro headed to Wales in the hope of ending their cup final jinx.

They came by car, train and three chartered planes from Teesside Airport. When they arrived they found the stadium's roof closed over, creating a magical atmosphere as both sets of fans vied for vocal supremacy. Bolton kicked off with smoke from the pre-match pyrotechnic display still swirling round the arena.

Boro repelled a dangerous early raid before playing the ball from one end of the field to the other and taking the lead with just one minute and 47 seconds on the clock. Bolton's back line was caught square as Bolo Zenden made a run on the left and was picked out with a great long ball from Mendieta. The Dutchman's low cross picked out Joseph Job at the back post and the Cameroon international slid in to give Jussi Jaaskelainen no chance.

With just under seven minutes played the advantage was doubled. Mendieta played a neat ball into Job on the edge of the penalty area, his turn caught Emerson Thome by surprise and he tripped the Cameroon international a yard inside the box. Referee Mike Riley had no hesitation in pointing to the spot, despite heated protests from Wanderers and a disbelieving smirk from offender Emerson Thome. Zenden slipped as he took the kick and made contact with both feet, but although Jaaskelainen got a touch with a trailing boot, he could not keep the ball out.

• PENALTY - Job is felled by Emerson Thome

But the drama was not over. Bolton were gifted a way back into the final with 22 minutes played. Kevin Davies turned away from Gareth Southgate on the edge of the Boro box but still had plenty to do. A low, angled drive looked harmless enough but Mark Schwarzer bundled the bobbling ball into his own net at the near post.

Youri Djorkaeff had several great chances but Schwarzer recovered from his earlier error to make a string of stunning saves, his nerve holding as those of the fans behind him were stretched to breaking point. Seconds from time Bolton pressed forward and it took a desperate lunge from Ugo Ehiogu to block a Stelios shot. Had the ball struck the big defender's hand? Bolton demanded a penalty. Boro hearts were in mouths. Mr Riley waved the appeals away.

The final whistle was blown and the 128-year wait was over. Seven years after he sank to his knees after Boro's relegation at Elland Road, Juninho danced a samba of delight.

• RIVERSIDE ROAR - Thousands of Boro fans made the most of the big day in Cardiff

The celebration inside the Millennium Stadium did justice to the 128-year wait as Boro fans and players alike turned a small corner of the Welsh capital into Little Teesside. Perhaps the loudest cheer was reserved for Gibson, when he took to the pitch and was picked out by cameras relaying pictures on to big screens. Tears flowed, embraces were shared and Boro fans began to plan for trips to Europe.

The Bolton sections quickly drained on to the Cardiff streets, but some stayed behind, sharing in their victors' unbridled outpouring of joy. It seemed nobody could begrudge Boro their day of glory after 128 years of so many near misses without ever having won that first piece of silverware.

Boro had created history by scoring the quickest ever goal in a League Cup final – so quick that Steve McClaren had missed it! "I was busy getting changed out of my suit and into the lucky tracksuit," he explains. "I thought I might as well stay in the dressing room if it was going to bring luck, but decided not to and as I took my seat we went 2-0 up."

McClaren pays tribute to the outstanding Schwarzer, who recovered from his horrendous gaffe to produce a breathtaking display. "You have two ways to go after something like that happens to you," says McClaren. "You can cave in completely or fight back, and Mark fought back and made two or three fantastic saves which kept us in the game."

McClaren believes it was not by chance that Boro burst out of the blocks to such devastating effect, but that the breathtaking opening was down to the meticulous planning that went into his side's pre-final programme. "Our coaching staff had prepared the players to ensure they hit the ground running at two o'clock," he says.

It seems harsh to single anyone out for special praise after such a superb team performance but skipper Southgate, the first Boro captain to lift a major trophy, had used every ounce of his vast experience to hold things together as Bolton piled on the pressure.

"I came to Middlesbrough to try to win a title and we'd got so close before, our hands were on it and then we let it go," he says. "It was in my throat, that ambition to win a title with Middlesbrough. For me, lifting that cup represented the same importance as winning the World Cup with Brazil."

For chairman Gibson the heartache of so many near misses, not just in recent years but throughout the club's long history, made the victory so much sweeter. "It was a very, very special moment for the town, the fans, everybody," he says. "The fans were absolutely magnificent, they retained faith in our football club, which has not been easy.

"The opening seven minutes were unreal, it was a fantasy to be two-up that early in the cup, we just sat there and were shell-shocked. Then the reality comes into it and we're thinking, 'Let's just get through to half-time'. I thought we were very strong in the second half and perhaps deserved to win it by more."

Riverside **X**

• MILLENNIUM MAGIC - Skipper Southgate leads the celebration

"You need heroes in a cup final and we had 12 or 13," says McClaren. "Mendieta and Juninho were magnificent but if there is one player I would mention it's Southgate. He has been the talisman of our football club since I came here and made him my first signing."

Teesside had never seen a day like the one when the Boro squad paraded through Middlesbrough on an open-top bus with the trophy before a crowd some estimates put at close to 200,000. Poignantly, the parade began near the club's former spiritual home, Ayresome Park, beside the cemetery where legions of fans who lived in hope of seeing such an occasion now rested.

Under a suitably steel-grey sky, fans young and old braved the cold and drizzle to line the streets. While reporters in their overcoats and long johns huddled together shivering,

hardier types among the crowd sported short-sleeved Boro shirts. Proud Teessiders who had never been to a game in their lives lined up alongside others who had long since lapsed. Now they were united with the current generation of Riverside regulars, some so young they'd only ever known the site where Ayresome once stood as houses.

Some fans perched precariously on windowsills to get a better view, while others appeared to have removed whole windows for the occasion, with entire families gathered in the curtainless openings. Babies too young to understand were held aloft like trophies so one day they could be told, "You were there".

Pubs on Linthorpe Road enjoyed unscheduled boom times, while lads on groaning bus shelters supped from carry-outs. Music blasted from a mobile PA system and the

crowd took up the chants of "Up the Boro" and "Pigbag". Most of the time the music couldn't be heard, drowned out by deafening cheers. The bus turned from Ayresome Street to Linthorpe Road, then into Borough Road, with thousands more fans around every corner, stretching all the way to the stadium.

Banners ranged from the hastily homemade to the lovingly crafted. One immaculately embroidered flag states "Middlesbrough - deep in my heart",

quoting the civil rights anthem adopted by the Boro faithful during their long wait in football's wilderness. "And on the eighth day God created Juninho" read another banner.

A well-dressed elderly lady on her own with a big smile leaned against a road sign on a piece of wasteland near the stadium. Not your typical football fan, but she had also waited a lifetime, in her own way. Perhaps she was there for a long-gone husband or son.

• PARTY TIME - Franck Queudrue and daughter enjoy the parade in Middlesbrough

Riverside X

• FAN-TASTIC - As many as 200,000 supporters gathered to enjoy the feeling of finally winning a major trophy

As the players' bus reached the brow of the hill on Shepherdson Way, the sun came out for the first time all day, smiling on the thousands in the Riverside car park. The players were clearly bowled over by what they were seeing on a day when a town so often unfairly maligned showed the world it felt good about itself.

Stunned skipper Southgate sensed the huge importance of the day for the town when he told the huge crowds: "This football club, Middlesbrough the town and Middlesbrough the football club are now winners!"

His words were greeted by deafening cheers from the crowd, who had earlier chanted the captain's name. "Last Sunday at Cardiff was emotional for everyone and I didn't think that could be matched, but coming here today will live forever in the memories of the players," he added.

Goalkeeper Mark Schwarzer struggled to find words to describe his feelings. "To be part of the team that wins a major trophy for the first time in the club's history is fantastic and being here and seeing all the supporters, words can't describe it," he said.

Fans favourite Juninho was overcome with a emotion as he held baby daughter Bruna in his arms. "This club deserves to win this title after the hurt we've had," he said. "Middlesbrough has wanted for so long. I'm glad to be here when Middlesbrough won their first title. I want to say thank you for your support to every single person here."

Ugo Ehiogu described the parade as a "life-changing experience", saying: "I don't know how long it will take me to come to terms with what I have just seen. You have no idea what a sense of satisfaction that gives the players, we really feel we have achieved something."

McClaren dedicated the team's success to the fans. "Everybody here and everybody who's followed on the route, this is for you!" he told them as he held the trophy aloft. People had told the manager and the players how much their achievement meant to Teesside. Now they all knew.

The day was about far more than mere football. It was about pride. It was the day the town's Latin motto "Erimus" became "Sumus" at last. No longer the hopeful "We shall be", but a triumphant "We are!"

Europe
2004-05

• HISTORIC TRIP - Boro's players line up for the club's first European away game at Banik Ostrava in September 2004

It might have taken almost 50 years for Boro to make their European debut, but there was no way that Steve Gibson would allow his club to settle for just a good night out. When Steve McClaren's side prepared for the visit of Banik Ostrava for their UEFA Cup first round game in September 2004, the chairman made it quite clear what he expected.

"I, like every other Boro fan, have been looking forward to this with much anticipation for a long time," said Gibson. "But as thrilled as we are to have qualified for the competition, I can assure you that we will not be happy to simply make up the numbers. Too many English sides have fallen at the first hurdles of the UEFA Cup in recent seasons, their European dream all too fleeting."

He need not have worried as McClaren's team progressed to the last 16 of the competition before finally succumbing to Portuguese giants Sporting Lisbon. Not a bad run for a side playing European football for the first time in its history, and a Continental record that could quickly be improved on after Boro made it into the UEFA Cup for the second time at the end of the 2004-05 season.

Of course it all began with the Carling Cup win in February 2004, with Boro the first English side to be guaranteed a European spot for the following campaign. A long summer of anticipation followed as fans and players alike counted down to the draw on Friday August 27.

Banik Ostrava's unfashionable status might have ~~ one or two raised eyebrows among supporters, but there was no chance that Boro's manager would underestimate a team that had been eliminated from the Champions League after winning the Czech title. "They have experienced a mixed start to the season but they are the current champions of their country and certainly will be no pushovers," said McClaren ahead of the first leg, in which Boro had been drawn at home on September 14.

While skipper Gareth Southgate had played UEFA Cup football during his Aston Villa days, and had also travelled to four major tournaments with England, the Ostrava game remains a favourite memory of his career. He said: "The first European match was a defining night for the club. The Arsenal semi-final had been fantastic the previous season, but the Banik Ostrava tie was a terrific occasion because it was unique for the fans."

A game of two halves may be a most English of football truisms, but the Ostrava fixture showed that it applies just as much to European soccer as the domestic variety. A first 45 minutes devoid of action gave way to a second period in which Jimmy Floyd Hasselbaink opened the scoring and Mark Viduka added two more by the 80th minute. Boro produced some 29 shots amid an electric atmosphere created by 29,746 fans - and that was a necessary cushion.

• AMBASSADORS - Steve Gibson and, below left, Michael Reiziger have their bags and are ready to travel

A fantastic David Bystron volley just 19 minutes into the away leg two weeks later put the cat among the pigeons for the 1,050 official travellers to Ostrava's Bazaly Stadium on a night of drama and passion. It was also a night that heralded the beginning of several first-team careers, with no less than six members of the previous season's FA Youth Cup-winners featuring in the squad due to - not for the last time in 2004-05 - an injury crisis. Indeed, although the tie was pretty much over, it was James Morrison who levelled the scores with his first senior goal in the 90th minute as Boro proceeded 4-1 on aggregate, despite having played the last 33 minutes with 10 men after Franck Queudrue's sending off for a second bookable offence.

RiversideX

• GREAT START - Szilard Nemeth grabs an early goal in the 3-0 group win over Partizan Belgrade

Southgate said: "It was crucial for us to get through that qualifier - what a damp squib the cup final would have seemed if we'd gone down at the first hurdle."

The Teessiders had come up with the goods in a difficult opening round and attention now turned to Nyon, Switzerland for the UEFA Cup's inaugural group stage draw. In previous years Europe's second trophy had been a knockout competition from beginning to end, but the success of the Champions League made a group stage format inevitable by 2004-05 - and that meant at least four more exciting nights for Boro fans.

The players were also wrapped up in the excitement of the European campaign, not least Southgate who had played in three UEFA Cup campaigns with Aston Villa. "It's things like the draw itself that make playing in Europe such an exciting experience. A mundane ordinary weekday can instead have a buzz of anticipation if you play for one of those clubs lucky enough to be in Europe. We were at the training ground when physio Chris Moseley told us who we had been drawn with for the group stages. We couldn't have asked for any more as we drew three big names that had a fabulous history in European competition and, importantly, would add the support that makes European football so special."

Boro found themselves in Group E - quickly nicknamed The Group of Death - alongside former European Cup Winners' Cup winners and Serie A giants Lazio, Spanish outfit Villarreal and former European Cup finalists Partizan Belgrade of Serbia and Montenegro. Also in Boro's pool were the Greeks, Egaleo, and it was the Athens side that Boro faced in their opening match of the second phase on October 21.

Alastair Brownlee,
Century FM commentator

"When we moved to the Riverside Stadium we were a club that probably averaged a home gate of around 16-17,000. At that stage we'd never been in a major cup final, never won a major piece of silverware and never been, apart from the Anglo-Italian Cup, into Europe at all. Now we've made it to the last 16 and there's no doubt that Europe provided us with some of the greatest memories of the last 10 years."

• EURO HERO - Bolo Zenden had plenty of European experience before joining Boro, and scored twice in the club's brilliant win against Lazio

Following the intense night in the Czech Republic, things were a little more sedate in front of 313 travelling fans at the Rizoupolis Stadium. Southgate recalled: "It was a surreal experience as the ground only had three sides, and the other side looked like the back of a school building. There were only 2,500 fans there - we thought it would be hostile in Athens, but it was only the pitch that caused any bother."

For the second European game in succession it was a homegrown player who came up with the goods for Boro, as sub Stewart Downing grabbed the only goal of a dour game as he confidently drove home in the 77th minute. Egaleo felt hard done by at the end, but it was a "professional performance" according to McClaren, who had rested some big names ahead of a Premiership clash with Portsmouth just three days later.

The hard-fought graft of Athens was soon followed by Boro's biggest test yet when Lazio came to the Riverside on November 4. Despite their stock having fallen somewhat due to financial difficulties, the visit of Lazio was still an enormous chapter in the club's history according to Gibson. He said: "When I took up the mantle a decade ago, the idea of facing a club of Lazio's stature in European competition was no more than a dream."

But the dream got even better when a former Barcelona, Chelsea and PSV Eindhoven star scored twice in a fantastic 2-0 win in front of a jubilant 33,991 crowd. If anything, the scoreline flattered the Romans, although they could have taken the lead through Antonio Filippini in the seventh minute. But Bolo Zenden opened the scoring in the 16th minute when he volleyed home from outside the area, and he doubled the lead in the second half after converting Downing's cross with a sublime header. "It was a perfect European night," said McClaren. "European nights are special, a little bit different. To bring Lazio here, I felt an expectancy in the town and it was a great performance, with great goals and a clean sheet. The biggest thing was the control we had. We didn't let Lazio play."

Riverside X

• MAN IN FORM - Stewart Downing enjoyed a successful European run with Boro

By now Boro were also a fixture in the Premiership's top five and, having beaten Liverpool the previous weekend, must have fancied their chances as they travelled - alongside an incredible 3,032 Teesside fanatics - to the previous season's semi-finalists, Villarreal, for matchday three. This time, however, it wasn't to be as they were outplayed and defeated 2-0 thanks to goals from Antonio Guayre and Rodriguez Javi Venta although, again, McClaren decided to rest players ahead of a Premiership game against Tottenham Hotspur.

Boro's boss had opted for a lone striker in Joseph-Desire Job in Spain, but a two-pronged attack was the preferred option for the final group game as McClaren's men sought to make sure of their place in the last 32 of the competition, preferably by winning the group. The stand-in duo of Job and Szilard Nemeth worked perfectly against Partizan as they had made it 2-0 by the 22nd minute, and a European night

wouldn't be a Boro European night without a youngster getting in on the action as Morrison finished the scoring with a stunning strike in the final moments.

So, in front of a 20,856 crowd, Boro had clinched the top spot in Group E ahead of runners up Villarreal, with Lazio eliminated having finished only fourth. Confidence was high, as Franck Queudrue added: "Why shouldn't we make the final? It will be hard, but we face hard games every week in the Premier League. With the team we have at the moment, we should be looking to go as far as possible."

Unfortunately "the team we have at the moment" would not be available as Boro resumed European activities in February, with an injury list that would have decimated any of the 32 teams that remained in the competition. Boro's third-round opponents were the Austrian champions of Grazer AK, with the first leg taking place away from home on February 17.

Boro might have expected to make an early breakthrough against a side that had not played for two months because of Austria's winter break, but it would be the second half before the game kicked into life. Zenden was again the hero as he put the visitors a goal to the good with a fine strike six minutes after the interval. But Mark Schwarzer made a rare mistake as he allowed Mario Bazina to equalise in the

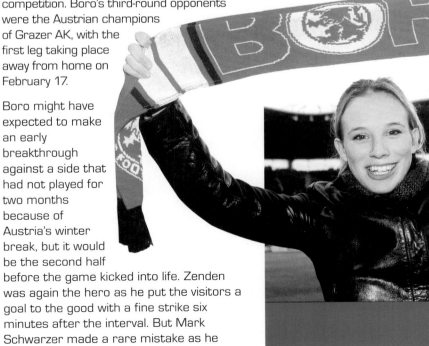

Kirsten O'Brien,
TV presenter and Boro fan

"I'd like to see us storm Europe, we did really well in the UEFA Cup and wouldn't it be fantastic to see us go even further? The fans seemed to really enjoy the new opportunity of watching foreign sides, and our players responded."

• KEEP IT TIGHT - Gareth Southgate keeps an eye on Sporting's Sà Pinto in the last 16

64th minute, much to the disappointment of the 1,142 away fans.

Just seconds later Jimmy Floyd Hasselbaink restored Boro's lead as he knocked home a Downing cross, but then Roland Kollmann concluded the scoring as he smashed home a free kick. A dramatic game set things up perfectly for another Riverside rollercoaster, with 20,371 fans experiencing all the highs and lows of European football on February 24. Volunteers had managed to clear 200 tonnes of snow from the Riverside pitch prior to the game, but they might have wished they hadn't bothered when Bazina made it 1-0 to the visitors just eight minutes into the game.

Ten minutes later Morrison scored his third UEFA Cup goal of the season when he was on hand to lash home after Grazer's goalkeeper had only been able to

parry a Downing shot. That strike failed to ignite Boro, and McClaren was forced to change from 4-4-2 to 5-3-1-1 as he attempted to shore things up and grab something on the break. At the top of that "Christmas Tree" was Hasselbaink, and it was the Dutchman who grabbed what seemed an unlikely winner on the hour as he turned and fired home from the edge of the area following a great move by Doriva, Zenden and Ray Parlour.

"I'm delighted with the result," said a relieved McClaren. "The first half was very difficult, as Graz came with a game plan, knocked every ball forward into the box and really caused us problems, hence the changes we made at half-time."

But it certainly wasn't all smiles as Boro prepared for the last-16 match with another European giant in the shape of Sporting Lisbon, who were to host the competition's final in May. Morrison had limped off with a hamstring strain at half-time against Grazer, and joined a long-term casualty list that included Mendieta, Viduka, George Boateng and Ugo Ehiogu.

Boro were playing two games per week with an under-strength squad, and tiredness was beginning to have a big effect on results with McClaren's side winning just one Premiership game in the first three months of 2005. That was a huge worry ahead of the first leg against Sporting on March 10, as 23,739 watched arguably one of the club's biggest-ever games.

Matters looked to be rolling along nicely as the game remained goalless at half-time, but then disaster struck and Boro were given a football lesson as they conceded three goals in the first 20 minutes of the second period. Despite a 79th minute overhead kick from Job - voted goal of the season by Boro's players - and Chris Riggott's close-range effort, there seemed little hope of making it to the quarter-finals in Portugal.

"By the time we got to the Sporting games we were simply running into the ground," said Southgate. "Their three goals effectively ruled us out of the tie. We did very well to get two goals back but it was too much to expect us to win 2-0 in Lisbon. It was a great experience out there. I have never before experienced the atmosphere that the fans of both sides created that night."

Riverside X

Seven days later a bruised and battered squad, along with 2,366 Boro supporters, set off for the Jose Alvalade Stadium where they performed stoically but were eventually beaten 1-0, with Lisbon winning the tie 4-2 on aggregate thanks to Barbosa's second goal of the tie. Even by Boro's standards it was a young 17-man group that was selected for the second leg with teenagers Tony McMahon, Danny Graham, Adam Johnson, David Wheater, Andrew Taylor and Jason Kennedy each involved.

Lisbon progressed to the final - beating Newcastle United in the quarter finals - in which they lost 3-1 to CSKA Moscow. But for Boro a first season in Europe had proved successful, with foundations laid for future glory nights in Continental competition. McClaren said: "We did well because it meant so much to the players and they responded. In the end the injuries cost us more than anything, and if we can make sure that doesn't happen again then we have a great chance in the future."

While supporters backed the European bid by snapping up tickets at home and abroad, the European season proved to be a success from the point of view of prestige rather than pure finance, according to chief executive Keith Lamb. He said: "The UEFA Cup is not the financial

cash cow of the Champions League. We don't lose money, but we don't make a lot of money either. We are in it to give fans the opportunity to see European competition, and give them the chance to travel. They were magnificent in the Czech Republic, Spain, Greece, Austria and Portugal. From a personal point of view there were some great experiences like going to the UEFA Cup draw in Monte Carlo. That was fantastic - little Boro rubbing shoulders with the big boys."

For chairman Gibson, Europe is now at the heart of Boro's future plans. He explained: "We are targeting the UEFA Cup as something that we can have major success in. I wouldn't like to go as far as to say that we will win, but I think that we could win it. What we are working towards, year on year, is being able to achieve a place in the top six and then maintain it. The first target has to be the UEFA Cup but we also want to be able to challenge for a Champions League spot, too."

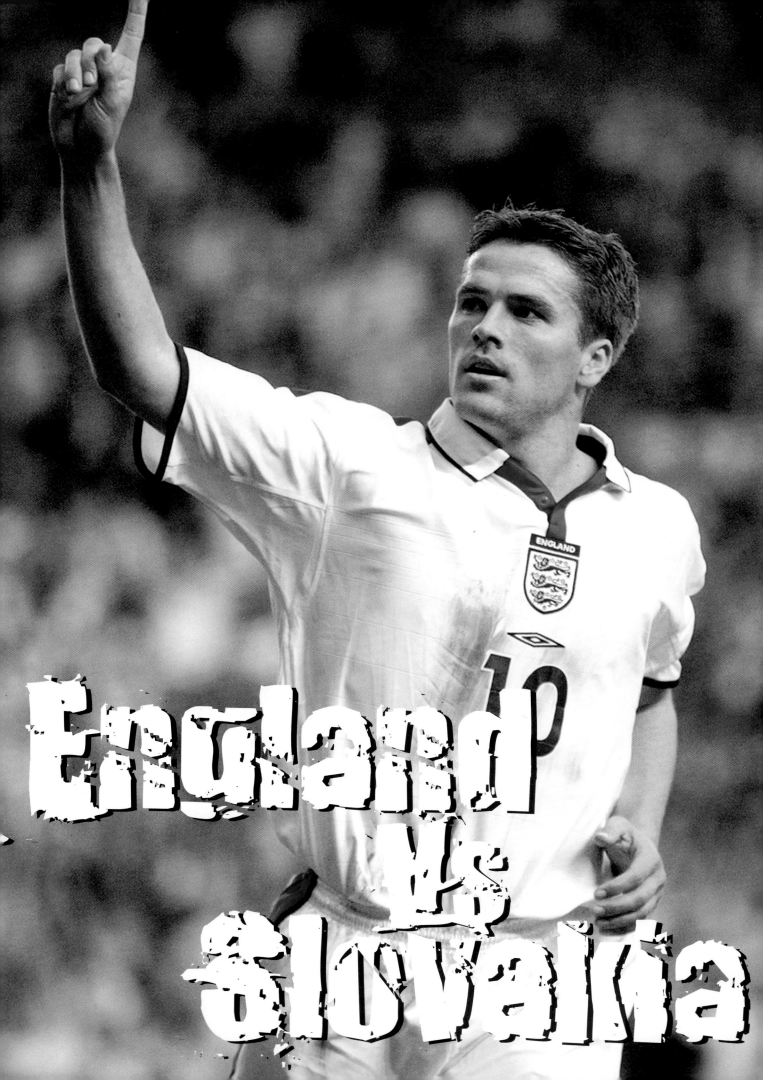

Riverside X

• NO INTRODUCTION NEEDED - England captain Michael Owen watches Boro skipper Gareth Southgate greet VIP guest Steve McClaren

One day, in the not too distant future, it might seem as though England's nationwide roadshow was but a dream. But it did happen. With Wembley closed for six years in the early part of the 21st century, a side overlooked by a Swede, Sven Goran Eriksson, took the Three Lions to the provinces. And in May 2003 it was the Riverside's turn – some 66 years after the last of three England matches at Ayresome Park – to host its first full international as England played Slovakia in a European Championships qualifier.

Already local rivals Newcastle and Sunderland had welcomed Beckham et al to their stadia – with Old Trafford, Anfield, White Hart Lane, Villa Park and Ipswich

Town's Portman Road among the 11 grounds that had preceded Middlesbrough's. But the choice of the Riverside was particularly appropriate for this game with Szilard Nemeth the Premiership's most prominent Slovak, and the Boro forward had given his country a surprise lead when the two sides met in Bratislava the previous September in a game which England eventually won 2-1.

Eriksson's team, which included Boro skipper Gareth Southgate, again had to come from behind to grab a win by the same scoreline on Teesside – but while England celebrated three points, the Riverside, which had sold out in a record 53 minutes, also proved a winner.

After a game in which he had scored both England's goals and captained his country, Liverpool's Michael Owen said: "It is a fantastic stadium and the atmosphere was just incredible. We've been up here a few days now and

• RIVERSIDE READY - The two teams line up ahead of the Euro 2004 qualifier

everything about the set-up they have got here at Middlesbrough is absolutely superb. The training facilities were second to none, the pitch was superb and the stadium is magnificent. It is a wonderful stadium well worthy of international football."

Southgate won his 55th cap as he partnered Matthew Upson in central defence, but his foul on Nemeth after 14 minutes led to Slovakia's opener with Vladimir Janocko curling home a free kick. Nemeth and Igor Demo could have each increased Slovakia's lead, but England clawed their way back into the game when Owen was brought down in the penalty

area in the 62nd minute and converted from the spot. Soon the Riverside was being treated to a classy display from England, with Steven Gerrard particularly outstanding in central midfield. But it was when the Liverpool man drifted out wide that he created Owen's winner as he crossed for his then Anfield colleague to head home.

Owen would later hit the crossbar, with Gerrard and Owen Hargreaves also coming close to extending England's lead, but 2-1 was enough for an ecstatic Teesside public.

And officials couldn't have been more pleased with the way things went, as chairman Steve Gibson said: "Everyone I have spoken to at the FA and in the media are full of praise for the way in which Middlesbrough Football Club staged the event."

RiversideX

While the game was entertaining enough, the evening was also memorable for the fantastic atmosphere following trouble at a game between England and Turkey at the Stadium of Light earlier in the year. That almost caused the Slovakia game to be played behind closed doors, with the Football Association eventually fined £68,000. UEFA described that as a 'clear warning' and the Slovakia game became a benchmark in the FA's anti-racism campaign with 35,000 leaflets handed out at the Riverside.

England's link with the Riverside hasn't just been confined to games at Boro's stadium in the last 10 years. A host of Boro players have worn their nation's colours since 1995, with Bryan Robson and Steve McClaren also linking up with the international set-up under Terry Venables and Eriksson.

Nick Barmby joined Boro in the summer of 1995 and in September of that year wore an England shirt against Colombia. The match finished goalless but is well remembered for the 'scorpion kick' as Columbia goalkeeper Rene Higuita bizarrely saved from a Jamie Redknapp shot. Barmby would go on to make eight appearances, and feature in Venables' Euro '96 squad, before switching to Everton. Robson was Venables' assistant during the future Boro manager's two years at the helm of the England side, and was tipped as a possible replacement when El Tel left his post with the Football Association after Euro '96.

Paul Merson was the next Riverside star to wear England colours, a massive achievement since Boro were in the First Division for the majority of the ex-Arsenal player's time at the club. Merson won five of his 21 caps while at the Riverside, and made Glenn Hoddle's World Cup 1998 squad, playing in the penalty shoot-out defeat against Argentina. Merson would play against Sweden on September 5 as England got their Euro 2000 qualification campaign underway, and just three days later quit Boro for Aston Villa.

One player who famously didn't make the World Cup 1998 was Paul Gascoigne, whose omission from Hoddle's plans for France made headlines worldwide. Gazza had joined Boro in March 1998 and made three international appearances in three months before the last of his 57 caps against Belgium in Casablanca on May 29.

• OPENER - Boro's Szilard Nemeth, left, helps celebrate Vladimir Janocko's goal

England 2 Slovakia 1

England: James, Mills (Hargreaves 43), Upson, Southgate, A Cole, P Neville, Gerrard, Scholes, Lampard, Rooney (Vassell 57), Owen

Subs not used: Robinson, Bridge, Terry, J Cole, Heskey

Slovakia: Konig, Petras, Hanek, Zeman, Zabavnik, Demo (Mintal 55), Labant (Debnar 39), Vittek, Michalik, Nemeth (Reiter 75), Janocko

Subs not used: Rzeszoto, Karhan, Kisel, Kozlej

Booked: Hanek, Vittek, Debnar

Attendance: 35,000

Ref: Wolfgang Stark (Ger)

Paul Ince was already an established international when he moved to the Riverside in 1999, having played 45 times for England while with Manchester United, Internazionale and Liverpool. But he added eight more caps while under Robson and Venables at the Riverside including all three of England's games at Euro 2000 against Portugal, Germany and Romania. The latter would be his final cap, as he was excluded from Eriksson's plans when the Swede took over the England hot-seat from Kevin Keegan.

Boro again increased their tally of internationals when they swooped for Aston Villa's defensive pair of Ugo Ehiogu and Southgate in 2000 and 2001

respectively. Ehiogu had made his England debut in 1996 against China and would have to wait until Eriksson's first game in charge – against Spain in February 2001 – before adding to his haul. The following year he would play against the Netherlands and Italy, but his defensive partner would go on to appear on a much more regular basis. Southgate had already played in a World Cup and two European Championships by the time he moved to Boro, and had amassed 42 caps. But he would play another 15 times in the next three years as he again made the England squad for World Cup 2002 and only failed to make Euro 2004 due to an injury. The defender made his last international appearance against Sweden in March 2004.

• ROCKLIFFE FOCUS - The nation's media descended on Boro's Rockliffe Park ahead of the Slovakia match

Riverside X

• CAPPED - Nick Barmby makes his first England appearance while a Boro player against Columbia

While Southgate's international days look to be over, Stewart Downing began his England career in February 2005 when he made a second half appearance against the Netherlands during a 0-0 draw at Villa Park. The young winger went on to make England's squad for the World Cup qualifiers against Northern Ireland and Azerbaijan the following month, and was part of the group that travelled on tour to the United States in summer 2005 but was ruled out with a knee injury.

But McClaren remained on the tour as a vital part of the international set-up as Eriksson's right-hand man. Boro's boss had first linked up with England as assistant to Peter Taylor in the then Leicester City manager's one game in charge in 2000. McClaren then remained under Eriksson through to the World Cup in 2002 before being replaced by Brian Kidd. But Kidd was forced to quit in 2004 due to illness, with McClaren returning for Euro 2004 and helping England to the quarter finals and through the World Cup qualifying campaign in 2004 and 2005.

The Euro 2004 game wasn't the Riverside's first, or last, taste of international football. Middlesbrough had hosted England's U-21s on three previous occasions dating back to the visit of Austria in November 1995. Just three months after the Riverside had opened, a young Jamie Pollock had appeared in midfield in the European Championships qualifier as Robbie Fowler and Neil Shipperley scored the goals in a 2-1 win. Pollock was replaced by a 20-year-old David Beckham in the second half, with Sol Campbell and Nicky Butt also playing for Dave Sexton's team in front of 13,496.

The U-21s returned to the Riverside in August 2000 as they smashed Georgia 6-1 in a friendly. Full backs Luke Young and Ashley Cole opened the scoring with Francis Jeffers and David Dunn making it four by half-time. Future Boro ace Jonathan Greening, then with Manchester United, and Watford's Tommy Smith completed the rout.

Just over a year later, in September 2001, it was goals galore again, but this time Jeffers attempted to make it a solo act with a hat-trick in a 5-0 win over Albania in front of 23,000 spectators. The striker had just moved from Everton to Arsenal for £10m, with Jermaine Defoe also getting on the scoresheet just three days after the full England team's famous 5-1 win over Germany. As if the feel-good factor around the Riverside could not have got any better, two Boro lads combined to grab the fourth for David Platt's team as Mark Wilson teed up Greening.

Following the senior side's debut at the Riverside, England U-21s came back for more twice within the space of seven months as Peter Taylor's team beat Ukraine and Azerbaijan. Carlton Cole grabbed two and Darren Bent a single strike against the former in a 3-1 win as Taylor began his second spell in charge of the Three Lions youth side in August 2004. Boro's own Stewart Downing made his third U-21s appearance that evening, and within six months had made his full debut against the Netherlands. In March 2005 it was the turn of the Azerbaijanis to taste defeat on Teesside as 19,095 saw John Welsh and Dean Ashton score in a 2-0 victory.

Greatest Players

1. Juninho – 70.5%*

Trying to conduct a fans' poll into Boro's greatest player isn't as easy as it might seem, and it's all because of 'the little fella'. Basically, it means running two votes. One with the Brazilian included, and then another one without so that the opposition actually pick up some votes!

This fabulous attacking midfielder joined Boro for the first time in October 1995 in a blaze of worldwide publicity, but despite having starred for Brazil against England in the Umbro Cup little was known about this mysterious Brazilian. Some nine years later and he made his last appearance for the club, by now a living legend and surely a contender for Boro's greatest player of all time, not just the Riverside era.

No player has been as influential as Juninho over the last 10 years although others have played more games, have cost more money or have scored more goals. He is now back in Brazil with Palmeiras, but despite more than a year flying by since he left Boro for the last time to join Celtic, there is little doubt that much of his heart remains on Teesside. He said: "I miss Middlesbrough, it's my second home because I had five great years there. The people were always very friendly and I never had any problems with adapting off the pitch because of the people. The club, the supporters and the people of Middlesbrough will be in my heart forever."

That connection was there from the start, as he was made to feel wanted by Bryan Robson and Keith Lamb, who would not give up on trying to sign him from Sao Paolo in 1995. When he had put pen to paper and jetted over to England, he was met by thousands of fans at the Riverside – it was then that he knew he had made the right move. He recalled: "I was shocked because that's not normal in Brazil. I was happy because I could see the excitement of the supporters. When you have support like

that, it's 100 per cent certain that you'll be happy."

It was tough to adapt to life on a different continent at first, but during his second season with the club in 1996-97 he was clearly one of the Premiership's outstanding performers as he scored 12 goals and set up countless others. Unfortunately the player's ambition to make Brazil's World Cup squad for 1998, meant he had a tough decision to make following the club's relegation in May 1997 – and he was soon moving to Atletico Madrid for a massive £12m. He said: "At the time I was disappointed with

• NUMBER ONE - Juninho enjoyed three spells with Boro

what had happened that year. We could have got into Europe and won a first cup for Middlesbrough and we ended up with nothing but relegation.

"I was receiving a lot of offers from clubs in England and Spain. The next year was the World Cup and I wasn't in the Brazil squad so I was worried if I continued playing for Middlesbrough in the First Division then the manager maybe wouldn't take me to the World Cup. That was the key reason I chose to move. If Middlesbrough had reached a European competition then maybe I would have stayed.

"But it wasn't only my decision to move. The club received a good offer for me. They had only paid £4.75m for me two years before and another club offered £12m so it was a wonderful profit for the club, who still had ambitions to build the training ground. I think it was an agreement between me and the club that it was the right time to go.

"I think Liverpool's manager was talking with my father and showed interest in keeping me in England but at the time the Spanish league was very popular in Brazil."

But the sun would not be brighter in Spain's capital, and within six months the player suffered a horrific leg injury and was ruled out of the World Cup. He would return to Boro on loan in 1999-2000, but suffered a frustrating time in a Boro side that was built on defence rather than attacking flair.

Some people say never go back, but Juninho joined Boro for the third time in

2002 shortly after winning the World Cup. Unfortunately he damaged his cruciate ligament in his first pre-season back, but he was able to show some of the old magic during 2003-04 as he finally helped Boro to a major title as they won the Carling Cup. However, he would not fully share in the glory as he had joined Celtic on a free transfer by the time Boro began their UEFA Cup run the following season. He said: "I didn't leave the way I would have wanted to. I achieved that title with Middlesbrough but couldn't play in Europe, and that's why I have bad feelings with Steve McClaren, who I respect as a coach.

"I was pushed into going to Celtic, because every supporter knows I wanted to play in Europe with Middlesbrough. Just before the holiday the manager told me that he was going to play with two strikers and he thought I wasn't going to play regularly. What that means is I'm not going to be in the first 11, and I didn't understand that because in the last season myself and Szilard Nemeth were the joint highest scorers."

While disappointed about his departure, Juni has wonderful memories of his time with Boro, and having played in three different sides, is an ideal judge of the way forward for the club. He added: "I went to Middlesbrough to try to win a title and we got so close, our hands were on it and then we let it go. It was in my throat, that ambition to win a title with Middlesbrough. It's true, for me, lifting that cup represented the same importance as winning the World Cup."

He added: "If you put the midfield and the strikers from the 96-97 team and then the defence from the 2004 team, then I think that would be the greatest Middlesbrough team ever. Maybe it would be the complete team, and that's what is needed on the pitch.

"Off the pitch I think Steve Gibson has got the club where he wants it. They have the best training ground in the world, it's fantastic. When you give that support to the players they respond by playing at their best and that's why we've achieved a place in European competition again in 2005-06."

* First vote completed includes Juninho, all other positions are based on poll not including Juninho

Riverside X

2. Gareth Southgate - 21.1%

The club captain already had 42 England caps and had enjoyed an illustrious career with Crystal Palace and Aston Villa when he joined Boro in 2001. He was Steve McClaren's first, and still most important, signing, and remains an integral feature of Boro's Premiership side as he reaches his 35th birthday during the 2005-06 season.

But it could all have been very different. Southgate had actually handed in a transfer request at Villa in 2000, and had his eye on a return to his native London.

He recalled: "I was aware that Chelsea's manager Gianluca Vialli was trying to sign me and had made a couple of bids already. I just assumed that I would end up there, however Villa basically decided that they didn't want to do business with Chelsea – and that was very frustrating for me. At that point Boro hadn't even entered my head although Ugo Ehiogu had moved to the club, and I also followed Boro's fortunes closer after Terry Venables' arrival in 2000-01."

Southgate eventually signed for £6.5m and, despite the years going by, this composed but commanding defender is still rated as one of the Premiership's best. He travelled to the 2002 World Cup with England while a Boro player and would have gone to Euro 2004 but for an injury. While some Villa fans questioned his decision to join Boro – was it really a step up for the player, they wondered – Southgate has no regrets about his Riverside years.

"It was a gamble, there's no doubt about that," he said. "Villa is historically a bigger club but I felt I was joining a club with better possibilities. I think the move was good for my reputation as I wanted to play in a back four, because many people thought I could only play in a three. I wanted to disprove the myth that surrounded me at the time.

"Just as important as all of that, I have enjoyed my football here, enjoyed an element of success and my decision to join has been vindicated."

• GAMBLE - Gareth Southgate suprised many when he moved to Boro from Aston Villa in 2001

3. Fabrizio Ravanelli - 13.6%

• SUPREME - Fabrizio Ravanelli scored 31 goals in one season with Boro

The Italian forward enjoyed – and endured – an amazing spell with the club, and despite the controversies, the fights and the bickering, he is the club's second highest scorer of the last 10 years. That's quite an achievement for a player that only competed one full season with Boro.

Ravanelli had started his career with Perugia in 1986, but came to international prominence after joining giants Juventus in 1992. He made more than 150 appearances for the Turin side, with his last game being the Champions League final of 1996 when he helped beat Ajax. He also played in Euro '96 that summer before signing on the dotted line for Boro. Keith Lamb recalls the club record £7m spent on the forward as being a watershed. He said: "I had to take a time-out at one point of the negotiations when I thought about the fee. Bryan Robson and myself walked out into the blinding sunshine of Rome. I said 'Bryan, do you realise, how much we are talking about -

£7m?'. Bryan said: 'He's worth it'. I called Steve Gibson and told him how much – but he said: 'If Bryan says we should do it then do it.' I just thought 'Christ!'"

The fee was repaid as he opened his Boro career with a hat-trick against Liverpool, and his 31 strikes would help the club to two cup finals, although they couldn't prevent relegation. Like Juninho, Ravanelli felt forced to leave the relegated side as he harboured ambitions to make the 1998 World Cup, and would join Marseille for £5.25m shortly after the start of the 1998-99 season.

But the goodwill which went with Juninho was not as forthcoming for Ravanelli, who had been quoted as making derogatory remarks about the club, and its facilities, and the town itself on several occasions. That caused some problems with his team-mates and a scuffle ensued before the start of the 1997 FA Cup final, with Ravanelli arriving at Wembley with grass stains on his suit.

Ravanelli, who scored in the 1997 Coca-Cola Cup final, said: "Every criticism that I made was directed at trying to improve things, a big constructive criticism. The only big regret I have is that because of all the speculation and misinterpretation I left on not very good terms with the fans. I love the people of Teesside, and my experience with them was dear to me."

4. Mark Schwarzer - 12.9%

A majestic goalkeeper who is the club's top appearance maker in the last 10 years after joining from Bradford City for £1.25m. The Australian is also the club's most capped player having made 28 appearances for his country since signing in 1997, but perhaps kept his most influential act in Boro's colours for the last game of 2004-05 when his penalty save against Manchester City earned a UEFA Cup place.

Schwarz has seen several stoppers come and go since he moved from West Yorkshire, with rivals such as Gary Walsh, Ben Roberts, Marlon Beresford, Mark Crossley and Carlo Nash all departing having failed to depose the 6ft 5in ace from the number one spot.

The stopper was born in Australia but has joint German nationality, and began to make a name for himself in

Riverside X

Europe having played for Dynamo Dresden and Kaiserslautern in the Bundesliga. He moved to Bradford for £250,000 in November 1996 but would move onwards and upwards to the Riverside just four months later. His standing was proved in 1998 when he signed a six-and-a-half year contract, and in 2005 agreed a new deal that will keep him at Boro for another three seasons.

Schwarzer has seen the club grow and grow in his years at the Riverside. He added: "The club I joined in 1997 was an exciting one. People always say it was one of the most entertaining sides we have ever had but it was certainly not the most successful. Today it is completely different. We have won the right to compete with the best, and we're ambitious to take things as far as we can."

• LONG STOPPER - Mark Schwarzer has been with Boro since 1997

5. George Boateng - 10.3%

• GOLDEN BOY - Boro midfielder George Boateng

A tough-tackling, all-action midfielder, it's no surprise that the Dutchman is such a big favourite with the fans. 'You are Boateng' is a regular chant, to the tune of Spandau Ballet's 'Gold', from the Riverside's stands as the ex-Aston Villa and Coventry ace puts in another man of the match performance.

Boateng was signed as a replacement for the similarly powerful Paul Ince, increasing the number of ex-Villa aces at the Riverside – including Gareth Southgate, Ugo Ehiogu and coaches Steve Harrison and Paul Barron. He began his career with Excelsior in the Netherlands before moving to the famous Feyenoord. He first moved to England in 1998 when he joined Coventry, then in the Premiership, and was snapped up by Villa the following year before a £5m move to Boro.

Boateng was voted player of the year by supporters in 2003-04 and his absence due to injury the following season almost put paid to the club's chances of a UEFA Cup finish. However, he returned just in the nick of time and a rare goal against Tottenham brought about an ultimately crucial three points.

Despite the glory and rewards of being a Premiership footballer, Boateng, born in Accra, Ghana, has never lost his passion for the beautiful game. He said: "For me, football is all about the smell of the grass, the sweaty shirts, the jokes and the adrenaline before the game. Whenever I've been injured I crave getting back, because time out reminds me how much I love the game."

6. Franck Queudrue - 8.7%

'Franck who?' was the cry around Teesside when the Frenchman was signed on loan from Lens at the start of Steve McClaren's first season with Boro. Information was sketchy – he was French and he was a left-sided defender. But with no international experience, would he really be up to Premiership standards?

But it would take little time for Queudrue to establish himself in Boro's defence and his transformation from man of mystery to fans' favourite is now complete after making the top 10 of our list. Perhaps the only questions still remaining about Franck is why is he yet to be picked by France? An easy-going and charitable nature off the pitch is in complete contrast to his attitude when he steps out on to it. The Paris-born defender was sent off an incredible six times in his first four seasons with the club, earning the dubious honour of being the only player to be dismissed three times in a Premiership season during 2002-03.

But his indiscretions are far outweighed by his positive contributions to Boro's success, and he scored a healthy five goals during 2004-05.

"I have improved the disciplinary side as my record was not good in my early time," he said. "But my main focus is on helping the team do well. If I can do my best then who knows about France? We are certainly getting noticed as a club in Europe these days. We are a highly-ambitious club with an ambitious manager and have a very big chance to achieve things."

• AMBITION - French defender Franck Queudrue wants success with club and country

Riverside X

7. Stewart Downing - 6.7%

- DEAL - England star Stewart Downing will stay at the Riverside until at least 2010

When Bolo Zenden signed a new contract with Boro in the summer of 2004, 19-year-old Stewart Downing thought his career with his hometown club could be over before it truly began. Having impressed while on loan at Sunderland the previous season, he had shown positive signs when given a first-team chance.

But left-winger Zenden was a Dutch international, surely Downing didn't have a chance? However, having scored against Newcastle on the opening day of 2004-05 he would then establish himself as one of the first names on the teamsheet after his mighty scoring performance at Manchester United's Old Trafford in October. Zenden was slotted into the centre of midfield as Downing's wing

wizardry became such an important part of Boro's rise up the Premiership table.

By February 2005 he was making his England debut against the Netherlands – the Pallister Park kid having become one of the country's most talked about talents. There were rumours that Manchester United were ready to take a chance on signing the youngster in the summer, but July of that year saw only a multimillion bid from Tottenham – which was immediately rejected by Boro.

Downing acted quickly to show exactly where his allegiances lay when he signed a new five-year contract within days of the Tottenham approach. Despite his lightning quick ascent to the top of the game, Downing feels there is still much hard work to be done. He said: "I don't think I've made it with Middlesbrough yet, let alone England. There's so much I've got to work on, and if I don't perform for Boro I know only too well I will be out of the team."

8. Craig Hignett - 5.6%

The man who scored the first ever Riverside goal is still fondly remembered on Teesside some 10 years later. The attacking midfielder had been snapped up from Crewe Alexandra in 1992 by Lennie Lawrence and proved himself to be one of the ex-Charlton boss's best captures as Boro attempted to stay in the Premiership and then during the following First Division season.

However, he struggled to find a starting place during Bryan Robson's first season but would make an immediate Premiership impact as he scored in the wins over Chelsea, Sheffield Wednesday and QPR as well as the draw against Bolton.

Roger Davenport Yarm

"Ravanelli was a revelation. What a way to start a career with a club than a hat-trick against Liverpool? Stories kept on being printed about him but we didn't know if it was just the media trying to stir things up, and it sounded as though his criticisms had a good effect in the end. That amount of goals in one season proves that he's Boro's greatest striker since Brian Clough.

Dave Brooks Richmond

"Uncle Festa he may have been, but there were few horrors when he was round in Boro's defence. It took him a while to win people over, but come rain or shine he always gave his best for the club and people responded to that."

But 12 consecutive starts would be brought to an end following the arrival of Juninho, and Hignett would be a bit-part player until the end of 1996-97 after Nick Barmby's departure. His being left out, with big-money signings Barmby and Juninho seemingly always picked ahead of him, was the cause of major frustration for the likeable Scouser. He recalled: "My philosophy was that if I was playing better than any other person then I should be in the side. But it didn't seem like it was that way for me, although I could see that the manager had paid £10m on those other two players."

Hignett would play a major role in Boro's promotion season of 1997-98 and scored twice against Oxford in his last ever game before departing to Aberdeen at the end of his contract.

He added: "I left the best way I could have. I had a few tears on the night of the Oxford game because I knew it was my last game, but they were happy tears because I knew we'd been promoted."

• FRUSTRATION - Craig Hignett was often left out by Bryan Robson

9. Bolo Zenden - 4.8%

• FREE TRANSFER - Bolo Zenden joined from Chelsea for nothing

While millions were splashed out on the likes of Ravanelli and Juninho in the early Riverside years, the Bosman ruling of December 1995 changed football's transfer market forever. It meant that, while some players such as Gareth Southgate, could still cost a lot of money, others could be brought in for nothing depending on their contract situation.

Perhaps Boro's most successful Bosman signing to date has been Dutchman Bolo Zenden, who initially joined on loan from Chelsea in 2003 before signing permanently the following year. He joined as an exciting left-sided midfielder following a successful career with PSV Eindhoven, Barcelona and then the Stamford Bridge side, and had also appeared at a World Cup and two European Championships with the Netherlands.

Zenden initially struggled to win over Boro's fans but his career seemed to turn after he scored a penalty in the Carling Cup final, and from then on he became a firm favourite. He would score eight goals the following season,

Riverside X

missing just two league games as he became established in the centre of midfield alongside fellow countryman George Boateng. Zenden would further endear himself as he hit an important penalty to equalise at home against Fulham as Boro's European dreams looked in tatters but perhaps his best Boro performance was the match-winning display against Lazio when he scored two tremendous UEFA Cup goals.

Zenden would leave Boro as he had joined them – on a free – in July 2005 when he signed for Liverpool.

10. Nigel Pearson - 3.7%

The skipper that led Boro out for the Riverside's first ever game was also the man that brought the Ayresome Park era to a close. Pearson lifted the First Division trophy at the end of 1994-95 and remained just as influential as a captain and defender during the early Riverside years.

• NEVER SAY DIE - Popular skipper Nigel Pearson

In total he played 139 times for Boro after signing from Sheffield Wednesday for £750,000. He had suffered with injuries during the previous few seasons with Wednesday, but fans will always remember him as a tough and commanding skipper – he missed just two games of the first Riverside season despite approaching his mid-30s.

Injury problems would return the following season, and Boro missed his presence as they were relegated. But Captain Marvel's own Captain Marvel was there to lead his team in both cup finals, and made his final Boro appearance as his club were promoted back to the Premiership at the end of 1997-98.

Pearson's defensive partner Derek Whyte explained Pearson's enduring appeal. He said: "Nigel was the best captain that I ever played for and it was a privilege to play alongside him. He was such an influential player to have in your side – as important to Boro as Roy Keane has been to Manchester United. He had a never-say-die attitude that rubbed off on everyone in the dressing room, and the fans also warmed to that."

11. Gianluca Festa - 3.5%

Se soltanto. That's how one says 'if only' in Italian. If only Boro had signed Gianluca Festa ahead of the 1996-97 season. The team would have probably stayed in the Premiership, they would have kept hold of Juninho and Ravanelli and could have gone on to world domination. Unfortunately, life and football are not that simple.

In many ways Festa was the last piece of the jigsaw puzzle for Bryan Robson, a talented defender signed at the peak of his powers from Internazionale – top of Serie A and in the semi finals of the UEFA Cup – to complement Boro's attacking talents. But his arrival came when Boro were already rooted to the bottom of the Premiership, and while matters improved in the second half of the season, it was too late.

Festa started life in the First Division with a goal on the opening day and any doubts about his commitment to life in England's lower leagues was dispelled as he was voted supporters' player of the season in 1997-98. He would

remain just as important until he finally left the club in 2002, having proved himself reliable – and capable of scoring the odd useful goal – as Boro began to concentrate on defence to establish themselves as a Premiership force.

Some 171 games after joining he departed for Portsmouth, but only after becoming a favourite, and will always keep Teesside in his heart. He said: "When I came I knew nothing about Middlesbrough and Middlesbrough knew nothing about me. We all had to get to know each other and the challenge for me was to prove myself. I look on coming to England as a positive experience – and a lot of that is down to the help I received at the club and in the local community."

• CHALLENGE - Gianluca Festa proved himself to Boro fans

12. Paul Merson - 3.5%

• REVELATION - Paul Merson was a hit on Teesside

Hero or villain? Having been voted one of the club's greatest players of the last decade it seems that the jury has delivered verdict on Paul Merson. He spent little more than one year at the Riverside but his influence was massive as he dragged the club kicking and screaming back into the Premiership after the disappointment of relegation in 1997.

Merson had been a prodigy at Arsenal when he first came on the scene in the late 1980s. But by the early 1990s he had begun a descent into drink and gambling problems that would stall his career. Mentor George Graham left Arsenal in 1995 and two years later he was allowed to leave Highbury for £4.5m by new boss Arsene Wenger.

The drop to the First Division could go either of two ways. But Merson was a revelation as he scored 12 goals in a mighty 45 league starts as Boro were promoted. Gone were the drinking celebrations that he had shared with Highbury crowds in years gone by, but it was soon more of a wake atmosphere as just three games into 1998-99 and he slapped in a transfer request.

Riverside X

For good measure the Riverside favourite had also hinted at disciplinary problems at the club, and his Boro career was over as he was sold to Aston Villa for a massive £7m.

Merson himself added: "I don't think I let anyone down at Middlesbrough. I am not being big-headed but I still believe that Boro wouldn't have got back into the Premiership that season if I hadn't gone to the club. I left because I was a sick man who had problems, that's all there is to it. It was nothing to do with the club, I could have been at AC Milan and I would still have left."

....

13. Emerson - 2.7%

Like London buses, you wait for one fantastic Brazilian and then two arrive on Teeside within months. In fact three South American stars joined Boro in 1996 and 1997 with Juninho and Emerson also joined by World Cup winner Branco, although the latter did not enjoy the success of the other pair.

• TOUGH - Emerson was a solid midfielder

While Emerson was overshadowed by his more famous countryman, he played just as big a role in helping focus the nation's attention on Teesside during the dramatic 1996-97 season. Indeed Emerson looked to have been more tutored in a European school of hard knocks than the beach soccer flair of his homeland. A strongly-built midfielder who dropped deep, Emerson's power was equalled by his cunning with the ball at his feet. As well as breaking down the opposition he could also score sublime goals, and it was a great shame that his time at the club was dogged by his failure to settle in England.

He went AWOL on a number of occasions, and even missed the 1997 Coca-Cola Cup semi-final at the Riverside as he attempted to convince his wife to return from Brazil to Boro. Eventually he was sold to Spanish side Tenerife for £4.25m, but only after he had played 22 game in the First Division following Boro's relegation.

Robson said: "Emmo was a great lad, all the other players got on with him and he was never late for training. He only let himself down once, and that was the Stockport game when he had gone to Brazil for family reasons."

....

14. Paul Ince - 1.8%

Ince, like Blackburn's Robbie Savage, pretty much sums up that old football saying about players that are loved by their own fans and hated by opponents. Crunching tackles, snapping at opponents and officials, a marathon-runner's stamina and no shortage of skill, it's hardly surprising that Ince was a favourite at all six of his clubs – but not liked in many other places. Indeed he is said to have departed three of

Donal Tully
Ireland

"Having arrived on Teeside as an unknown, few expected Franck Queudrue to become anything more than a fringe player. His goalscoring home debut dismissed those presumptions immediately and he has since proved himself one of the clubs best ever signings. Franck's boundless energy, confrontational style, ability to initiate attacks from deep, decisive tackles and 100 per cent determination make him such an asset."

Anthony Ryles
Stockton

"Juninho is quite simply the best and the greatest player to grace the Premiership. If he played for Manchester United people would be saying he was the best player in the world. Only the Riverside faithful can appreciate how consistently brilliant he was, we will never again see a player whose ability matches his commitment to such high levels. A statue of Juninho outside the Riverside is the least the little fella deserves."

his previous clubs, West Ham, Manchester United and Liverpool, on bad terms so that 'love' is pretty much only found at Inter, Boro and current club Wolves.

One of England's finest midfielders of the last 20 years, Ince was the lynchpin at the heart of his country's success at Euro '96 and also played at World Cup 1998 before moving to the Riverside the following year from Anfield. He played a key role in turning Boro from their previous incarnation as an entertaining yo-yo side into an established Premiership force. He brought experience and bite to the centre of the park, and also a great deal of professionalism as he maintained his high performance levels despite losing the captaincy to Gareth Southgate in 2001.

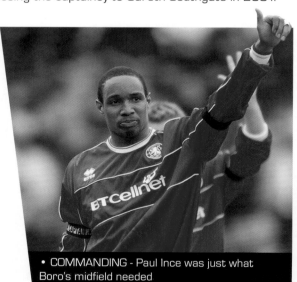

• COMMANDING - Paul Ince was just what Boro's midfield needed

15. Jimmy Floyd Hasselbaink - 1.2%

A hit at whichever club he has played, the Dutch striker added all-important goals to Boro's defensive security when he joined in 2004. From having one of the Premiership's least successful strike forces in recent years, all of a sudden Boro were fourth highest scorers in the top division during 2004-05.

While Bolo Zenden, Mark Viduka, Stewart Downing and Szilard Nemeth scored some vital goals, it was Hasselbaink who led the charts with his fantastic haul of 17 goals in his first Boro season. Included among that was a brilliant hat-trick at Blackburn, and a number of superb strikes from free kicks. The most famous of those was the vital opener at Manchester City on the final day of the season, as Hasselbaink – who had endured a thin period for a couple of months – beat David James with a typical thunderbolt.

Born in Surinam, Hasselbaink first played in the Premiership for Leeds in the mid-1990s before moving to Atletico Madrid. But he would then enjoy four seasons with Chelsea before being deemed surplus to requirements after Roman Abramovich had spent millions on Crespo, Mutu, Drogba and Kezman.

Chelsea's loss was Boro's gain and Steve McClaren was quick to please the fans with a striker that has always scored goals – and never gives up. "I want to be angry on the field and tired when I get home after games," he said. "That's when I know I've enjoyed it and have done my job. I'm only ever happy when I'm scoring goals. If I have 20, I want to score 25."

• FREE - Jimmy Floyd Hasselbaink was a great success after moving to the Riverside from Chelsea

Boro's greatest team

This side was voted for by fans on the official club website www.mfc.co.uk.

Supporters voted for their favourite player in each position from the last 10 years, and the results show who is regarded as the best of the Riverside era.

Goalkeeper

Mark Schwarzer ran away with the competition as he grabbed 87.7 per cent of votes, with Mark Crossley in second spot with 6.5 per cent. Despite having made only a handful of first-team appearances, Brad Jones also polled 1.7 per cent, which shows how highly supporters rate the young Aussie.

Defence

Current players Franck Queudrue and Gareth Southgate were comfortably selected to play in the Riverside's best back line. Frenchman Queudrue took 79.5 per cent of the left-back vote while Christian Ziege (10.6) and Colin

Cooper (4.9) were also heavily backed. Southgate took a mighty 62.6 per cent of votes for central defence, and was joined in the centre by Nigel Pearson, who was the main man for 12 per cent. Cooper was again in the running with 6.1 per cent, while Gary Pallister took 5.7 per cent.

Right back was one of the closest races, with the No. 2 shirt a tough choice for supporters who had idolised players from Neil Cox through to Stuart Parnaby. Tony McMahon gathered an astonishing 28.1 per cent despite having still to play a full Premiership season, but the overall winner was Gianluca Festa (29.2), a central defender who also had spells at right-back. Danny Mills, a loan signing in 2003-04, grabbed 17.2 per cent with Curtis Fleming receiving 12.8 per cent.

Midfield

This area was broken into two sections – defence and attack. It was no surprise to see Juninho grab 70 per cent of votes, but it was a tighter contest for his partner just behind the forwards. Indeed only a 10th of one per cent separated Paul Merson (5.8) and Craig Hignett, with the former just squeezing into the all-star team. Bolo Zenden (4.9) and Stewart Downing (4.5) were also close, with Paul Gascoigne (1.5) only seventh – which shows some of the attacking talents Boro have been treated to in the last decade.

George Boateng swept to 60.6 per cent of votes cast in the deeper role, and Brazilian Emerson just beat off Robbie Mustoe (9.8), Paul Ince (9.2) and Zenden (9.0) to join him just in front of defence.

Attack

It takes a special player to score 30-plus goals in a season, and that's exactly why, nine years on, Fabrizio Ravanelli was the runaway winner of the poll to find Boro's best forward of the Riverside era. Despite the controversy that surrounded him, Boro fans have put his goals before his words and 65.1 per cent chose him as their number nine. Jimmy Floyd Hasselbaink came second with 13.7 per cent, while perhaps a surprise third choice was Marco Branca (5.2), with the Riverside's top scorer Hamilton Ricard (4.5) and Croatian legend Alen Boksic (4.3) also in the running.

Most memorable games

1. BORO 2 Bolton 1 - 35.6%

CARLING CUP FINAL
FEBRUARY 29, 2004
MILLENNIUM STADIUM (72,634)

Glory at last! After 128 years in the waiting, Boro grabbed their first major silverware on an unforgettable afternoon at the Millennium Stadium in Cardiff. And how Teesside celebrated.

This was the final that had everything - great goals, a wonderful atmosphere under the stadium's closed roof . . . and a nail-biting finish as the minutes ticked down to the final whistle with Boro within touching distance of victory. Joseph-Desire Job expertly converted from Bolo Zenden's cross after only two minutes. Then, five minutes later, Zenden doubled the advantage from the penalty-spot after Emerson Thome had fouled Job. An uncharacteristic mistake by Mark Schwarzer let in Kevin Davies as Bolton sensed a comeback, but Boro comfortably held out to lift the trophy.

BORO 2 **(Job 2, Zenden 7 (pen)**: Schwarzer, Mills, Ehiogu, Southgate, Queudrue, Mendieta, Boateng, Doriva, Zenden, Juninho, Job (Ricketts 65).
Subs (not used): Jones, Riggott, Maccarone, Downing.
Booked: Boateng, Ricketts.

Bolton 1 **(Davies 21)**: Jaaskelainen, Hunt (Stelios 87), N'Gotty, Thome, Charlton, Frandsen (Pedersen 63), Campo, Okocha, Nolan (Moreno 78), Djorkaeff, Davies.
Subs (not used): Poole, Barness.
Booked: Campo, Charlton, Frandsen.
Referee: M Riley

• VICTORY - Juninho beats Bruno N'Gotty

2. BORO 2 Lazio 0 - 20.4%

UEFA CUP SECOND ROUND, GROUP E
NOVEMBER 4, 2004
RIVERSIDE STADIUM (33,991)

• GLORY, GLORY NIGHT - Bolo Zenden celebrates his opener

This home win over the Italian giants was the highlight of Boro's first ever European campaign following the Carling Cup triumph. Boro took the lead after 16 minutes when Lazio failed to clear a Stewart Downing cross and Bolo Zenden smashed home a powerful volley.

The pair also had a hand in the second when Zenden headed home brilliantly from a Downing cross on 71 minutes. Despite a poor showing from Lazio, a memorable Boro performance meant fans went home dreaming of European glory as their side stayed top of UEFA Cup Group E.

BORO 2 **(Zenden 16, 71)**: Schwarzer, McMahon, Southgate, Riggott, Queudrue, Parlour, Boateng, Zenden, Downing, Hasselbaink (Job 81), Viduka.
Subs (not used): Nash, Cooper, Doriva, Morrison, Wilson.

Lazio 0: Casazza, Oddo, Lopez, Couto, Seric, Filippini, Dabo, Giannichedda (Melara 14), Cesar Aparicido (Manfredini 64), Di Canio, Delgado (Rocchi 50)
Subs (not used): De Angelis, Pandev, Sannibale, Torroni.

3. BORO 2 Liverpool 0 - 16.3%

COCA-COLA CUP SEMI-FINAL, SECOND LEG
FEBRUARY 18, 1998
RIVERSIDE STADIUM (29,828)

Bryan Robson's First Division side was 1-0 down coming into this semi-final second leg, but still managed to claim a final place in style. Many fans remember this night for the amount of red and white flags being proudly waved by the Boro faithful, which made for one of the most exciting atmospheres the Riverside has seen.

The game itself featured yet another perfect start. After only two minutes, Mikkel Beck was fouled inside the box and Paul Merson converted from the spot. Marco Branca then doubled the lead just a couple of minutes later. Boro's commanding performance was typified by the fact that Liverpool had only two efforts on goal all night, with Boro going to Wembley 3-2 on aggregate.

BORO 2 (Merson 2 (pen), Branca 4): Schwarzer, Kinder, Festa, Vickers, Pearson, Mustoe, Hignett (Baker 74), Branca, Beck, Merson, Townsend.
Subs (not used): Fleming, Ormerod.
Booked: Branca, Townsend.

Liverpool 0 James, Jones, Harkness, Bjornebye, Matteo, (Leonhardsen 46), Carragher, Ince, Berger (Riedle 65), McManaman, Fowler, Owen
Subs (not used): Friedel.
Booked: Ince, McManaman, Riedle.

• GREAT START - Paul Merson opened the scoring after two minutes

4. BORO 3 Chesterfield 3 - 10.5%

FA CUP SEMI FINAL
APRIL 13, 1997
OLD TRAFFORD (49,640)

• DRAMA - Gianluca Festa puts Boro in front against Chesterfield

This FA Cup semi-final at Old Trafford against Second Division opposition was packed full of incident from the start. Chesterfield took a two-goal lead and Boro were facing an even bigger task when Vlad Kinder was sent off.

But they bounced back with goals from Fabrizio Ravanelli and Craig Hignett, who slotted home a penalty after a foul on Juninho.

Extra time soon came and Gianluca Festa headed Boro into the lead, only for Jamie Hewitt to grab an equaliser right at the death. This was justice for the Spireites, who had an effort controversially ruled out, even though it had crossed the line.

BORO 3 (Ravanelli 64, Hignett 70 (pen), Festa 100): Roberts, Vickers, Emerson, Kinder, Mustoe, Beck (Blackmore 39), Juninho, Ravanelli, Fleming, Festa, Hignett (Moore 115).
Subs (not used): Whyte.
Booked: Blackmore, Roberts.
Sent off: Kinder.

Chesterfield 3 (Morris 54, Dyche 60 (pen), Hewitt 119): Mercer, Hewitt, Jules, Curtis, Williams, Dyche, Davies, Holland (Beaumont 74), Morris, Howard, Perkins (Carr 84).
Subs (not used): Leaning.
Booked: Curtis, Jules.

Riverside X

5. BORO 3 Liverpool 3 - 8.6%

PREMIERSHIP
AUGUST 17, 1996
RIVERSIDE STADIUM (30,039)

This home game was Fabrizio Ravanelli's debut in English football – and he marked it with a hat-trick as Boro earned an opening-day point after trailing three times. The ex-Juve man's first was from the spot and cancelled out Stig-Inge Bjornbye's early goal.

John Barnes then put the visitors back ahead only for Ravanelli to convert Neil Cox' low cross. In the second half, Robbie Fowler put Liverpool in front once more but, 10 minutes from time, Boro's new £7m striker completed his hat-trick and the home fans went wild.

BORO 3 (Ravanelli 26 (pen), 36, 81): Miller, Cox, Whyte, Vickers, Pearson, Emerson, Barmby, Mustoe, Juninho (Moore 83), Ravanelli, Fleming.
Subs (not used): Walsh, Whelan, Hendrie, Hignett.
Booked: Emerson.

Liverpool 3 (Bjornebye 4, Barnes 29, Fowler 65): James, Babb, Bjornebye, McAteer, Wright, Matteo, McManaman, Collymore, Fowler, Barnes, Thomas.
Subs (not used): Warner, Jones, Ruddock, Thompson, Carragher.
Booked: McManaman, Wright.

• BIG MAN - Fabrizio Ravanelli is congratulated by Juninho as he scores a debut hat-trick

6. Manchester Utd 2 BORO 3 - 4.8%

PREMIERSHIP
DECEMBER 19, 1998
OLD TRAFFORD (55,152)

• GREAT DAY - Dean Gordon tackles Manchester United's Ryan Giggs

Bryan Robson once claimed this to be the best result of his managerial career and, although that verdict may have changed after his heroics with West Brom in 2004-05, this was still a remarkable result.

Boro managed to go three goals up, with first-half strikes from Hamilton Ricard and Dean Gordon, the latter hitting a spectacular effort. In the second half, it was 3-0 when a Ronny Johnsen error allowed Ricard to tee up Brian Deane – but the final half hour saw a remarkable comeback from United with goals from Nicky Butt and Paul Scholes almost enough to level matters.

Man Utd 2 (Butt 62, Scholes 70): Schmeichel, P Neville (Solskjaer 78), Irwin, Johnsen, G Neville, Butt, Beckham (Scholes 64), Keane, Giggs, Cole, Sheringham.
Subs (not used): Blomqvist, Van Der Gouw, Brown.
Booked: Beckham.

BORO 3 (Ricard 23, Gordon 31, Deane 59): Schwarzer, Gordon, Vickers, Festa, Pallister, Mustoe (Moore 72), Deane, Maddison (Beck 83), Townsend, Ricard, Cooper.
Subs (not used): Blackmore, Roberts, Stockdale.
Booked: Festa.

156

7. Boro 2 Chelsea 0 - 3.5%

PREMIERSHIP
AUGUST 26, 1995
RIVERSIDE STADIUM (28,286)

Etched in history for one simple reason – it was the Boro's first game at the then-named Cellnet Riverside Stadium and boasted the club's highest attendance for 14 years. A strong Chelsea outfit, including Ruud Gullit and Mark Hughes, were beaten comfortably by a lively Boro side, who took the lead just before half time.

Nick Barmby strode down the left and teed up Craig Hignett whose strike became the first goal at the new stadium. Just 15 minutes from the end, Barmby did it again and this time set up Jan-Aage Fjortoft, and the match was beyond the glamorous visitors.

BORO 2 **(Hignett 39, Fjortoft 76)**: Miller, Pearson, Vickers, Whyte, Cox, Pollock, Mustoe, Hignett, Morris, Barmby, Fjortoft.
Subs not used: Whelan, Moreno, Kavanagh.
Booked: Barmby, Morris, Pollock.

Chelsea 0: Kharin, Sinclair, Gullit, Johnsen, Clarke, Lee, Wise, Peacock, Myers, Hughes, Stein (Newton 80).
Subs not used: Hitchcock.
Booked: Clarke, Johnsen, Sinclair, Spencer, Wise.

• HISTORY MAN - Jan-Aage Fjortoft celebrates his goal with Nick Barmby

8. BORO 3 Banik Ostrava 0 - 2.3%

UEFA CUP FIRST ROUND, FIRST LEG
SEPTEMBER 16, 2004
RIVERSIDE STADIUM (29,746)

• MOBBED - Mark Viduka scored twice in Boro's first European match

Another big night in the club's history, as Boro's debut in European competition went better than many imagined. Against the Czech champions, Boro looked in fine form and, despite a goalless first half, never looked in serious trouble.

Jimmy Floyd Hasselbaink opened the scoring for the home side when George Boateng's deflected shot fell to him. Mark Viduka grabbed the next, finishing well after good play from Szilard Nemeth. With 10 minutes left, Bolo Zenden's cross from the left was met by Viduka, who added his second. The great result and atmosphere will live long in the memory of many fans.

BORO 3 **(Hasselbaink 57, Viduka 63, 80)**: Schwarzer, Parnaby, Southgate, Riggott, Queudrue, Nemeth, Boateng, Parlour, Zenden, Viduka, Hasselbaink.
Subs (not used): Nash, Job, Downing, Doriva, Cooper, Morrison, McMahon.
Booked: Parlour.

Banik Ostrava 0: Raska, Pospech, Dvornik (Velkoborsky 15), Besta, Drozd, Latal, Bystron, Zubek, Cizek, Matusovic (Papadopulos 87), Licka (Lukes 66).
Subs not used: Konig, Zavadil, Hoffmann, Zurek.
Booked: Velkoborsky.

9. BORO 4 Oxford United 1 - 1.1%

FIRST DIVISION
MAY 3, 1998
RIVERSIDE STADIUM (30,228)

The game that sealed Boro's promotion back to the Premiership after a season in the First Division. Going into the game, it was necessary for Boro to win if they were to maintain their place ahead of rivals Sunderland in the promotion spot just behind champions Nottingham Forest.

However, a goalless first half, combined with Sunderland being ahead in their game, meant nerves were jangling at the Riverside. Then Alun Armstrong calmed everyone down when he opened the scoring just three minutes after half time. Armstrong then added another while Craig Hignett scored his last two goals for the club to ensure that Boro pipped the Black Cats to promotion by a single point.

BORO 4 (Armstrong 47, 48, Hignett 57, 63): Schwarzer, Fleming, Harrison, Festa, Pearson, Townsend, Mustoe, Gascoigne, Armstrong (Ricard 67), Merson, Hignett.
Subs not used: Kinder, Beck.

Oxford Utd 1 (Banger 70): Whitehead, Robinson, Marsh, Gray, Davis, Gilchrist, Murphy (Banger 67), Smith, Francis (Cook 85), Powell (Remy 63), Beauchamp.

• WE ARE GOING UP - Robbie Mustoe, Craig Hignett, Mark Schwarzer and Mikkel Beck applaud the fans after promotion is sealed

10. BORO 1 Leicester City 1 - 0.9%

COCA-COLA CUP FINAL
APRIL 6, 1997
WEMBLEY (76,757)

• STRUGGLE - Emerson tussles with Emile Heskey

This was the first time Boro had made a major cup final in their 122-year history. It was also the first of three successive domestic finals, which sadly all ended in disappointment.

Tens of thousands of Boro fans travelled to Wembley but witnessed something of a dull 90 minutes as both sides halted each other's attacks until the fifth minute of extra time. Fabrizio Ravanelli got on to the end of a Juninho pass and drove home what looked a likely winner. But Emile Heskey hit an equaliser three minutes from time, with the Foxes winning the Hillsborough replay 1-0.

BORO 1 (Ravanelli 95): Schwarzer, Cox, Pearson, Emerson, Mustoe, Beck, Juninho, Ravanelli, Fleming, Festa, Hignett.
Subs not used: Vickers, Moore, Blackmore.
Booked: Beck, Cox, Juninho.

Leicester 1 (Heskey 118): Keller, Grayson, Whitlow (Robins 105), Walsh, Izzet (Taylor 108), Lennon, Claridge, Parker, Heskey, Kaamark, Prior.
Subs not used: Poole.
Booked: Heskey, Kaamark, Prior.

Greatest
Goals
of the Riverside Era

From Nick Barmby's opener at Arsenal in 1995 to Jimmy Floyd Hasselbaink's amazing free kick at the end of 2004-05, the Riverside years have seen some fantastic goals. While goals involving the whole team – or a simple tap-in at the far post – count equally, it is those moments of individual brilliance that rate most highly in this fans' poll to find the best of the 630 goals scored by Boro in the last 10 years. So whether it's some Brazilian magic courtesy of Juninho and Emerson, a Dutch master or Croatian cracker, these are YOUR favourite goals since the Riverside opened its doors. But we start with a goal that was just the Job.

1. JOSEPH-DESIRE JOB – 37.7%

V SPORTING LISBON
UEFA CUP ROUND OF 16 - MARCH 10 2005
RIVERSIDE STADIUM

• SPECTACULAR - Joseph-Desire Job, right

Some goals will never be forgotten for their importance. Others remain forever imprinted on the memory because of their sheer brilliance. Joseph-Desire Job's awesome overhead kick against Sporting Lisbon falls firmly into the second category. It was truly spectacular.

There looked to be nothing on when Bolo Zenden nonchalantly chipped a left-foot free-kick deep into the Sporting penalty box. With his back to goal, Job's best hope looked to be a knock-down header for one of his team-mates to run on to. Instead, he produced a once-in-a-lifetime goal that sent a previously downbeat Riverside into raptures.

The fact that it was ultimately as meaningless as it was wondrous does not detract from Job's scissor kick extraordinaire. It was one of those rare goals that those Boro fans who saw it will

never forget. Many will one day tell their grandchildren: "I was there the night Joseph Job scored his overhead kick."

Had it not been so special, Job's strike would have warranted no more than a passing mention in a review of Boro's first UEFA Cup campaign. Boro were 3-0 down and facing Riverside humiliation against their experienced European visitors. The goal arrived out of the blue, sparking renewed hope of an unlikely comeback. It inspired team-mates and fans to believe the unbelievable, that Boro could still win through against all the odds.

Another goal from Chris Riggott caused the Sporting defence to push the panic button, but the Portuguese held on for a 3-2 first leg win despite several late scares. However, Boro – and particularly Job - had kept the tie alive for the second leg in Lisbon. Ironically, with the scores delicately balanced at 0-0 a week later, the Cameroon international would miss a far easier chance that might just have tipped the tie Boro's way.

The super-strike, the run-away winner of our fans' poll to choose the greatest goal of the Riverside era, was naturally special to Job himself. "I wanted the ball for about five seconds before, but it was only then that Bolo picked me out," he said. "The main thing is to get the ball on target. It was a nice goal to score."

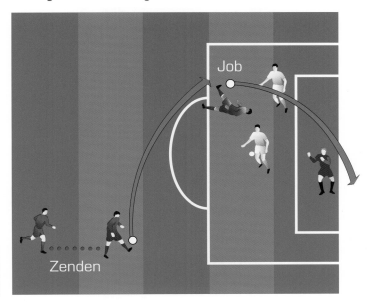

2. JIMMY FLOYD HASSELBAINK - 18.8%
V MANCHESTER CITY

PREMIER LEAGUE - MAY 15 2005
CITY OF MANCHESTER STADIUM

Bang! This was what you call an unstoppable shot. The man scientifically proven to have the hardest shot in English football pulled one of his best ever out of the bag just when Boro required it most.

• WALLOP! - The Dutchman has the hardest shot in football.

• WOW! - There's no stopping Jimmy Floyd Hasselbaink at Manchester City

Needing a point from the season's final game to qualify for a second successive European campaign, Boro were on the back foot during the opening 20 minutes as a Manchester City energized by the permanent managerial appointment of Stuart Pearce launched wave after wave of attacks. It seemed only a matter of time before they would make a breakthrough. But they hadn't banked on Jimmy.

Brought down by Robbie Fowler midway inside the City half, Hasselbaink's most likely scenario seemed to be a chip into the box. But Boro's top scorer had only one thing on his mind as he placed the ball down and took aim. With all the confidence of a man who had scored with three free-kicks already that season, Jimmy let rip with a shot that blasted in off the underside of David James' crossbar.

Sky TV's speed guns had previously clocked Jimmy's pocket rockets at an amazing 80.4mph, the sort of oomph that could cost three points on your licence on the A19. But this was more like Formula One. The incredible strike, his 16th of the season, lifted the pressure off Boro, at least until Kiki Musampha's goal in the opening seconds after half-time. But hard-hitting Hasselbaink – with a little help from the hand of Mark Schwarzer – had put Boro in Euro ecstasy once again.

3. JUNINHO – 14.6%

V CHELSEA
PREMIER LEAGUE - MARCH 22 1997
RIVERSIDE STADIUM

Dazzling, dynamic and awe-inspiring. It says something about this goal that it polled so many votes more than eight years after the ball nestled in Chelsea's net.

After a nightmare run that had left relegation looking inevitable, Boro – and Juninho - were suddenly on a roll going into this crucial game. Three successive league wins and 11 goals had taken Bryan Robson's team to within sight of safety.

But the Blues proved a tough nut to crack, the game remaining scoreless until the 53rd minute. Then Juninho wove a little more of his magic. Like many great goals, there initially seemed to be little threat. But this was Juninho at his peak and anything was possible.

Playing a swift one-two with Emerson, the little Brazilian jinked his way past two opposing defenders, sped into space and played a perfect pass to Mikkel Beck. The Dane played his part perfectly, holding up the ball to give his team-mate time to race into the box and then delivering a wonderful cross into the box. And there was Juninho, his marker left for dead, racing into the six-yard area to dispatch a diving header low into the net. What a player! What a goal!

• OH YES - Juninho is congratulated by Mikkel Beck after his incredible goal

4. EMERSON - 5.6%

V SUNDERLAND
PREMIER LEAGUE - OCTOBER 14 1996
ROKER PARK

• MY GOAL - Emerson hit a cracker at Roker Park

There was something about Emerson and the spectacular. The enigmatic Brazilian did nothing by halves. Whether on or off the pitch, he had a penchant for grabbing the headlines. Blessed with skill, strength and a samba-style goal celebration, his strikes were perhaps his piece de resistance.

A month earlier he had issued warning of his long-range shooting ability with a spectacular effort in Boro's 7-0 Coca-Cola Cup drubbing of hapless Hereford. Even if Sunderland had taken heed, there was little they could have done about this strike, bar bricking up their goal.

Curtis Fleming started the move, cutting in from the left wing before playing a short ball inside to Nick Barmby. When the England star failed to control the ball, the chance looked to have gone. But a Sunderland defender carelessly played the ball out of the box... straight into Emerson's path. The Brazilian did not need a second invitation.

Emerson launched a net-busting, 30-yard rocket high into the net. Cue ecstatic celebrations.

5. EMERSON – 4.0%

V SUNDERLAND
DIVISION ONE - SEPTEMBER 28 1997
STADIUM OF LIGHT

Just as he had marked Roker Park's last ever Wear-Tees derby with a trademark blast, Emerson repeated his magic in Boro's first match at the newly opened Stadium of Light. Sunderland fans must have hated him.

Almost 12 months from his first visit to Boro's North-East rivals, Emerson gave Peter Reid's side another taste of his Brazilian blend. This time, the two sides were vying for promotion after both had suffered the heartbreak of relegation the previous summer. Emerson would be long gone by the time the Teessiders would ultimately beat Sunderland to the second automatic promotion spot in a dramatic end-of-season finish. But this was a key moment.

Paul Merson made a darting run along Sunderland's left flank before cutting the ball back from the touchline to the onrushing Emerson. The ball sat up perfectly for the midfielder to launch a volley past the home side's stranded 'keeper and into the net. Boro were on their way to an important 2-1 win in the backyard of their neighbours and rivals.

• HEARTBREAKER - Brazilian Emerson volleyed home

6. GAIZKA MENDIETA – 3.1%

V WOLVES
PREMIER LEAGUE - NOVEMBER 1 2003
RIVERSIDE STADIUM

• UNSTOPPABLE - Gaizka Mendieta is congratulated by Colin Cooper

Goals have been hard to come by for Gaizka Mendieta since the Spanish superstar made the move to English football during the summer of 2003. But this long-range rocket would have stood out even had he averaged 20 goals a season.

As two Wolves defenders allowed themselves to become distracted by Danny Mills, Juninho played a short free-kick inside to Mendi. Two quick touches took the midfielder to the right-hand corner of the Wolves box, from where he launched an unstoppable shot into the top corner of the net.

It was Mendieta's first Premier League goal and gave notice to opponents that he was still capable of reproducing the form that had made Lazio pay £28.9 million for him just two years earlier.

7. ALEN BOKSIC – 3.0%

V LEICESTER CITY
PREMIER LEAGUE - APRIL 21 2001
FILBERT STREET

He might not have been everyone's cup of tea, but there was no disputing that Alen Boksic had world-class ability. Bryan Robson and Steve McClaren struggled to get the best out of the sulky Croatian, but the striker saved most of his best displays for Terry Venables.

This stunning goal, the second in a 3-0 away win, made Boro all but safe from the threat of relegation which had hung over the club for the past eight months. Coming a week after another memorable three-goal success, at Arsenal, the welcome three points lifted Boro into 15th, their highest league position since late October.

Receiving the ball on the halfway line, Boksic initially simply made up space as he ran towards the Leicester penalty area. But when the home side's defence failed to close him down, his goalscoring instinct told him there was only one way to go – and yet it took something very special to put Boro two-up.

A sudden turn of speed took him past a Foxes defender to the edge of the City box, from where he lobbed the ball with perfect precision into the home side's net.

• SALUTE - Alen Boksic lobbed home at Leicester City

8. MARCO BRANCA - 2.7%

V SWINDON TOWN
DIVISION ONE - MARCH 11 1998
RIVERSIDE STADIUM

• MEMORABLE - An acrobatic goal courtesy of Marco Branca

Overhead kicks always look spectacular, even when – as usual – they end up in the back of the stand instead of the back of the net. But when everything goes right and the result is a goal, wow!

Italian striker Marco Branca had announced his arrival in English football a month earlier by scoring against Liverpool just two minutes into his Boro debut in the semi-final of the Coca-Cola Cup. But this goal suggested he was capable of overshadowing the achievements of even his fellow countryman Fabrizio Ravanelli.

From just outside the six-yard area, Branca acrobatically launched himself into the air to meet Curtis Fleming's left-footed, right-wing cross. The goal completed a six-goal rout to send Boro back into top spot.

9. BOLO ZENDEN – 2.7%

V LAZIO
UEFA CUP GROUP STAGE - NOVEMBER 4 2004
RIVERSIDE STADIUM

A magical night on which Boro announced their arrival on the European scene against one of the giants of Italian football was capped by two stunning goal from Bolo Zenden. An exquisite header would follow later, but this stunning strike calmed nerves and set the ball rolling for a great win.

When the Lazio defence failed to deal with Stewart Downing's left-wing cross, an attempted clearance flicked up invitingly off Mark Viduka's outstretched foot. From the edge of the box, Zenden struck a perfect low volley into the net, sending the Boro fans wild with delight.

Later crowned the Supporters Club's player of the year, Zenden was in the middle of a goal streak that saw him score five times in six games, including one against his next employers, Liverpool.

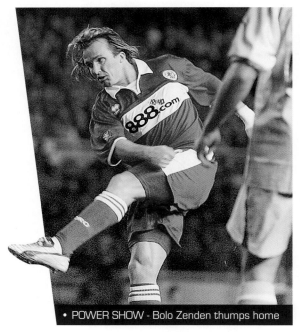

• POWER SHOW - Bolo Zenden thumps home

10. JUNINHO – 2.2%

V EVERTON
PREMIER LEAGUE - MAY 14 2000
GOODISON PARK

• DARTING - Juninho startled Everton's defence

This is what you call signing off in style. For much of Juninho's second spell with Boro, on loan from Atletico Madrid, he flattered to deceive, but this was a reminder of the Brazilian at his best.

The teams had little but pride to play for as the curtains closed on the Premiership season. With Boro a goal up with just three minutes left on the clock, Juni received the ball fully 40 yards out. From there, he set off virtually walking it into the net.

A sudden change of gear and a darting run took him past two startled Everton players. A quick one-two with Brian Deane left two more for dead. Juni was inside the box with the 'keeper to beat. Many would still have panicked and missed, but the "The Little Fella" coolly slotted his shot inside the post to clinch a 2-0 win.

RiversideX

11. MASSIMO MACCARONE – 1.8%

V BIRMINGHAM CITY
PREMIER LEAGUE - MARCH 20 2004
RIVERSIDE STADIUM

This was one of those games in which everything goes right. Three weeks earlier, Massimo Maccarone had cried tears of pain as his team-mates danced around the Millennium Stadium pitch, the Carling Cup held aloft. Left on the bench for the full 90 minutes, Boro's record signing had missed out on one of the biggest days of his career.

But the £8.15 million Italian proved he was oozing with bouncebackability with this amazing strike in a truly remarkable game. Boro had already shared five goals in an incredible half, when Maccarone collected the ball wide on the right. It was too much to expect another goal in the seconds that remained of the first half.

But the struggling striker thought otherwise, cutting inside his marker before striking a beautiful shot into the Birmingham net from a seemingly impossible angle. The match would eventually finish 5-3, with Maccarone's goal the best of the eight.

• WONDER GOAL - Massimo Maccarone is congratulated by Jonathan Greening

12. GEREMI – 1.8%

V LEEDS UNITED
PREMIER LEAGUE - MARCH 15 2003
ELLAND ROAD

• CHIP - It was a belter for Geremi at Leeds

Another player with an eye for the spectacular, Geremi wasn't always at his best on Boro's travels, but this day was different. Facing their old boss Terry Venables – and future star Mark Viduka – Steve McClaren's side turned on the style for a 3-2 win as they continued on an eight-game unbeaten run.

Boro had already bounced back from an early Viduka goal to lead 2-1 when Geremi received a lay-off from Jonathan Greening. Fully 25 yards out from goal, the Cameroonian loan star looked up, beat an opponent and placed a delicate chip under the crossbar for an immaculate goal.

Rob Dodsworth Darlington

"Joseph Job's goal against Lisbon has to be the best – we were 3-0 down but it still managed to bring me off my seat. I also liked Mark Viduka's two goals against Manchester City in 2004-05, and the way he pulled the ball back from behind him for the first was sublime."

Andy Cooke London

"Juninho ran the Leicester game, and the goal was the icing on the cake. In my mind he beats the whole of their team - I'm sure he didn't, but the pace of dribbling and super cool finish showed him to be on a different technical level to anyone else on the pitch. It ended up being a bit of a double-edged sword, this goal, because it probably led to Martin O'Neill man-marking Juninho out of the Coca-Cola Cup final later on in the same season."

Captains

Three international stars and a no-nonsense professional have been the four permanent skippers of Boro since the move to the Riverside. In years gone by the club had seen a variety of personalities lead their team-mates out to battle, from George Hardwick to Tony Mowbray, Brian Clough to Gordon Jones and George Elliott to Stuart Boam.

- LEADER - Boro skipper Nigel Pearson greets Chelsea captain Dennis Wise at the 1997 FA Cup final

But few of them could match the inspirational qualities of Nigel Pearson, the club's skipper at the time of the move to the new stadium and the man who led Boro out for that first Riverside game against Chelsea. Pearson had joined the club from Sheffield Wednesday in 1994 as one of Bryan Robson's first recruits following his arrival on Teesside.

He was already coming up to his 31st birthday when he was identified by Robson as the man to shore up Boro's defence, and the £750,000 fee paid to the Owls seemed a massive outlay for a man who had suffered knee problems and two broken legs.

But the manager known as "Captain Marvel" during his playing career had no problems identifying a great skipper, and that was proved when Pearson lifted the First Division championship in May 1995. He had struck up a solid defensive partnership with Steve Vickers during that first season, which remained the same during the first Premiership season.

Pearson was approaching his 33rd birthday during the 1995-96 campaign but he managed to play in all but two of Boro's Premiership games with Player of the Year Vickers starting 32 games himself.

The Nottingham-born defender also began the first three games of 1996-97, but was then ruled out for a month through injury. He then returned for another three games before suffering a horrific neck injury in a collision with Wimbledon's Marcus Gayle. That problem kept him out until February 1997 and he would again resume first-team duties.

He occupies a special place in Boro folklore because, as well as leading out the team in their very first match at the Riverside, he also skippered the club in their first-ever major Wembley cup finals in 1997 plus the Coca-Cola Cup final return trip the following season. He failed, however, to add to the League Cup winners' medal he had claimed in 1991 while with Wednesday.

Pearson missed the start of the 1997-98 season, back in the First Division, but would again force his way back into the first team despite the addition of Gianluca Festa. He would make a total of 29 starts as Boro made their way back to the Premiership. Pearson would wear the captain's armband for the last time as Oxford United were defeated 4-1 in the final game of the season.

He finally retired at the age of 35 that summer and would later become manager of Carlisle United and enjoy a coaching spell with the FA before reuniting with Robson at West Bromwich Albion in 2004-05. Pearson became assistant manager at The Hawthorns and the two old Boro boys helped the West Midlands side avoid relegation in a dramatic finale to the Premiership season.

Team-mate Vickers said: "Nigel represented everything that a captain should be – on and off the pitch. He was a

natural leader and I think everyone saw that. He was also an excellent motivator in the dressing room."

Pearson's successor joined ahead of the 1997-98 season, and would wear the armband for the first time against Birmingham in February of that season before being installed as club skipper the following campaign. Andy Townsend had played at the World Cup in 1994 as an integral part of the Republic of Ireland squad and would eventually win 70 caps. He had enjoyed a successful career with Southampton, Norwich City and Chelsea but became recognised as one of the Premiership's best left-sided midfielders when he joined Aston Villa in 1993. He won two League Cup crowns while with Villa, and was a Premiership runner-up, but moved to Boro as a 34-year-old and would play 88 games in his three seasons with the club. Part of Townsend's "captain duties" included living with Paul Gascoigne for a short spell after the star joined in 1998, but his influence on the field was just as impressive when he started 35 of Boro's 36 Premiership games in 1998-99. He signed a new one-year deal in summer 1999, but he would start just three more times for the Riverside club as he moved on to West Brom for £200,000 in September 1999.

"Andy led the side by example and was a leader with a lot of experience," recalled Robson. "He held the midfield together for us in what could have been a difficult season in the First Division and then showed he still had class when we got into the Premiership."

• GREAT LEADER - Paul Ince in conference with Bryan Robson during 2000-01

There was no shortage of potential skippers following Townsend's departure, as Boro included several experienced players including Robbie Mustoe, Gianluca Festa, Colin Cooper and Gary Pallister. But the obvious candidate was newly-signed Paul Ince, who had joined from Liverpool after falling out with Gerard Houllier. Ince was still based on Merseyside and made the 300-mile round trip every day to Rockliffe and never gave less than 100 per cent in training and matches during his three Boro seasons. Despite his presence being most keenly felt in midfield, the ex-Manchester United and Internazionale star also scored some important goals in his first season, in which he started 32 league games, including one in the 2-1 win against Arsenal.

Ince was a key part of England's squad at Euro 2000, having also captained his country before wearing the armband at Anfield and the Riverside.

While 2000-01 was tough for Boro, as they fought against relegation, Ince was in outstanding form as joint manager Terry Venables recalled: "Ince was terrific. I had

• EXPERIENCE - Andy Townsend was an experienced skipper at the Riverside

Riverside X

worked with him at England level and knew what I would be getting in terms of grit, determination and skill. But by the time we were at Boro together he was in his 30s and had even more experience, but had lost none of his desire."

Ince, now 35, continued to defy age as he started 31 games in 2001-02, but by that time he had been replaced as skipper by Gareth Southgate, who had joined from Villa. New boss Steve McClaren felt Ince lost none of his influence despite losing the armband. He said: "At the beginning I was sceptical about Paul Ince because I wanted to bring in Gareth as skipper and I knew that could be an ego problem for such a big player.

"He was a player who we had to convince, but in the end he was probably the best of the group that season. He was a key player and, what I call, an 'emotional leader' because he was such a winner and had a massive influence on others around him."

Southgate had been captain of Villa for several years when he made the £6.5m move to Teesside, after a year on the transfer list. While Boro struggled during the early games, Southgate oozed class

and would start all but one game as he rekindled his defensive partnership with ex-Villa team-mate Ugo Ehiogu. He then missed just two games in 2002-03, and the following season became the first Boro skipper to lift a major trophy when he captained his team to Carling Cup glory.

As he approached his 35th birthday the legs showed little sign of tiring as he missed just five of Boro's 52 games in 2004-05, and that's why the manager still rates him as the most important player at the club. McClaren said: "Gareth will always be the best signing I've made, and he was my first priority when I joined. He's the kind of leader that is so respected by the fans and the players, and is incredibly competitive inwardly.

"I've been at clubs before at which there has been a leader on and off the field – at Manchester United it was Roy Keane. Gareth was the best example of that I could think of that was available at the time. He's an example on and off the field. His performances have been incredible, but his temperament and the way he goes about things are tremendous."

Boro's best Riverside captain (%)

Gareth Southgate	69.8
Nigel Pearson	23.5
Paul Ince	5.1
Andy Townsend	1.6

Alan Keen, MP for Feltham & Heston

"Gareth is an outstanding player, captain and man and I think all Boro fans have been delighted to have him as our leader over the last few years."

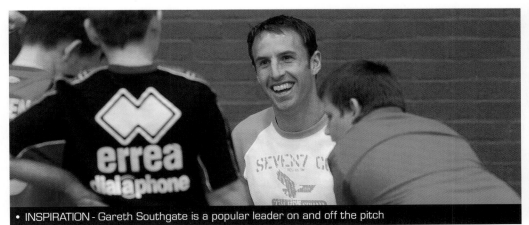

• INSPIRATION - Gareth Southgate is a popular leader on and off the pitch

greatest seasons

There may be a few moans and the odd groan at the Riverside, but Boro's supporters obviously don't look back with too great a tint in their glasses. While fans often pine for the 'good old days', Boro's faithful know when they're on to a good thing – and that's exactly why they decided that the last two campaigns have been the greatest of the Riverside era.

The ninth and 10th seasons at the Riverside certainly proved dramatic – with gold at the end of the rainbow as Europe was achieved on both occasions. One saw a cup final and the lifting of major silverware for the first time, while the other witnessed the club's highest ever Premiership finish. Both achievements were reached with the usual Boro tension – with many, presumably uncomfortable, supporters having to spend the nine months from August 2004 to May 2005 on the edge of their seats.

"There were so many times when I was convinced we had blown it," said Trevor Yarnton of Stockton. "I actually left the stadium early for the first time in my life when we were losing against Southampton, and almost did the same thing against Fulham after they went a goal ahead. But I decided to stick around and will on the team, and it paid off when we managed to equalise. After that I thought it was a dead cert that we would get the seventh spot, until Franck's handball at Manchester City. I was listening on the radio and could hardly listen. I don't know how people in the stadium could watch, never mind the players.

"I think the elation that came with Schwarz's save made it all worthwhile. How boring would it have been if we'd scored two in the first five minutes? It's not the Boro way!"

The emphasis on thrills and spills is evident in the fact that – league position-wise – the least successful Riverside season is third in the fans' poll. Back in 1996-97 it was all about attacking football, big characters and goals. Ravanelli, Juninho and Emerson were three of the highest profile players in the Premiership, and boss Bryan Robson one of the most famous men in the game.

Maureen McSorley, of Middlesbrough, said: "We made it to two cup finals, lost them both and were relegated. It was gutting, I just couldn't believe what happened to us. Talk about highs and lows, it felt like we were top of the world with international players and by the following August we were playing at Tranmere. I wondered if we would recover from it, but the promotion season got the place buzzing again."

Strangely, a season in which Boro escaped relegation was deemed the worst of the Riverside's first 10 years. Even with the charismatic Terry Venables involved, and with Tel, Robbo, Alen Boksic and Paul Ince helping Boro stay in the Premiership, fans obviously have bad memories of 2000-01. With not even a cup run to spice things up, that strained campaign received no votes in the poll

"It was an awful year, even though we stayed up in the end," said Andy Balfour, of Carlisle. "There was an awful atmosphere around the place and I think there was a feeling that Robson would not last, which was very sad. Some fans turned on him and the team, and because we knew Venables wouldn't stay for the long-term, we didn't know for just how long relegation had been put off. That has to be the worst season of recent times, but it shows how far we've come because 10 years earlier it would have been a massive achievement to stay in the top division."

While players and managers come and go it's the fans who stay with the club for a lifetime. While the Riverside has seen great matches, fantastic goals and wonderful players, as well as some dreary days, the supporters have remained constant. And, following two of the club's most successful years ever, they might finally be receiving their just rewards.

Greatest Season

1	2004-05	60.5%
2	2003-04	20.2
3	1996-97	12.8
4	1995-96	3.2
5	1997-98	2.1
6	1998-99	0.4
=	1999-00	0.4
8	2002-03	0.3
9	2001-02	0.1
10	2000-01	0

Most disappointing results

As well as the highs, there have been terrible lows during the last 10 years. The most famous of these are represented in supporters voting for cup final defeats and the grim relegation at Elland Road in 1997. There's also a fair few dismal trouncings at the hands of Arsenal and local rivals Newcastle.

But the match voted the most disappointing of all took place in January 2005, and fans do not remember the Premiership trip to Norwich's Carrow Road as a point gained.

1. Norwich 4 Boro 4 - 27.6%

Carrow Road, 22/01/05

Premiership

• NIGHTMARE - Adam Dury equalises for Norwich in the dying seconds

How could it possibly have gone wrong? Boro approached the last 10 minutes of this game with the score at 4-1, despite Damien Francis giving the home side the lead in the first half. Two goals each from Jimmy Floyd Hasselbaink and Franck Queudrue had put Boro into a position no team could slip from.

But the Boro defence decided to fall asleep at a time when Norwich found a new urgency. With 10 minutes left, Dean Ashton headed home and then in injury time Leon McKenzie and Adam Drury each scrambled the ball into the net to complete an impossible recovery.

Boro were quite literally stunned into silence after the match. Boss Steve McClaren said: "There was no grand speech after the game. There was total silence. We've missed an opportunity. At 4-1 everybody agrees that we were in no trouble. We were in total control and then these things happen. You look for all kinds of reasons. Did the players switch off? Did they get complacent after going 4-1 up?"

Skipper Gareth Southgate added: "I haven't been involved in a game like that - not since I was a kid I think."

2. Boro 1 Leicester 1 - 27.4%

Wembley, 6/04/97

Coca-Cola Cup

A tight Coca-Cola Cup Final from the off, both Boro and Leicester played out a very dull 90 minutes by cancelling each other out.

Indeed, Leicester were so determined to frustrate Bryan Robson's team that they stuck a man-marker on Juninho.

The little Brazilian did manage to wriggle free five minutes into extra-time though, as his run set up Fabrizio Ravanelli who smashed home what looked like the winner.

Sadly, it wasn't meant to be as Emile Heskey took the tie to a replay with an equaliser three minutes from time.

Ravanelli fumed: "The cup was here, was ours. We had it in our hands and then we threw it back."

Boro lost the Hillsborough replay to a Steve Claridge goal - the first of three cup final defeats for Boro in 12 months.

• OH NO! - Emile Heskey scores for Leicester to make it 1-1

3. Leeds 1 Boro 1 - 22.2%

Elland Road, 11/05/97
Premiership

• TEARS - Curtis Fleming is comforted at Elland Road

A game that wouldn't have been as disappointing if Middlesbrough had been able to put out a team in a December fixture against Blackburn.

Injuries and illnesses meant they couldn't and they were docked three points by the FA and needed a win in this last-day clash to stand any chance of playing Premiership football the following season.

Brian Deane put Leeds ahead in the first half and, with just over 10 minutes left, Juninho equalised.

Every fan's memory of this day is the little Brazilian's tears at full time as he sat on the Elland Road turf contemplating his future at the First Division's newest club.

Juninho recalled: "It was bad moment because I knew our team was a lot better than a lot of the teams in the Premier League. That's why I was so disappointed."

4. Boro 0 Chelsea 2 - 12.4%

Wembley, 4/05/97
FA Cup

If watching the Coca-Cola Cup slip away and relegation become a reality wasn't enough for Boro fans, this just added to the misery of 1996/97.

It is also an encounter etched into history, as Robert Di Matteo's thunderbolt after 43 seconds remains the fastest goal ever scored in an FA Cup final.

Boro recovered to stage something of fightback and, despite Robbie Mustoe and Fabrizio Ravanelli being subbed with injuries, got the ball into the Chelsea net - however Gianluca Festa's header was ruled out as he was deemed offside.

Eddie Newton grabbed a second for Chelsea late in the second half and had lost their second major final of the season.

"Losing in the FA Cup final still hurts," said ex-Boro defender Gianluca Festa.

• SECONDS AWAY - Roberto Di Matteo puts Chelsea ahead at Wembley

Riverside X

5. Portsmouth 5 Boro 1 - 5.3%

Fratton Park, 15/05/04

Premiership

• IMPRESSIVE - Future Boro star Yakubu scored four times

After winning the Carling Cup in February of the 2003/04 season, Boro concentrated on reaching a league finish higher than their previous best of ninth.

But it wasn't meant to be and they slumped to 11th after this hammering from Harry Redknapp's boys - a result that was Boro's heaviest away defeat for five years.

A certain Nigerian striker named Yakubu grabbed four goals and Teddy Sheringham got the other in a rout that made Bolo Zenden's first-half strike nothing more than a pointless consolation.

Not the best way to end a season, as boss Steve McClaren admitted: "It was totally unacceptable and there's no excuses."

6. Boro 1 Bolton 4 - 2.1%

Riverside Stadium, 17/02/96

Premiership

In their first Premiership season under Bryan Robson, Boro went through something of a slump from the end of December to the middle of February.

This was their eighth successive defeat and the heaviest home defeat of the season.

Bottom club Bolton Wanderers took the lead early on in the first half but, when Jamie Pollock pulled one back soon after, things looked rosy for Boro fans.

However, Bolton took control in the second half with three more goals and Boro's awful league run continued.

"We've been going through a tough time," explained Nick Barmby after the game. "But the players are still trying their hardest."

• SHOCKER - Bryan Robson had to endure another defeat as Boro lost at home to Bolton

7. Boro 1 Newcastle 4 - 1.9%

Riverside Stadium, 8/09/01

Premiership

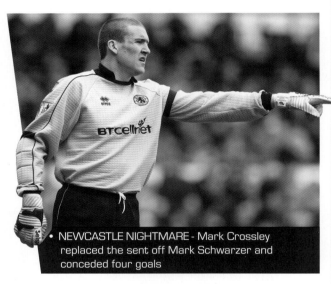

- NEWCASTLE NIGHTMARE - Mark Crossley replaced the sent off Mark Schwarzer and conceded four goals

Steve McClaren's first season in charge began with four successive defeats including this home loss against local rivals Newcastle United.

Middlesbrough got off to a great start when Colin Cooper's deflected header beat Shay Given.

But any hopes of a first win of the season were lost when Mark Schwarzer brought down Laurent Robert in the box, resulting in a red card for the keeper and Alan Shearer's equaliser from the spot.

Mark Crossley came on for 10-man Boro but couldn't stop later strikes from Nikos Dabizas, Robert and - yet again - Shearer.

It was the 50th Tyne-Tees derby and Newcastle's biggest win in the fixture.

"The sending off was a defining moment and it was always going to be very difficult after that," said McClaren.

8. Boro 0 Leicester 3 - 1.2%

Riverside Stadium, 18/11/00

Premiership

Boro's sixth straight defeat of the season came just a few weeks before the club's decision to bring in former England manager Terry Venables to help Bryan Robson.

The portents coming into the game didn't bode well for the home team. Boro hadn't won at the Riverside since March and also hadn't kept a clean sheet all season.

The reasons why were plain to see when they found themselves 2-0 down in the opening 15 minutes with Muzzy Izzet scoring from the spot and Trevor Benjamin heading home.

Darren Eadie scored in the second half to keep Boro in the bottom three.

"It was an all-too-familiar story," said Robson. "We gifted our opponents the points through a series of individual errors you just can't afford to make at this level."

- ON TARGET - Muzzy Izzet blasts home a penalty

Riverside X

9. Boro 1 Arsenal 6 - 0.5%

Riverside Stadium, 24/04/99

Premiership

• EASY - Kanu scored two of Arsenal's six goals

Another depressing home defeat, this time to a quality Arsenal side who terrorised Boro from the kick-off.

Marc Overmars' penalty gave the Londoners the lead after only four minutes when Nicolas Anelka was fouled.

Anelka went on to grab two goals himself, as did Kanu - one of them an audacious back-heel from outside the box - while Patrick Viera took advantage of the slack defending to grab one for himself.

Alun Armstrong got one back with three minutes left but by then, Boro's humiliation was complete.

The result remains their heaviest Premiership defeat, and boss Bryan Robson said: "It always hurts to lose heavily."

10. Boro 1 Derby 4 - 0.4%

Riverside Stadium, 15/01/00

Premiership

A young striker called Malcolm Christie scored two goals in this home Premiership clash against Boro, who endured a miserable day at the Riverside.

Christie gave the visitors the lead with less than 10 minutes gone and another goal from him, as well as strikes from Dean Burton and Craig Burley, put the game out of sight.

Hamilton Ricard also missed a penalty in the second half but Andy Campbell grabbed a consolation for Boro with 20 minutes left.

This was Bryan Robson's side's second successive defeat in what was to be a run of six straight league games without a win.

Campbell said: "It was great to get a goal, but it didn't mean anything because it was such an awful performance and result."

• BRACE - Malcolm Christie scored twice for Derby

Alistair Griffin
Pop star and Boro fan

"The FA Cup final was a low, especially coming after the League Cup and relegation. The cup finals were typical Boro - coming so close and just missing out. Even with a change of stadium and our superstars, we just couldn't change our luck."

Adrian Adamson
Ormesby

"For me the most disappointing result of the Riverside era was the St Valentine's Day massacre when we lost 4-0 at home to Aston Villa. I had a feeling of dread going to the stadium that day - but the result was worse than I imagined. This was closely followed by being beaten at home by Southampton during 2004-05, which almost caused me not to renew my season ticket."

Most Controversial players

Riverside X

Most Controversial Players

Controversy is never far from the surface in this highly charged business and Boro have had their fair share of players who have courted adverse publicity. We asked the Boro fans for their choice of most controversial player and it was, perhaps, no surprise who came out top!

1. Christian Ziege - 28.2%

Ziege polled 28.2% of all votes cast and is still seen by many fans as a traitor following, not so much his leaving for Liverpool, but rather the way in which it was reported that the transfer deal was put together. It was alleged that the Reds had made an illegal approach for the player.

Chairman Steve Gibson was so incensed that he pursued the matter through the courts; maybe his was one of the votes!

The German looked to have rescued his career when Boro salvaged him from a troublesome spell in Italy with AC Milan. He greatly impressed during 1999-00, but was soon crossing the country to sign for Liverpool after a fee was offered that triggered a release clause in his contract.

• GET-OUT-CLAUSE - Christian Ziege

2. Emerson - 17%

• HOME AND AWAY - Emerson regularly flew back to South America

Emerson was called many things by many people: he was the epitome of an enigma.

As powerful and classy a midfielder as Boro had had on their books for some time, he never played for the club again after going AWOL over Christmas during 1997-98.

He arrived with the kind of fanfare that surrounds Brazilians on Teesside, but departed more in the Branco-mould than Juninho. Emerson greatly impressed when out on the field, but his wife failed to settle in England and he was regularly forced to jet back to Brazil.

A booking at Bury in December 1997 brought a suspension, and a flight from Teesside brought Emerson a break on the beach. Bryan Robson took exception and Emerson moved on the following summer without kicking a ball in anger again.

180

3. Fabrizio Ravanelli - 15.9%

Tact and diplomacy didn't arrive with Fabrizio Ravanelli when he joined from Juventus. He'd just moved from a side which had won the European Cup to one in transition.

Language conversion from Italian to English in one form or another has been around for some time, so "lost in translation" became a bit limp for Boro fans when used as an excuse to explain interviews with Rav each time he returned home. A great finisher, but not liked by everyone in the dressing room.

Chairman Steve Gibson likened him to "a Ferrari without a garage", while others felt he was a sandwich short of a picnic.

4. Alen Boksic - 14.3%

Another classy finisher, but fans often evaluate commitment with wages – and the figures reported to have been paid for the Croatian hitman had many Boro fans gasping. A large percentage thought he should have put in more appearances to justify his tag as the largest wage earner the club has known.

There were occasions when it appeared he simply didn't want to play – such as prior to the Old Trafford trip in 2002, when he would score the winning goal – and he was also something of an unknown quantity to his fellow Boro players.

Having enjoyed his best spell under Terry Venables in 2000-01, he completed the first Steve McClaren season before retiring midway through 2002-03.

5. Paul Merson - 8.6%

"Merse" arrived having achieved almost everything in the game and was a class act after making the move from Arsenal. But it doesn't matter how good a player you are, fans are unforgiving when you badmouth their club.

He was the driving force behind Boro's promotion in 1997-98, but within weeks of the start of the following Premiership season he had demanded a move to Aston Villa, citing personal problems and bad influences at Boro.

Merson had previously suffered drink and gambling problems, but blaming the club rather than himself at the time didn't go down well with fans and former teammates.

• HERO TURNED VILLAIN - Paul Merson's departure left a bad taste in Boro mouths

Riverside X

6. Paul Gascoigne - 7.5%

A surprise inclusion given his natural ability to entertain, but he was quite probably a nightmare to coach! You never knew quite what was coming next with Gazza, a race along the A19 or self-taught coach-driving lessons! But he was good in the dressing room and did more for charitable causes than most people will ever hear about.

Perhaps it was his extraordinary life away from the Boro which led fans to vote for him. Perhaps it was the expectations following a fantastic career with Newcastle, Tottenham, Lazio, Rangers and England.

He joined in 1998 as the club was achieving promotion, but his time at the Riverside was dogged by injury – the most famous his broken arm, suffered when elbowing Aston Villa's George Boateng in February 2000. He didn't play for the club again before leaving for Everton.

7. Branco - 6.9%

Branco arrived as a World Cup winner and fans were entitled to expect better than they got. He never seemed at home on Teesside and never showed the form which brought him the ultimate prize in the game when wearing the yellow and blue of his homeland.

Just a couple of years after winning the World Cup in the United States, he was making his Boro debut against Everton in March 1996. With Juninho and, soon, Emerson also on Boro's books there shouldn't have been a problem on paper. But he would make just 11 appearances before departing with stinging words about Boro's coaching staff.

8. Marco Branca - 1.6%

A player with much potential, but another who didn't figure as often as fans would have liked. After making an explosive start to his Boro career with two goals against Sunderland – which should have guaranteed hero status – and another against Liverpool, he followed that with a couple against Swindon and a hat-trick against Bury.

The Italian, who had made his debut in February 1998, hit nine goals in 11 games but made his last appearance in April of the same year before an argument ensued about the player's fitness and he was forced to retire.

• SMILE PLEASE - Paul Gascoigne meets a young fan while with Boro

Worst players

The fans were asked to name the biggest flop of the last 10 years – and the nominations ranged from international stars to honest professionals.

Coming out in joint first place was Brazilian Branco, and amazingly a second World Cup winner also made the list, with Christian Karembeu in 10th spot. Michael Ricketts, a big money signing of 2003 who failed to impress before departing for Leeds, was equal with Branco in the fans' poll.

Local lad Phil Whelan found himself in third spot, having made 30 appearances from 1995-97, followed by three international stars and the Riverside era's leading scorer.

Alen Boksic and Paul Gascoigne – who had been teammates at Lazio – both failed to deliver what was expected of them at Boro considering their fantastic careers, while Mikkel Beck also disappointed some fans following an impressive Euro '96 with Denmark.

In joint sixth spot is Hamilton Ricard, who scored a mighty 44 goals for the club from 1997-02. But some fans felt he should have grabbed many more. Alan Wright, the full back who had enjoyed a long career with Aston Villa before signing in 2003, played just twice for the club and was voted eighth in our list.

Brian Deane, another forward, made ninth spot despite his 17 goals in 79 starts, while those who finished just outside the top 10 included Michael Debeve, Fabio, Jamie Pollock, Allan Johnston, Ricardinho and Tony Vidmar.

Players and Statistics

The Players

Everyone of Boro's first team players in the first
10 years of the Riverside

Alun Armstrong (1998-2000)

From Stockport County, £1.6m
To Ipswich Town, £800,000
Apps: 33 - **Goals:** 9

Scored on his debut against Sunderland and will always
be remembered for two goals against Oxford which
helped secure promotion to the Premier League in
1997-98. Sadly, back and Achilles tendon injuries
hampered his progress and he moved on to Ipswich in
December 2000, later playing for Darlington.

Steve Baker (1997-2002)

From Youth
To Scarborough, Free
Apps: 13 - **Goals:** 0

A tough-tackling defender who represented the
Republic of Ireland at U-21 level despite hailing from
Pontefract. Performed a memorable man-marking
job on dangerman Steve McManaman in the 1998
Coca-Cola Cup semi-final, but experienced a
frustrating time with injuries, spending loan spells at
Huddersfield, Darlington and Hartlepool.

Nick Barmby (1995-96)

From Tottenham Hotspur, £5.25m
To Everton, £5.75m
Apps: 49 - **Goals:** 10

Became the first current England international to
join Boro since Steve Bloomer 90 years earlier
when he signed for a record-shattering fee in
August 1995. Finished top scorer in his first
season but became less effective after the
arrival of Juninho and Bryan Robson sold him to
Everton just 14 months after signing him.
Went on to play for Liverpool and Leeds before
joining hometown club Hull City.

Michael Barron (1993-97)

From Youth
To Hartlepool Utd, Free
Apps: 1 (10) - **Goals:** 0

A talented centre-back, Barron was handed
his debut as an 18-year-old by Lennie
Lawrence against Portsmouth in November
1993, playing out of position at right-back.
His only Premier League game was two
years later when he replaced Steve
Vickers for a 2-0 defeat against Everton.
Went on to establish himself as a regular
at Hartlepool after initially moving to
Victoria Park on loan.

Statistics

BIG SPENDERS

Boro's top 10 purchases in the last decade

Massimo MACCARONE	Empoli	Jun 2002	£8.15m
Ugo EHIOGU	Aston Villa	Oct 2000	£8m
YAKUBU	Portsmouth	Jul 2005	£7.5m
Fabrizio RAVANELLI	Juventus	Jul 1996	£7m
Gareth SOUTHGATE	Aston Villa	Jul 2001	£6.5m
Nick BARMBY	Tottenham	Aug 1995	£5.2m
George BOATENG	Aston Villa	Jul 2002	£5m
JUNINHO	Sao Paulo	Oct 1995	£4.75m
Paul MERSON	Arsenal	Jul 1997	£4.5m
Mark VIDUKA	Leeds	Jul 2004	£.4.5m

BIG SELLERS

Boro's top 10 sales in the last decade

JUNINHO	Atletico Madrid	Jul 1997	£12m
Paul MERSON	Aston Villa	Sep 1998	£7m
Nick BARMBY	Everton	Oct 1996	£5.75m
Christian ZIEGE	Liverpool	Aug 2000	£5.5m
Fabrizio RAVANELLI	Marseille	Sep 1997	£5.25m
EMERSON	Tenerife	Jan 1998	£4.2m
Christian KAREMBEU	Olympiakos	May 2001	£3.7m
Jonathan GREENING	West Brom	Jul 2004	£1.25m
Neil COX	Bolton	May 1997	£1.2m
Keith O'NEILL	Coventry	August 2001	£1m

PLAYERS USED

In all competitions season-by-season

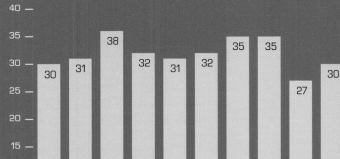

95-96	96-97	97-98	98-99	99-00	00-01	01-02	02-03	03-04	04-05
30	31	38	32	31	32	35	35	27	30

Mikkel Beck (1996-99)

From Fortuna Cologne, Free
To Derby County, £500,000
Apps: 117 - Goals: 31

The first player to join Boro under the Bosman ruling, the Danish international failed to live up to his reputation. Was openly criticised by strike partner Fabrizio Ravanelli on the pitch when he failed to perform and was equally unpopular with sections of the crowd. He did, however, play a major part in Boro's 1998 promotion success.

Chris Bennion (1999-2002)

From Youth
To Scunthorpe Utd, Free
Apps: 1 - Goals: 0

Former Scottish schoolboy international goalkeeper who was handed his full debut by Bryan Robson during an injury crisis for a 2-1 Worthington Cup win over Macclesfield Town in September 2000. It remained his only senior appearance for the club and Steve McClaren allowed him to join Scunthorpe. Became a regular in the League of Ireland with first Shelbourne and then Dundalk.

Marlon Beresford (1998-2002)

From Burnley, £400,000
To York City, Free
Apps: 14 - Goals: 0

Much-travelled goalkeeper who earned a reputation as something of a penalty-saving expert. Was signed after nine goals conceded in two games threatened to derail Boro's 1998 promotion challenge. Despite impressing when called upon, he found opportunities at the Riverside few and far between. Was named in the Division Two team of the year in 1994 while with Burnley and repeated the feat with Luton in 2005.

Clayton Blackmore (1994-99)

From Manchester Utd, Free
To Barnsley, Free
Apps: 35 (65) - Goals: 2 (4)

Welsh international who was one of Bryan Robson's first signings. Known as a squad player at Old Trafford, he failed to shake off the tag at the Riverside despite his versatility – he could play in midfield or at full-back. Was loaned to Bristol City in 1996 but was recalled during an injury crisis and appeared in the Coca-Cola Cup final replay and FA Cup final in 1997.

George Boateng (2002-)

From Aston Villa, £5m
Apps: 100 - Goals: 3

Powerful and tough tackling Dutch international midfielder who manager Steve McClaren once described as the "rock" that held his midfield together. Born in Ghana and introduced to English football by Coventry City, Boateng was a key member of Boro's 2004 Carling Cup-winning side.

Alen Boksic (2000-03)

From Lazio, £2.5m
Retired
Apps: 77 - Goals: 22

Controversial striker who was a world class talent on his day but was all too often missing through niggling injuries, calling many to question his commitment to the club. Boksic earned a huge reputation within the game while at Marseille, Lazio and Juventus. Highlights of the Croatian's stint on Teesside included two goals in a win at Newcastle and a stunning chip at Leicester.

Marco Branca (1998-99)

From Internazionale, £1m
Retired
Apps: 14 - Goals: 10

An inspired signing, the experienced Italian scored just four minutes into his debut, against Liverpool in the Coca-Cola Cup semi-final. He added nine league goals in 11 games to galvanise Boro's promotion challenge but due to injury he made only one appearance, as a substitute, after the club's return to the top flight. He left the club in acrimony after specialists stated his knee could no longer stand up to the rigours of professional football.

Riverside X

Branco (1996)

Free agent
Released
Apps: 11 - Goals: 2

A Brazil legend with more than 80 caps and a World Cup winner's medal to his name, Branco arrived at the Riverside in a blaze of publicity. Although he showed flashes of his ability, his brief spell on Teesside was a major disappointment and he looked badly out of condition. He was released with eight months left on his contract, delivering a stinging tabloid attack on the club's coaching staff as he went.

Jamie Cade (2002-03)

From Youth
To Colchester Utd, Free
Apps: 1 - Goals: 0

Pacy former England youth international forward who made just one full appearance for the club, as a substitute in a 3-1 Carling Cup defeat at Ipswich Town in November 2002. Scored two goals in a successful loan spell at Chesterfield but struggled to hold down a first-team place after making a permanent move to Colchester and was released in 2005, joining Crawley.

Andy Campbell (1995-2002)

From Youth
To Cardiff City, £950,000
Apps: 71 - Goals: 7

Lightning-quick Middlesbrough-born striker who was the first 16-year-old to play in the Premiership. An England U-21 international, his first goal came against Sunderland in the 1997 Coca-Cola Cup and one of his best a close-range header in the 2-0 FA Cup win over Manchester United in 2002. Scored a play-off final winner for Cardiff at the Millennium Stadium but struggled to establish himself in the first team.

GREAT YEAR

The most Boro goals in a season by a single Boro player

31	Fabrizio RAVANELLI	1996-97
18	Hamilton RICARD	1998-99
16	Jimmy Floyd HASSELBAINK	2004-05
	Paul MERSON	1997-98
15	Mickel BECK	1997-98
	JUNINHO	1996-97
14	Hamilton RICARD	1999-00
12	Alen BOKSIC	2000-01
11	Mickel BECK	1996-97
10	Marco BRANCA	1997-98
	Brian DEANE	1999-00
	Craig HIGNETT	1997-98

GOALSCORERS X+

Players that have scored more than 10 Boro goals during the Riverside era

1	Hamilton Ricard	44
2	Juninho	34
3	Fabrizio Ravanelli	32
4	Mikkel Beck	31
5	Szilard Nemeth	28
6	Craig Hignett	24
7	Alen Boksic	22
=	Joseph-Desire Job	22
9	Brian Deane	19
10	Jimmy Floyd Hasselbaink	16
=	Massimo Maccarone	16
=	Paul Merson	16
=	Robbie Mustoe	16
14	Bolo Zenden	15
15	Gianluca Festa	12
16	Emerson	11
17	Nick Barmby	10
=	Marco Branca	10
=	Noel Whelan	10

• HITMAN - Jimmy Floyd Hasselbaink

Benito Carbone (2002)

From Bradford City, Loan
Apps: 13 - Goals: 1

Gifted forward who enjoyed a memorable loan spell at the Riverside during an eventful career that included spells at nine Italian clubs plus five in England. Set up Alen Boksic's winner in the 1-0 win at Manchester United and impressed throughout his short Boro spell, but Steve McClaren sprang a surprise by choosing not to make the move permanent and the tiny playmaker instead returned to Italy.

Malcolm Christie (2003-)

From Derby County, £3m
(joint deal including Chris Riggott)
Apps: 26 - Goals: 7

Lively striker who began his career with Nuneaton Borough before being snapped up by Derby. Steve McClaren brought the England U-21 international to the Riverside along with defender Chris Riggott for an initial £3m fee, which could eventually rise to £5m. Has suffered major injury setbacks with a broken foot following a twice broken leg but hoped to return to action in the 2005-06 season.

Brian Close (2002-04)

From Youth
To Darlington, Free
Apps: 1 - Goals: 0

Combative Northern Ireland youth international who was equally at home in midfield or at right-back. Made just a single first-team appearance, as a substitute in a 3-1 Carling Cup defeat at Ipswich Town in November 2002, replacing Carlos Marinelli. Became a first-team regular at Darlington, joining the thriving ex-Boro colony at the Williamson Motors Stadium.

Colin Cooper (1984-91, 1998-)

From Youth (1984); Nottingham Forest, £2.5m (1998)
To Millwall, £300,000 (1991)
Apps: 180 (379) - Apps: 5 (13)

Evergreen defender who was a mainstay of Bruce Rioch's double promotion-winning side in the late 1980s before following the manager to Millwall. His career flourished after a move to Nottingham Forest, where he won two England caps. Returned to Boro in 1998 and once again established himself as a crowd favourite as he defied the advancing years with his tireless commitment to the cause.

Neil Cox (1994-97)

From Aston Villa, £1m
To Bolton Wanderers, £1.2m
Apps: 83 (128) - Goals: 3 (4)

Boro's first £1m man, Cox was a mobile and physical defender who loved to gallop forward to assist the attack. Began his career with Scunthorpe, he won England U-21 caps at Villa before being signed by Bryan Robson. Was reported to have been at the centre of a skirmish involving controversial Italian Fabrizio Ravanelli on the morning of the 1997 FA Cup final. Moved on to Bolton before captaining Watford and joining Cardiff City in 2005.

Mark Crossley (2000-03)

From Nottingham Forest, Free
To Fulham, £500,000
Apps: 28 - Goals: 0

Known as "Norm" within the game, Wales international Crossley was rated as one of the Premiership's top goalkeepers while at Nottingham Forest before falling out of favour at the City Ground and joining Boro on a free. Was largely an understudy to Mark Schwarzer but impressed during an extended run in the 2001-02 season, and was always popular with the fans.

• UNDERSTUDY - Mark Crossley

Riverside X

Michael Cummins (1995-2000)

From Youth
To Port Vale, Free
Apps: 2 - Goals: 0

Irish U-21 international defender or midfielder who made his only Boro start at wing-back in a 4-0 defeat against West Ham on the last day of the 1998-99 season. He was spotted playing for Eire U-16s against England and also starred in the 1997 World Youth Cup in Malaysia, helping his country to the semi-finals.

Andrew Davies (2002-)

From Youth
Apps: 17 - Goals: 0

Confident and proficient defender, the England youth international made his Boro debut in November 2002 in a League Cup defeat at Ipswich. Had two spells on loan with QPR in 2004-05 season before joining Derby County for a six-month loan spell prior to the start of 2005-06.

Brian Deane (1998-2001)

From Benfica, £3m
To Leicester City, £150,000
Apps: 95 - Goals: 19

Experienced striker who made Boro his fourth English club when returning from a spell with Benfica. Boro fans remembered him from his days with Leeds – he scored in the last game of the 1996-97 season which saw Boro relegated. Scored on Riverside debut against Nottingham Forest.

Michaël Debeve (2002)

From Lens, Free
To Amiens, Free
Apps: 6 - Goals: 0

From the northern French town of Abbeville, Debeve had not played outside his homeland until joining Boro for three months. A steady midfield player, he made six appearances, the best by some way coming in the 1-0 defeat against Arsenal in FA Cup semi-final at Old Trafford.

ONE HIT WONDERS

Players that have made just one first-team appearance in the last 10 years

Sean Kilgannon	2 minutes	Newcastle Utd	(Premiership) 2-05-00
John Eustace	3 minutes	Liverpool	(Premiership) 8-02-03
Jamie Cade	24 minutes	Ipswich Town	(League Cup) 6-11-02
Brian Close	24 minutes	Ipswich Town	(League Cup) 6-11-02
Fabio Moreira	90 minutes	Huddersfield Town	(First Division) 28-10-97
Chris Bennion	90 minutes	Macclesfield Town	(League Cup) 19-10-00

Does not include current Middlesbrough players

THE 100 CLUB

Players that have more than 100 appearances in the Riverside era

1	Mark Schwarzer	318
2	Robbie Mustoe	251
3	Steve Vickers	228
4	Colin Cooper	180
=	Curtis Fleming	180
6	Gianluca Festa	171
7	Gareth Southgate	162
8	Juninho	155
9	Franck Queudrue	150
10	Szilard Nemeth	135
=	Hamilton Ricard	135
12	Phil Stamp	132
13	Ugo Ehiogu	121
14	Mikkel Beck	117
15	Jonathan Greening	109
16	Joseph-Desire Job	111
17	Paul Ince	106
18	Nigel Pearson	104
19	Craig Hignett	103
20	Robbie Stockdale	102
21	George Boateng	100

• MOST GAMES - Mark Schwarzer

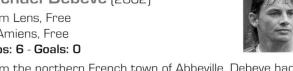

Andy Dibble (1998)

Free agent
Released
Apps: 2 (23) - Goals: 0

Goalkeeper who spent two spells with Boro, the first on loan when the club was still at Ayresome Park in 1991, the second on a short-term contract after Boro had moved to the Riverside. Welsh international with considerable experience in the domestic game having played for 15 different clubs.

Doriva (2003-)

From Celta Vigo, Free
Apps: 64 - Goals: 1

Dependable midfield player who signed initially on loan from Spanish side Celta Vigo. The Brazilian has played in Italy and Portugal as well as Spain, but describes the Premiership as the world's top league. Has confessed to loving Teesside, settled in the area with family. Signed one-year contract in summer 2005.

Craig Dove (2002-04)

From Youth
To Rushden and Diamonds, Free
Apps: 2 - Goals: 0

Hartlepool-born player who was a regular scorer at Academy and reserve-team level. Played for England from U-16 to U-19 levels. Joined Rushden and Diamonds following a loan spell with York. Converted to midfield, he joined Chester City in summer 2005.

Stewart Downing (2001-)

From Youth
Apps: 78 - Goals: 7

The pride of Pallister Park who made his full England debut late in the game against the Netherlands at Villa Park in February 2005. Had represented his country at youth levels and U21. Gifted and exciting left-winger who spent six weeks on loan with Sunderland late in 2003.

Ugo Ehiogu (2000-)

From Aston Villa, £8m
Apps: 121 - Goals: 8

Commanding central defender who became Boro's record signing when joining from Aston Villa. Injury prevented inclusion in the provisional England squad for World Cup 2002. Lasted just seven minutes of his Boro debut at Charlton, but became a key Boro defender and appeared in the 2004 Carling Cup final success.

Emerson (1996-98)

From Porto, £4m
To Tenerife, £4.2m
Apps: 70 - Goals: 11

Gifted, powerful and entertaining midfielder who formed a unique understanding with Juninho and Fabrizio Ravanelli. Incurred the wrath of Bryan Robson when going AWOL over Christmas 1997 and never played for the club again. Scored final goal in the 3-0 FA Cup semi-final replay win over Chesterfield in 1996-97, and played in both cup finals that season.

John Eustace (2003)

From Coventry City, Loan
Apps: 1 - Goals: 0

Midfielder who was brought in as cover for a month and played in just one game. In fact played just three minutes of a 1-1 draw with Liverpool at Anfield, enough time though to be shown a yellow card!

Gianluca Festa (1997-2002)

From Internazionale, £2.7m
To Portsmouth, Free
Apps: 171 - Goals: 12

Fiercely loyal servant to the club and popular central defender. From Cagliari, he always was annoyed at being labelled Italian – he was Sardinian! Big favourite with the fans who had the misfortune to score an own goal as Arsenal beat Boro 1-0 in the 2002 FA Cup semi-final at Old Trafford.

Riverside X

Jan-Aage Fjortoft (1995-97)

From Swindon Town, £1.3m
To Sheffield United, £700,000
Apps: 42 (50) - Goals: 9 (12)

Norwegian striker with a record of a goal every four games. Was record signing when purchased by Bryan Robson, playing the last seven games as Boro clinched promotion in their final season at Ayresome. Scored the second goal in the opening game at the Riverside, a 2-0 win over Chelsea.

Curtis Fleming (1991–2001)

From St Patrick's Athletic, £50,000
To Crystal Palace, £100,000
Apps: 180 (316) - Goals: 4 (4)

Irish international defender who played predominantly at right-back. Was awarded a deserved testimonial before moving to Crystal Palace after a loan spell with Birmingham. Signed by Colin Todd, he played under Lennie Lawrence, Bryan Robson, Terry Venables and Steve McClaren.

Chris Freestone (1994-97)

From Arnold Town, £15,000
To Northampton Town, £75,000
Apps: 12 (13) - Goals: 2 (2)

Striker signed from part-time amateur club after impressing in the Nottinghamshire leagues. Was victim of fierce competition for places when contesting at various times with the likes of Ravanelli, Fjortoft, Beck and Hendrie, but scored against Sheffield Wednesday on his full Premiership debut.

Paul Gascoigne (1998-2000)

From Glasgow Rangers, £3.45m
To Everton, Free
Apps: 48 - Goals: 4

One of the most gifted footballers of the modern era and an England legend. He was once alleged to be the second most photographed person in Britain behind Princess Diana. Donated 1998 Coca-Cola Cup final medal to Craig Hignett, whose subs place he felt he took. Failed to reproduce his best form before injuries and other problems ended his Boro career.

ALL AROUND THE WORLD

Players from 21 countries have worn a Boro shirt in the last 10 years

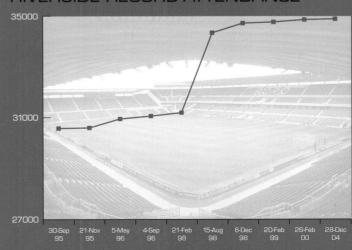

• ITALIAN JOB - Marco Branca

9	Ireland
6	Brazil
5	Australia
	Italy
	Scotland
4	Netherlands
3	France
	Wales
2	Cameroon
	Slovakia
1	Argentina
	Austria
	Bolivia
	Colombia
	Croatia
	Denmark
	Germany
	Nigeria
	Norway
	Spain
	Portugal
England	62

RIVERSIDE RECORD ATTENDANCE

Jason Gavin (1996-2003)

From Youth
To Bradford City, Free
Apps: 40 - Goals: 0

Dublin-born defender who carried high hopes of a career in the top league. It never quite worked out for him, though he made 40 appearances for Boro. Following loan spells with Hartlepool, Grimsby and Huddersfield, he then joined Bradford City permanently. Moved back to Ireland to play for Shamrock Rovers in 2005.

Geremi (2002-03)

From Real Madrid, Loan
Apps: 34 - Goals: 7

Cameroon international midfielder who made his mark in just one season at the Riverside. Injury ended his stay with Boro six weeks early. There were hopes he would sign permanently but he elected to join Chelsea when moving from the Bernabeu. Top class exponent of the art of free-kick taking.

Dean Gordon (1998-2002)

From Crystal Palace, £900,000
To Coventry City, Free
Apps: 71 - Goals: 5

Left-back who liked to overlap, a natural gift given he started life as a winger. Out of favour when Franck Queudrue joined. After a superb first season at the Riverside, serious injury curtailed his career. Moved to Cyprus with Apoel Nicosia in 2005.

Danny Graham (2003-)

From Youth
Apps: 17 - Goals: 2

Joined Academy late after moving from Northern League football with Chester-le-Street Town Juniors. Prolific goalscorer at Academy and reserve-team level. Made Premiership debut at Old Trafford in October 2004, scoring first senior goal in next match, against Coventry in the Carling Cup. February 2005 brought first Premiership goal, versus Charlton.

Jonathan Greening (2001-04)

From Manchester Utd, £2m
To West Bromwich Albion, £1.25m
Apps: 109 - Goals: 4

Scarborough-born midfielder who joined from Manchester United after starting his career with York City. Was named Supporters' Player of the Season in his second season at the Riverside and was involved in an England training camp that year. Moved to the Hawthorns in the summer of 2004.

Craig Harrison (1996-2000)

From Youth
To Crystal Palace, £200,000
Apps: 32 - Goals: 0

Left-back whose career was cut short by illness. Hard-tackling left-back, gifted natural left-footer who was a product of Redheugh Boys Club. Was Boro's young player of the year during 1997-98 promotion success. Peritonitis with added complications brought a premature end to a promising career.

Jimmy Floyd Hasselbaink (2004-)

From Chelsea, Free
Apps: 45 - Goals: 16

Powerful striker with a deadly shot who was snapped up after previous successful spells with Leeds United, Atletico Madrid and Chelsea. A Dutch international, Hasselbaink grabbed 16 goals in his first Riverside season including a hat-trick against Blackburn and a free-kick strike that ultimately clinched a UEFA Cup place at Manchester City.

John Hendrie (1990-96)

From Leeds Utd, £500,000
To Barnsley, £250,000
Apps: - 17 (235) Goals: 1 (56)

Was initially signed as a winger under Colin Todd, but by the time the club moved to the Riverside the Scot had become a fully-fledged striker. Scored twice in the last ever game at Ayresome Park. Helped Barnsley to the Premier League, partnering his old Boro strike partner Paul Wilkinson.

Riverside X

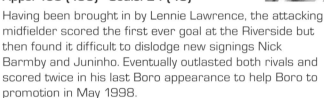

Craig Hignett (1992-98)

From Crewe Alexandra, £500,000
To Aberdeen, Free
Apps: 103 (196) - Goals: 24 (48)

Having been brought in by Lennie Lawrence, the attacking midfielder scored the first ever goal at the Riverside but then found it difficult to dislodge new signings Nick Barmby and Juninho. Eventually outlasted both rivals and scored twice in his last Boro appearance to help Boro to promotion in May 1998.

Mark Hudson (2000-03)

From Youth
To Chesterfield, Free
Apps: 2 - Goals: 0

The midfielder, who could operate in the centre and on the left, was handed his Premiership debut as a substitute against Liverpool on Boxing Day 2000. But Hudson would fail to make a start for Boro and would eventually leave the club for Chesterfield in 2003 after loan spells with the Spireites and Carlisle.

Paul Ince (1999-2002)

From Liverpool, £1m
To Wolves, Free
Apps: 106 - Goals: 8

Was already an international star before his three seasons at the Riverside, but became a talismanic captain who is best remembered for helping the side stay in the Premiership in 2000-01. Formerly with Manchester United, Internazionale and Liverpool, the tough-tackling midfielder won 53 England caps, and played at Euro 2000 while with Boro.

Joseph-Desire Job (2000-)

From Lens, £3m
Apps: 111 - Goals: 22

The Cameroon international was brought in from French football in 2000 and made a scoring debut against Coventry. The forward made just 17 appearances in his first two campaigns, and went to Metz on a season loan, but would return to favour and scored in the 2004 Carling Cup final. Loaned to Al-Ittahad of Saudi Arabia early in 2005-06.

GOOD DAY

Boro's biggest wins in the last decade

6-0	Swindon (H)	11/03/98
6-1	Derby (H)	5/03/97
5-1	Derby (H)	3/11/01
	Tottenham (H)	3/05/03
4-0	Blackburn (A)	16/10/04
	Coventry (H)	7/09/96
	Derby (H)	13/01/01
	Sheff Wed (H)	3/10/98
	West Brom (H)	23/04/05
	Bury (H)	11/04/98
	Reading (H)	13/12/97

BAD DAY

Boro's thrashings in the last 10 years

1-6	Arsenal (H)	24/04/99
1-5	Arsenal (A)	20/11/99
	Liverpool (A)	14/12/96
	Portsmouth (A)	15/05/04
0-5	Chelsea (A)	4/02/96
	QPR (A)	4/03/98
0-4	Arsenal (H)	18/08/01
	Arsenal (H)	24/08/03
	Everton (A)	26/12/95
	Nottingham F (A)	1/03/98
	Southampton (A)	28/09/96
	West Ham (A)	16/05/99

LEAGUE FORM

Boro's finishing positions

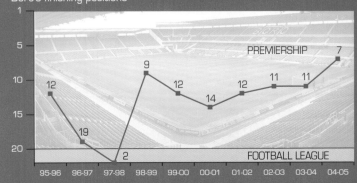

Allan Johnston (2001-04)
From Glasgow Rangers, £600,000
Released
Apps: 24 - Goals: 1

The Scottish international had gained Premiership experience with Sunderland before signing for Steve McClaren in September 2001. The left winger scored on his home debut against West Ham but struggled to become a first choice at the Riverside, with his most memorable game the FA Cup semi-final against Arsenal.

Brad Jones (2003-)
From Youth
Apps: 7 - Goals: 0

Born in Australia but made on Teesside, the Academy graduate goalkeeper looks set for a distinguished career at the Riverside. Made his debut in December 2003, but came to the fore with some fantastic displays at the end of 2004-05 as he deputised for fellow countryman Mark Schwarzer.

Juninho (1995-97, 1999-2000, 2002-04)
From Sao Paulo, £4.75m (1995);
Atletico Madrid, Loan (1999),
£3.8m (2002)
To Atletico Madrid, £12m (1997);
Celtic, Free (2004)
Apps: 155 - Goals: 34

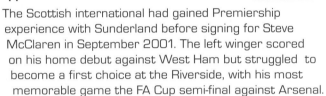

A club legend who initially signed as Brazilian Player of the Year in 1995, but departed after relegation in 1997 for a record fee. Returned on loan in 1999-2000 and signed permanently in 2002 before leaving for Celtic two years later. A quick and extremely skilful midfielder with tricks that could stagger any opponent.

• FRENCH FLAIR -
Christian Karembeu (left)

Christian Karembeu (2000-01)
From Real Madrid, £2.1m
To Olympiakos, £3.7m
Apps: 36 - Goals: 4

The creative midfielder was already a World Cup, European Championships and Champions League winner when he signed, bringing a touch of glamour with his model wife Adriana. Put Boro ahead at Old Trafford and scored a winner against Liverpool, but would depart after just one season in which he flattered to deceive.

Graham Kavanagh (1991-96)
From Home Farm, Free
To Stoke City, £500,000
Apps: 7 (48) - Goals: 1 (4)

Boro beat off Liverpool to sign Kavanagh in 1991, but he would play just seven games during the Riverside era as his 1995-96 season was ruined by injury. The Ireland international midfielder started the following campaign in the reserves before departing for Stoke following a successful loan spell. Back in the Premiership with Wigan in 2005.

Jason Kennedy (2005-)
From Youth
Apps: 1 - Goals: 0

A youth product, and part of the 2004 FA Youth Cup-winning team, the midfielder worked his way into the first-team picture towards the end of the Academy's fantastic 2004-05 season. Made the squad against Sporting Lisbon and Arsenal before his debut as a sub against Fulham.

Sean Kilgannon (2000-02)
From Youth
To Dunfermline, Free
Apps: 1 - Goals: 0

Played just one first-team game for Boro, a 2-2 home draw with Newcastle at the Riverside in May 2000. The left-sided player could feature in midfield or defence, and was released to join Scottish side Dunfermline in March 2002 after a successful loan spell.

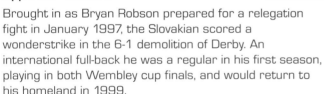

Vladimir Kinder (1997-99)

From Slovan Bratislava, £1m
Released
Apps: 50 - Goals: 5

Brought in as Bryan Robson prepared for a relegation fight in January 1997, the Slovakian scored a wonderstrike in the 6-1 demolition of Derby. An international full-back he was a regular in his first season, playing in both Wembley cup finals, and would return to his homeland in 1999.

Craig Liddle (1994-98)

From Blyth Spartans, Free
To Darlington, £50,000
Apps: 31 (34) - Goals: 0

Made his Premiership debut in the same game as Juninho in a draw with Leeds in November 1995, a year after Boro rescued him from the dole queue. Played in both defence and midfield during the first Premiership season, but his chances were limited after that and he moved on to skipper Darlington.

Massimo Maccarone (2002-)

From Empoli, £8.15m
Apps: 64 - Goals: 16

The club's record signing was brought in from Italy, despite the interest of a host of top European sides including Chelsea, after storming the European U-21 Championships in 2002. He began his Riverside career with two goals in only his second game, but was loaned out to Parma and then Siena in 2004-05.

Neil Maddison (1997-2001)

From Southampton, £250,000
To Darlington, Free
Apps: 67 - Goals: 4

His versatility had already shone in his time at Southampton, before he was used all over the park to boost Boro's promotion bid in 1997-98. Played in the Coca-Cola Cup final but his days were numbered with the arrival of players such as Andy Townsend, Paul Ince and Paul Gascoigne in midfield.

THE PREMIER LEAGUE

How long, how many and how few since 1995

Most consecutive clean sheets: Seven – 26.10.03 to 13.12.03 (Tottenham (a) 0-0, Wolves (h) 2-0, Villa (a) 2-0, Liverpool (h) 0-0, Man City (a) 1-0, Portsmouth (h) 0-0, Charlton (h) 0-0).

Most consecutive clean sheets (home): Four – 9.1.99 to 14.3.99 (Arsenal 0-0, Leicester 0-0, Tottenham 0-0, Southampton 3-0); 31.8.02 to 5.10.02 (Blackburn 1-0, Sunderland 3-0, Birmingham 1-0, Bolton 2-0); 1.11.03 to 13.12.03 (Wolves 2-0, Liverpool 0-0, Portsmouth 0-0, Charlton 0-0).

Most consecutive clean sheets (away): Four – 27.9.03 to 30.11.03 – Southampton 1-0, Tottenham 0-0, Villa 2-0, Man City 1-0.

Most consecutive wins: Five – 16.9.95 to 21.10.95 (Coventry (h) 2-1, Man City (a) 1-0, Blackburn (h) 2-0, Sheffield Wednesday (a) 1-0, QPR (h) 1-0).

Most consecutive wins (home): Four - 31.8.02 to 5.10.02 (Blackburn 1-0, Sunderland 3-0, Birmingham 1-0, Bolton 2-0); 9.3.04 to 12.4.04 (Tottenham 1-0, Birmingham 5-3, Bolton 2-0, Southampton 3-1). 20.11.04 to 28.12.04 (Liverpool 2-0, Man City 3-2, Aston Villa 3-0, Norwich 2-0). Run is five if include 3-0 win over Partizan Belgrade in the UEFA Cup.

Most consecutive wins (away): Three – 16.10.04 to 14.11.04 (Blackburn 4-0, Charlton 2-1, West Brom 2-1).

Most consecutive defeats: Eight – 26.12.95 to 17.2.96 (Everton (a) 0-4, Notts F (a) 0-1, Villa (h) 0-2, Arsenal (h) 2-3, Southampton (a) 1-2, Chelsea (a) 0-5, Newcastle (h) 1-2, Bolton (h) 1-4).

Most consecutive defeats (home): Five – 1.1.96 to 2.3.96 (Villa 0-2, Arsenal 2-3, Newcastle 1-2, Bolton 1-4, Everton 0-2).

Most consecutive defeats (away): Eight – 20.10.02 to 18.1.03 (Charlton 0-1, Newcastle 0-2, Chelsea 0-1, WBA 0-1, Arsenal 0-2, Villa 0-1, Blackburn 0-1, Fulham 0-1) Run is 10 if include 1-3 defeat at Ipswich in Worthington Cup and 0-1 defeat at Chelsea in FA Cup.

Most consecutive draws: Four – 20.1.01 to 10.2.01 (Liverpool (a) 0-0, Everton (a) 2-2, Man City (h) 1-1, Aston Villa (a) 1-1). Run was five if 0-0 home draw with Wimbledon in FA Cup is included.

Most games unbeaten: 11 – 3.10.98 to 19.12.98 (Sheffield W (h) 4-0, Blackburn (h) 2-1, Wimbledon (a) 2-2, Notts F (h) 1-1, Southampton (a) 3-3, Charlton (a) 1-1, Coventry (h) 2-0, Arsenal (a) 1-1, Newcastle (h) 2-2, West Ham (h) 1-0, Man United (a) 3-2. Note: team of 2000-01 went 10 Premier League games unbeaten, (12 in league and cup) under Terry Venables.

Carlos Marinelli (1999-2003)

From Boca Juniors, £1.5m
Released
Apps: 53 - Goals: 4

The Argentine midfielder was hailed as a future international star when he joined the club as a 17-year-old. Blessed with fantastic ball skills, his workrate was often questioned but he enjoyed his best run in the first team in 2001-02. Scored on the opening day of 2003-04 but never played for the club again and was with Torino in 2005.

Tony McMahon (2004-)

From Youth
Apps: 19 Goals: 0

Came through the ranks of Boro's Academy and lifted the FA Youth Cup as skipper in 2004. The right-back was then thrust into the limelight when he made an impressive first-team debut at Manchester United's Old Trafford in October 2004 and became a first-team regular while just 18 years old.

Gaizka Mendieta (2003-)

From Lazio, Free
Apps: 46 - Goals: 3

Had cost Lazio £28.9m just two years before he joined Boro on loan in 2003, making the deal permanent the following year. The two-times Champions League finalist with Valencia is a Spain international who enjoyed an impressive second half of 2003-04 on the right of midfield but missed most of the following season with a knee injury.

Paul Merson (1997-98)

From Arsenal, £4.5m
To Aston Villa, £7m
Apps: 58 - Goals: 16

Joined from Arsenal in 1997 and helped Boro storm their way back to the Premiership as the First Division's Player of the Year. The attacking midfielder/forward was then picked for England's World Cup '98 squad, playing against Argentina, but would make just three more Boro appearances before controversially leaving for Aston Villa.

Alan Miller (1994-97)

From Arsenal, £425,000
To West Bromwich Albion, £500,000
Apps: 18 (64) - Goals: 0

Played a key role in the championship success of 1994-95 before losing the jersey to Gary Walsh in the first season at the Riverside. Enjoyed a run as first choice at the start of the 1996-97 season before loss of form led to his sale.

Danny Mills (2003-04)

From Leeds Utd, Loan
Apps: 37 - Goals: 0

Combative right-back who won a Carling Cup winners' medal during his successful season on loan from Elland Road. The hard-working England defender's aggressive style made him a target for opposition fans and referees. He relaunched his career at Manchester City after failing to agree a permanent contract at the Riverside.

Alan Moore (1991-2001)

From Rivermount
To Burnley, Free
Apps: 26 (161) - Goals: 0 (17)

Despite much early promise, Moore's Boro career was largely unfulfilled. His Boro career was effectively over by the time the club moved to the Riverside. The talented winger was a key part of the 1994-95 promotion season but injuries and lack of form held him back thereafter.

Fabio Moreira (1997-98)

Free Agent
Released
Apps: 1 - Goals: 0

Few Boro careers were briefer than that of Emerson's cousin. Midfielder Fabio came over from Brazil to keep Emerson company but, despite impressing for the reserves, never looked Premiership material. He made a single first-team appearance against Huddersfield.

Chris Morris (1992-97)

From Celtic, £600,000
Retired
Apps: 29 (106) - Goals: 2 (4)

Morris arrived from Parkhead in tandem with Derek Whyte after a trophy-laden career in Scotland. The attack-minded full-back was part of the Boro side that slipped out of the inaugural Premier League in 1992-93. After returning from a serious knee injury, he found himself behind Curtis Fleming and Neil Cox in Bryan Robson's plans.

James Morrison (2003-)

From Youth
Apps: 24 - Goals: 4

The Darlington-born midfielder made a hugely-impressive start to his senior career when only 17 years old after helping Boro win the FA Youth Cup for the first time. He marked his UEFA Cup debut by scoring a vital equaliser against Banik Ostrava in the club's first-ever European trip. Tipped for a very bright future.

David Murphy (2001-04)

From Youth
To Hibernian, Free
Apps: 8 - Goals: 0

Local lad Murphy appeared to have the world at his feet when he made a scoring debut against Northampton in the Worthington Cup in September 2001. But the left-sided defender was plagued with a succession of injuries and slipped behind more established players for his position.

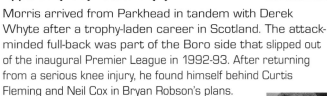

Robbie Mustoe (1990-2003)

From Oxford Utd, £375,000
Released
Apps: 251 (367) - Goals: 16 (31)

Mustoe's remarkable Boro career spanned the first eight years of the Riverside when he became one of the club's most reliable and respected players. The busy midfielder joined a struggling Second Division outfit playing in front of 6,000 crowds and ended his Boro days before 30,000-plus gates, excelling for five managers.

Most games unbeaten (home): 12 - 24.8.02 to 11.1.03 (Fulham 2-2, Blackburn 1-0, Sunderland 3-0, Birmingham 1-0, Bolton 2-0, Leeds 2-2, Liverpool 1-0, Man City 3-1, West Ham 2-2, Chelsea 1-1, Man United 3-1, Southampton 2-2) Run ended by 5-2 defeat to Aston Villa 28.1.03.

Most games unbeaten (away): Seven – 22.4.00 to 30.9.00 (Chelsea 1-1, West Ham 1-0, Everton 2-0, Coventry 3-1, Derby 3-3, Man City 1-1, Southampton 3-1). Run ended with 1-0 defeat at Charlton on 21.10.00. Seven - 27.9.03 - 10.1.04. (5 league, 2 cup) – Southampton 1-0, Tottenham 0-0, Wigan (cup) 2-1, Villa 2-0, Man City 1-0, Tottenham (cup) 1-1, Blackburn 2-2. Run ended with 4-1 defeat at Arsenal.

Most games without a win: 13 – 26.12.95 to 19.3.96 (Everton (a) 0-4, Forest (a) 0-1, Villa (h) 0-2, Arsenal (h) 2-3, Southampton (a) 1-2, Chelsea (a) 0-5, Newcastle (h) 1-2, Bolton (h) 1-4, Coventry (a) 0-0, Everton (h) 0-2, West Ham (a) 0-2, Forest (h) 1-1, Villa (a) 0-0). Run ended with a 1-0 win at Leeds on 30.3.96.

Most games without a win (home): 11 – 10.4.00 to 25.11.00 (Man United 3-4, Newcastle 2-2, Watford 1-1, Tottenham 1-1, Leeds 1-2, Everton 1-2, Villa 1-1, Newcastle 1-3, Arsenal 0-1, Leicester 0-3, Bradford City 2-2). Run ended on 16.12.2000 with 1-0 win over Chelsea in Terry Venables' first game in charge.

Most games without a win (away): 11 – 28.10.95 to 19.3.96 (Man United 0-2, Wimbledon 0-0, QPR 1-1, Blackburn 0-1, Everton 0-4, Nottm F 0-1, Southampton 1-2, Chelsea 0-5, Coventry 0-0, West Ham 0-2, Aston Villa 0-0). Run ended with a 1-0 win at Leeds on 30.3.96.

Most consecutive scoring games: 21 – 4.3.00 to 16.10.00. Note: run is 23 games if cup games are included

Most consecutive scoring games (home): 15 - 24.8.02 to 19.4.03 (Fulham 2-2, Blackburn 1-0, Sunderland 3-0, Birmingham 1-0, Bolton 2-0, Leeds 2-2, Liverpool 1-0, Man City 3-1, West Ham 2-2, Chelsea 1-1, Man United 3-1, Southampton 2-2, Aston Villa 2-5, Everton 1-1, Newcastle 1-0, Charlton 1-1, WBA 3-0). Run ended with 2-0 home defeat to Arsenal 19.4.03

Most consecutive scoring games (away): 11 – 5.2.00 to 30.9.00. Run ended with 1-0 defeat at Charlton on 2.10.00. Run was 12 if include cup game at Macclesfield.

Most goals in one game at Riverside: 8 - Boro 5 Birmingham 3.3.04.

Carlo Nash (2002-04)

From Manchester City, £100,000
To Preston North End, £175,000
Apps: 5 - Goals: 0

As cover goalkeeper for the consistent Mark Schwarzer, Nash rarely enjoyed the limelight. He arrived as replacement for Fulham-bound Mark Crossley and spent two frustrating seasons in the reserves before moving back to his native Lancashire and enjoying a Championship play-off final appearance with Preston.

Szilard Nemeth (2001-)

From Inter Bratislava, Free
Apps: 135 - Goals: 28

The Slovakian striker was Bryan Robson's last signing, having been strongly recommended by Head Coach Terry Venables. But by the time he arrived on Teesside, Steve McClaren had taken over as manager. A prolific striker for his country, Nemeth has proved adaptable in right midfield when necessary.

Keith O'Halloran (1994-97)

From Youth
To St Johnstone, £50,000
Apps: 5 (7) - Goals: 0

The Irish midfielder was very much a fringe player who enjoyed few chances at senior level. He eventually moved to Cardiff on loan before finding success with Perth side St Johnstone, helping them return to the Scottish Premier League.

Keith O'Neill (1999-2001)

From Norwich City, £700,000
To Coventry City, £1m
Apps: 42 - Goals: 0

Dublin-born O'Neill was an early casualty of Steve McClaren's rebuilding plans. After showing early promise, the versatile left-sided player was hit by a succession of injuries that limited his appearances. Turned out as a winger, striker, midfielder and wing-back. Now involved in a Christmas crackers businness.

Paul Okon (2000-2001)

From Fiorentina, Free
To Leeds Utd, Free
Apps: 30 - Apps: 0

The classy Australian midfielder had suffered a serious knee injury in Italy that limited his pace, but he was an excellent passer. Denied a place in the 2000 Olympics in his native Sydney by a foot injury. Showed his best form at sweeper under Terry Venables.

Anthony Ormerod (1996-2001)

From Youth
Released
Apps: 24 - Goals: 0

Skilful winger who showed much promise when he broke into Bryan Robson's 1997-98 promotion side. Injuries prevented further progress and he was loaned out to Carlisle and York before pursuing a non-league career.

Gary Pallister (1998-2000)

From Billingham Town, Free (1984);
Manchester Utd, £2.5m (1998)
To Manchester United £2.3m (1989);
Retired
Apps: 61 (249) - Goals: 1 (7)

Immensely talented defender whose Boro career spanned two distinct eras, with the 22-cap centre-half initially coming through the club's ranks before departing for Manchester United for £2.3m in 1989. Bryan Robson brought Billingham's finest back in 1998, but a back injury eventually forced the four-time Premiership winner to retire.

Ray Parlour (2004-)

From Arsenal, Free
Apps: 41 - Goals: 0

Vastly-experienced midfielder who played more than 400 games for Arsenal before switching to the Riverside. Quickly forged an excellent partnership with George Boateng and his know-how was invaluable during the inaugural UEFA Cup campaign. The former England player's desire and commitment remains as strong as ever.

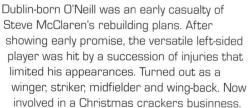

Riverside X

Stuart Parnaby (1999-)

From Youth

Apps: 64 - Goals: 0

Excelled in both midfield and defence as a youth player before specialising at right-back. The former England U-21 international would surely have made many more appearances but for injuries. Won an important vote of confidence at the end of 2004-05 when he was picked ahead of Michael Reiziger.

Nigel Pearson (1994-98)

From Sheffield Wednesday, £750,000
Retired

Apps: 104 (139) - Goals: 2 (5)

Big-hearted skipper who was a key figure in the early Riverside years and led Boro out during their three Wembley cup finals of 1997-98. Courageously fought back against injuries to lead by example at the heart of defence, where he added much-needed steel to Bryan Robson's flair teams. Helped Boro win promotion in his final match.

Jamie Pollock (1991-96)

From Youth
To Osasuna, Free

Apps: 40 (193) - Goals: 2 (19)

Few players were as proud to wear the Boro shirt as Stockton boy Pollock, who never lacked commitment and was fearless in the tackle. The energetic midfielder was an influential figure in the final years at Ayresome Park but enjoyed just one season at the Riverside before heading for a brief period in Spain. Now retired from the game, he owns a glass-making business on Teesside.

Franck Queudrue (2001-)

From Lens, £2.5m

Apps: 150 - Goals: 9

Skilful left-back with a thunderbolt free-kick who has been a major success since an initial eight-month loan from Lens. He was secured on a permanent deal in summer 2002 and became a key member of the 2004 Carling Cup team. Worked hard to conquer early disciplinary problems.

FA CUP

1995-96		
R3	Notts County	2-1
R4	Wimbledon	0-0 0-1
1996-97		
R3	Chester City H	6-0
R4	Hednesford Town H	3-2
R5	Manchester City A	1-0
QF	Derby County A	2-0
SF	Chesterfield	3-3 3-0
F	Chelsea	0-2
1997-98		
R3	QPR A	2-2 2-0
R4	Arsenal H	1-2
1998-99		
R3	Manchester Utd A	1-3
1999-00		
R3	Wrexham A	1-2
2000-01		
R3	Bradford City A	1-0
R4	Wimbledon H	0-0 1-3
2001-02		
R3	Wimbledon A	0-0 2-0
R4	Manchester Utd H	2-0
R5	Blackburn Rovers H	1-0
QF	Everton H	3-0
SF	Arsenal	0-1
2002-03		
R3	Chelsea A	0-1
2003-04		
R3	Notts County H	2-0
R4	Arsenal A	4-1
2004-05		
R3	Notts County A	2-1
R4	Manchester Utd A	0-3

Fabrizio Ravanelli (1996-97)

From Juventus, £7m
To Marseille, £5.2m
Apps: 50 - Goals: 32

Controversial but prolific striker who struck 31 goals – including 15 in 15 cup games – during the most dramatic season in Boro's entire history. Having scored in the 1996 Champions League final, he struck a debut Riverside hat-trick and later fired Boro's first ever Wembley goal.

Michael Reiziger (2004-05)

From Barcelona, Free
To PSV, Free
Apps: 25 - Goals: 1

Vastly experienced Dutch international, who earned a reputation as one of Europe's finest right-backs during illustrious spells with Ajax and Barcelona. Recovered from a major shoulder injury to regain his place in the Boro side during 2004-05, but returned to the Netherlands with PSV at the start of 2005-06.

Hamilton Ricard (1998-2002)

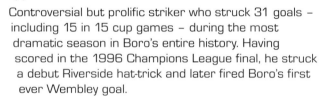

From Deportivo Cali, £2m
To CSKA Sofia, Free
Apps: 134 - Goals: 44

Swept aside the fans' initial concerns to finish successive seasons as the club's top scorer. Boasting power and close control, he punctuated frustrating performances with goals out of nothing. Scored more goals for the club than any other player in Boro's first decade at the Riverside. Fell out of favour under Steve McClaren and spent 2004-05 with APOEL in Cyprus.

Michael Ricketts (2002-04)

From Bolton Wanderers, £2.5m
To Leeds Utd, Free
Apps 38 - Goals: 4

Boro fans were excited when Steve McClaren signed Ricketts minutes before the January transfer deadline in January 2002. The big striker's scintillating goalscoring displays with Bolton had won him an England cap a year earlier, but he never came near repeating that form at the Riverside. Looked overweight and out of touch before McClaren finally lost patience and released him to Leeds.

Chris Riggott (2002-)

From Derby County, £3m
(joint deal including Malcolm Christie)
Apps: 61 - Goals: 5

Once rumoured to be a £7m target for Liverpool, the former England U-21 central defender was snapped up along with Derby team-mate Christie on transfer deadline day in January 2002. Has impressed during several first-team runs as he looks to challenge Gareth Southgate and Ugo Ehiogu for a regular starting place.

Ben Roberts (1993-2000)

From Youth
To Charlton, Free
Apps: 25 (26) - Goals: 0

Will be forever remembered as the goalkeeper who conceded a goal just 42 seconds into an FA Cup final. Roberts never quite fulfiled his early promise, which saw him play in two major cup finals before his 21st birthday. An England U-21 international, from Boro he moved to Charlton and then Brighton, from where injury forced him into retirement in 2005.

• IMPRESSIVE -
Chris Riggott

Riverside X

Bryan Robson (1994-1998)

From Man United, Free
Retired
Apps: 5 (26) - Goals: 0 (1)

Boro's player-manager became the oldest player to appear for the club's first team when facing Arsenal during an injury crisis on New Year's Day 1997. Announced his retirement from the playing side in 1998 after an incredible career that saw him win 90 England caps and achieve League, FA Cup, League Cup and European glories with Manchester United.

Mark Schwarzer (1997-)

From Bradford City, £1.25m
Apps: 318 - Goals: 0

Arguably Bryan Robson's best ever signing, Schwarzer is now in his ninth season as Boro's first choice goalkeeper. Weeks after clinching Boro's UEFA Cup qualification by saving Robbie Fowler's penalty in the last game of 2004-05, the Australian surpassed Wilf Mannion as the most capped player in Boro's history. No player has made more appearances for Boro during the Riverside era.

Gareth Southgate (2001-)

From Aston Villa, £6.5m
Apps: 162 - Goals: 4

Perhaps Steve McClaren's finest signing, Southgate succeeded Paul Ince as captain before leading Boro to Carling Cup victory in February 2004, the club's first ever major silverware. An outstanding central defender, with poise and timing, he is also Boro's most-capped England international since Wilf Mannion.

Phil Stamp (1993-2002)

From Youth
To Hearts, Free
Apps: 132 (154) - Goals: 8 (8)

Hard-running attacking midfielder who never fully established himself as a first choice in the side during a long stay with his hometown club. A series of niggling injuries held back his progress before he finally fell out of favour under Steve McClaren. Perhaps best remembered for his quote, used on Boro's FA Cup final record, "Yer jokin' aren't yer!"

LEAGUE CUP

1995-96		
R2/1	Rotherham Utd H	2-1
R2/2	Rotherham Utd A	1-0
R3	Crystal Palace A	2-2 2-0
R4	Birmingham City H	0-0 0-2
1996-97		
R2/1	Hereford Utd H	7-0
R2/2	Hereford Utd A	3-0
R3	Huddersfield Town H	5-1
R4	Newcastle Utd H	3-1
QF	Liverpool H	2-1
SF/1	Stockport County A	2-0
SF/2	Stockport County H	0-1
F	Leicester City	1-1 0-1
1997-98		
R2/1	Barnet H	1-0
R2/2	Barnet A	2-0
R3	Sunderland H	2-0
R4	Bolton Wanderers H	2-1
QF	Reading A	1-0
SF/1	Liverpool A	1-2
SF/2	Liverpool H	2-0
F	Chelsea	0-2
1998-99		
R2/1	Wycombe Wanderers H	2-0
R2/2	Wycombe Wanderers A	1-1
R3	Everton H	2-3
1999-00		
R2/1	Chesterfield A	0-0
R2/2	Chesterfield H	2-1
R3	Watford H	1-0
R4	Arsenal H	2-2
R5	Tranmere Rovers A	1-2
2000-01		
R2/1	Macclesfield Town H	2-1
R2/2	Macclesfield Town A	3-1
R3	Wimbledon A	0-1
2001-02		
R2	Northampton Town H	3-1
R3	Blackburn Rovers A	1-2
2002-03		
R2	Bradford City A	4-1
R3	Ipswich Town A	1-3
2003-04		
R2	Brighton H	1-0
R3	Wigan Athletic H	3-1
R4	Everton H	0-0
R5	Tottenham Hotspur A	1-1
SF/1	Arsenal H	1-0
SF/2	Arsenal A	2-1
F	Bolton Wanderers	2-1
2004-05		
R3	Coventry City H	3-0
R4	Liverpool A	0-2

Robbie Stockdale (1998-2004)

From Youth
To Rotherham Utd, Free
Apps: 102 - Goals: 2

Redcar-born right-back who made his Boro debut as an 18-year-old, one of several young players to make the first-team breakthrough during the 1997-98 promotion campaign. Although never first choice under Bryan Robson, he was given his most sustained run of games in Steve McClaren's first year in charge but lost out following the emergence of Stuart Parnaby.

Mark Summerbell (1995-2002)

From Youth
To Carlisle Utd, Free
Apps: 59 - Goals: 2

Summerbell's hard-tackling performances in central midfield for Boro's reserves earned him a first-team call-up, but he remained a fringe player throughout his time with the club. Hit the crossbar on his debut against Spurs in 1996, also scoring his first goal for the club with a header against the same side early in 2000-01.

Michael Thomas (1998)

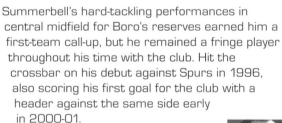

From Liverpool, Loan
Apps: 10 - Goals: 0

A career best remembered for his injury time winner that clinched the 1989 title for Arsenal at Anfield was on a downward spiral by the time he joined Boro on loan during the second half of the 1997-98 promotion season. However, the experienced midfielder played a steady if unspectacular role before returning to Liverpool.

Andy Townsend (1997-99)

From Aston Villa, £500,000
To West Bromwich Albion, £100,000
Apps: 88 - Goals: 4

Vastly experienced left-sided midfielder, who won 70 caps for the Republic of Ireland during a distinguished career. Played a steadying role in helping Boro to promotion and a third successive cup final in his first season at the Riverside, before succeeding the retired Nigel Pearson as club captain as Boro re-established themselves in the Premiership.

Steve Vickers (1993-2001)

From Tranmere Rovers, £700,000
To Birmingham City, £425,000
Apps: 228 (310) - Goals: 5 (11)

Boro's Player of the Year in the club's first season at the Riverside, ahead of big-money superstars Juninho and Nick Barmby. Signed by Lennie Lawrence long before the Riverside Revolution was even a dream, Vickers was a dependable central defender under Bryan Robson and Terry Venables. Helped the club to two promotions and played in the 1998 Coca-Cola Cup final.

Tony Vidmar (2002-03)

From Glasgow Rangers, Free
To Cardiff City, Free
Apps: 15 - Goals: 0

Signed as a central defender early in the 2002-03 season, Vidmar displayed his versatility with several impressive displays as an attacking left-back, most notably in a 1-0 home win over league leaders Liverpool. A vastly experienced Australian international, he stood in for both Franck Queudrue and Ugo Ehiogu, but never played again after a 5-2 defeat to Aston Villa.

Mark Viduka (2004-)

From Leeds Utd, £4.5m
Apps: 21 - Goals: 7

A prolific goalscoring record with Leeds United persuaded Steve McClaren to part with £4.5m during the summer of 2004. The striker initially looked the part, scoring twice in Boro's first ever UEFA Cup match against Banik Ostrava, but niggling back and hamstring injuries took their toll, Viduka playing only 10 minutes during the season's final five months.

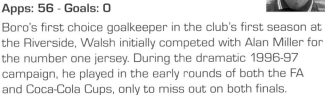

Gary Walsh (1995-97; 2000)

From Manchester Utd, £250,000 (1995);
Bradford City, Loan (2000)
To Bradford City, £250,000
Apps: 56 - Goals: 0

Boro's first choice goalkeeper in the club's first season at the Riverside, Walsh initially competed with Alan Miller for the number one jersey. During the dramatic 1996-97 campaign, he played in the early rounds of both the FA and Coca-Cola Cups, only to miss out on both finals. Returned for a three-game loan spell during a 'keeper crisis in 2000-01.

David Wheater (2005-)

From Youth
Apps: 1 - Goals: 0

A central defensive member of Boro's victorious FA Youth Cup-winning side in 2004, Redcar-born Wheater also played in the previous year's final against Manchester United while still a schoolboy. An England youth international, he made his first-team debut during the final two minutes of Boro's UEFA Cup defeat to Sporting Lisbon in March 2005.

Noel Whelan (2000-03)

From Coventry City, £2.25m
To Millwall, Free
Apps: 73 - Goals: 10

Whelan is best remembered at the Riverside for his coolly struck winner in the north-east derby at Sunderland during Steve McClaren's first season in charge. Mainly playing in an attacking midfield role, he struggled to win a regular starting place during his three years with the club due to a combination of form and injuries.

FOREIGN LEGION
Percentage of foreign players in Boro's squad

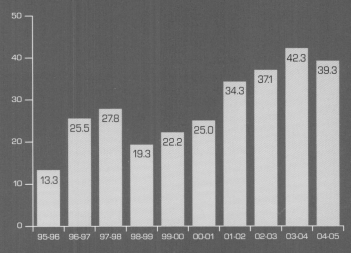

LOCAL HEROES
Homegrown players in Boro's squad

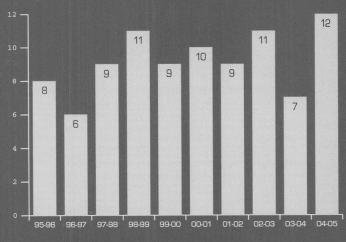

TRANSFER TRAIL
Boro's spending through the Riverside era

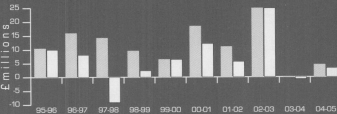

TOTAL GROSS SPEND: £115.8 million   TOTAL NET SPEND: £62.99 million

Note: Gross spend is total spending on new signings
Net spend is total outgoings minus income for transfer sales

202

Phil Whelan (1995-97)

From Ipswich Town, £300,000
To Oxford Utd, Free
Apps: 30 - Goals: 1

University graduate Whelan failed to make the grade for Boro. Signed from Ipswich on transfer deadline day during the 1994-95 promotion campaign, he was unable to play that season as his registration was late going through. A tall central defender, he struggled at the highest level and became a boo-boy target. Missed games in his first full season after suffering a broken jaw in an incident outside a Middlesbrough pub.

Derek Whyte (1992-97)

From Celtic, £900,000
To Aberdeen, £200,000
Apps: 66 (196) - Goals: 1 (3)

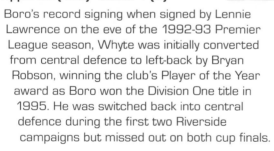

Boro's record signing when signed by Lennie Lawrence on the eve of the 1992-93 Premier League season, Whyte was initially converted from central defence to left-back by Bryan Robson, winning the club's Player of the Year award as Boro won the Division One title in 1995. He was switched back into central defence during the first two Riverside campaigns but missed out on both cup finals.

Paul Wilkinson (1991-96)

From Watford, £500,000
To Barnsley, Free
Apps: 6 (202) - Goals: 0 (67)

A striker whose goal clinched Boro's place in the first ever Premier League season, back in 1992, was no more than a periphery figure by the time the club returned to the top flight in the Riverside's opening season. "Wilko" was Boro's top scorer in the three seasons preceding Bryan Robson's arrival, but played only due to an injury crisis in 1995-96.

Luke Wilkshire (1997-2003)

From Youth
To Bristol City, £250,000
Apps: 23 - Goals: 1

Recruited to Boro's Academy from his native Australia as a 15-year-old, Wollongong-born Wilkshire worked his way through the youth and reserves to make his first-team debut in March 2002. The attacking midfielder appeared in the FA Cup semi-final against Arsenal that same season but eventually dropped down a couple of divisions to join Bristol City.

Mark Wilson (2001-05)

From Manchester Utd, £1.5m
To Dallas Burn, Free
Apps: 24 - Goals: 2

Big things were expected of Wilson when he joined the club in a deal that also saw Jonathan Greening make the move from Manchester United. Sadly, he failed to impress and became something of a forgotten man at the Riverside, regularly sent on loan. A fine display in a 3-1 home win over his old side in December 2002 stood out.

Dean Windass (2001-02)

From Bradford City, £600,000
To Sheffield Utd, Free
Apps: 46 - Goals: 3

Brought in to help Boro stave off the threat of relegation in 2000-01, shortly after scoring a thumping header for Bradford at the Riverside. Big-hearted Windass was the only signing during Terry Venables' time in charge. He became a regular sub under Steve McClaren the following season, switching between the front line and midfield.

Riverside X

Bolo Zenden (2003-05)

From Chelsea, Free
To Liverpool, Free
Apps: 88 - Goals: 15

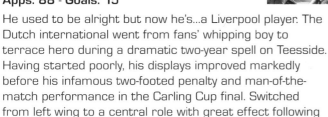

He used to be alright but now he's...a Liverpool player. The Dutch international went from fans' whipping boy to terrace hero during a dramatic two-year spell on Teesside. Having started poorly, his displays improved markedly before his infamous two-footed penalty and man-of-the-match performance in the Carling Cup final. Switched from left wing to a central role with great effect following the emergence of Stewart Downing.

Christian Ziege (1999-2000)

From AC Milan, £4m
To Liverpool, £5.5m
Apps: 34 - Goals: 7

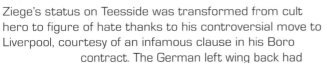

Ziege's status on Teesside was transformed from cult hero to figure of hate thanks to his controversial move to Liverpool, courtesy of an infamous clause in his Boro contract. The German left wing back had previously enjoyed an excellent first season with the club, crowned the club's player of the year after winning an international recall.

• INFAMOUS -
Christian Ziege

GOALS GOALS GOALS

Boro's for and against in the league since 1995

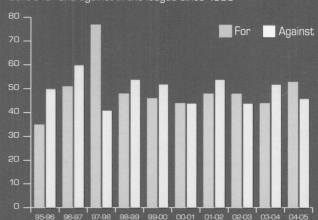

Legend: For / Against

X-axis: 95-96, 96-97, 97-98, 98-99, 99-00, 00-01, 01-02, 02-03, 03-04, 04-05

MR DURABLE

The most appearances in a Riverside season

55	Paul MERSON	1997-98
48	Bolo ZENDEN	2004-05
	Fabrizio RAVANELLI	1996-97
47	JUNINHO	1996-97
	Gianluca FESTA	1997-98
	Gareth SOUTHGATE	2004-05
46	Robbie MUSTOE	1996-97
45	EMERSON	1996-97
	Mark SCHWARZER	1997-98
44	Nigel PEARSON	1995-96
	Mark SCHWARZER	2003-04
	Gareth SOUTHGATE	2001-02
	Andy TOWNSEND	1997-98

All statistics relate to Boro appearances and goals in all competitions during the Riverside era, August 1995 to May 2005 only.

Figures in brackets indicate total number of Boro appearances and goals when a player was with the club before the move to the Riverside.

PLAYERS • STOP PRESS

Emanuel Pogatetz (2005-)
From Bayer Leverkusen, £1.8m

The Austrian international had come to Steve McClaren's notice when impressing against Boro in the 2004-05 UEFA Cup during a loan spell with Grazer AK. Equally at home at left-back or in central midfield, he had to wait to make his Boro debut due to a ban imposed by the Russian Football Union after an incident during his final game on loan with Spartak Moscow. Formerly with Sturm Graz, Karnten and Aarau.

Fabio Rochemback (2005-)
From Barcelona, Undisclosed Fee

Capped seven times by Brazil as a Barcelona player, the midfield playmaker made his Boro debut in a 2-1 win over Arsenal in September 2005. Started out in his homeland with Internacional before moving to Spain. Hugely impressive during a two-year loan-spell with Sporting Lisbon, helping them knock both Boro and Newcastle out of the 2004-05 UEFA Cup.

Abel Xavier (2005-)
Free Agent

Vastly experienced defender, who joined Boro following a short spell with Italian side, Roma. A Portuguese international, a previous spell in England saw him play for both Everton and Liverpool, while he has also played for clubs in Portugal, Spain, Italy, Holland, Turkey and Germany. Made Boro debut against Arsenal in September 2005, following Michael Reiziger's transfer to PSV.

Yakubu (2005-)
From Portsmouth, £7.5m

Joined Boro just over 12 months after scoring four goals against Steve McClaren's side for his former club, Portsmouth. Only Thierry Henry scored more Premier League goals than Yakubu in the period 2003-05. Spotted by Portsmouth after impressive European appearances for Israeli side, Maccabi Haifa. Previously with Hapoel Kfar-Saba. Scored first Boro goal in 2-1 win over Arsenal in September 2005.

Adam Johnson (2005-)
From Youth
Apps: 1 – Goals: 0

Tricky winger who was thrown in at the deep end by his local club when making his first-team debut as a late substitute in the UEFA Cup tie away to Sporting Lisbon in March 2005, aged just 17. Less than 12 months earlier he had been unable to win a place in Boro's starting line-up for the FA Youth Cup final. Made his Premier League debut against Arsenal in September 2005.